The Healing SEMINARS

Kauai 1989 & Chicago 1990
by **Herb Fitch**

Copyright © 2019 by Bill Skiles.

ISBN Softcover   978-1-950580-76-7

All rights reserved. No part of this book may be reproduced or transmitted in any form or by any means, electronic or mechanical, including photocopying, recording, or by any information storage and retrieval system without express written permission from the author, except in the case of brief quotations embodied in critical reviews and certain other non-commercial uses permitted by copyright law.

This book remains the property of The Mystical Principles Group http://www.mysticalprinciples.com

Unauthorized publishing of any of the content is forbidden without first contacting the Mystical Principles site owner.

Printed in the United States of America.

To order additional copies of this book, contact:
Bookwhip
1-855-339-3589
https://www.bookwhip.com

The Healing SEMINARS

Kauai 1989 & Chicago 1990
by **Herb Fitch**

PART I
The Chicago Preparation For Healing Seminar
Kauai 1989

&

Part II
Chicago Healing Seminar
Chicago 1990

Transcribed, Edited and Compiled
2011 - 2013

Bill Skiles

TABLE OF CONTENTS

PART I

THE CHICAGO PREPARATION FOR HEALING SEMINAR KAUAI 1989

Foreword I By Bill Skiles	3
Tape 1 New Dimensions In Spiritual Healing	5
Tape 2 Breaking the Illusion Of Power	19
Tape 3 Hard Sayings	33
Tape 4 Are You Still A Body Prisoner?	46
Tape 5 Life Before Birth	60
Tape 6 The Infallible Healer	74
Tape 7 Spiritual Supply	86
Tape 8 Freedom From Mind	97

PART II

CHICAGO HEALING SEMINAR CHICAGO 1990 BY HERB FITCH

Foreword II By Bill Skiles	111
Class 1 Physician, Heal Thyself!	113
Class 2 Heal The Sick	134
Class 3 The Mirage Of Me	152
Class 4 Raise The Dead	167
Class 5 A Moment In Infinity	183
Class 6 Light Bodies	198
Class 7 My Time Has Come	210
Class 8 Living The God Life	226

PART I

THE CHICAGO PREPARATION FOR HEALING SEMINAR KAUAI 1989

FOREWORD I

By Bill Skiles

> *"Jesus answered and said unto them, Go and shew John again those things which ye do hear and see: The blind receive their sight, and the lame walk, the lepers are cleansed, and the deaf hear, the dead are raised up, and the poor have the gospel preached to them. And blessed is he, whosoever shall not be offended in me." John 11:4-6*

"The power and scope of spiritual healing are virtually unknown in our mental and material world. Most people know it only by name and usually by hearsay. Exactly what is spiritual healing? What makes it so different? Why is it totally unlike any other type of healing known to the world?.. We will find all the answers, I hope, in these tapes which are to follow." Herb Fitch

This series of talks which were mailed out to students in 1989, were a preparation for the "Chicago Healing Seminar," which took place the following year in 1990. These talks were some of the deepest talks Herb ever made and they certainly deliver on his promise to take us into what he termed, "New Dimensions in Healing."

A serious student will have a meditation and step out of the mind before playing each talk. Thereafter, the student will "let" the Spirit within reveal what they are to hear and uncover from the treasures that are so freely offered.

I invite you to make this journey now and to prepare for even greater and deeper revelations in the classes which later came forth and became the "Chicago Healing Seminar." May you not be offended by the Truth.

Bill Skiles
Robbinsville, NC
11/27/11
Link: http://www.mysticalprinciples.com

TAPE 1
NEW DIMENSIONS IN SPIRITUAL HEALING

Herb: From the island of Kauai, greetings from spirit to spirit, soul to soul. It is truly joy to welcome you again to this new series of important healing tapes to help prepare you for the infinite way healing seminar next Easter.

By now you should have your invitation to the seminar and if not then you want one or another one perhaps for your friend. Please get in touch with me at my home.

[Herb Fitch's mailing address followed]

Our healing seminar will begin next Easter on a Thursday night April 12th 1990 and will extend to April 16th. It will take place just outside Chicago at a very lovely resort called Oakbrook Hills Hotel and Conference Center. And I know that our work here will be very very special.

We're going to learn to practice new dimensions in spiritual healing. Many infinite way students do not have a specific idea about the nature and the method of spiritual healing or just what spiritual healing can be and cannot be. Many friends call for a spiritual healing usually there are those who call when everything else has failed. Then there are others who lean heavily on spiritual healing and on the practitioner and all too often they expect only mundane results, not spiritual unfoldment. This seminar will be special in that its purpose will be to make you self sustaining, confident that you are functioning under perfect divine law. To accomplish this we must say many things that we cannot say to normal students. Things that are only appropriate when the issues that we face appear to be life and death. We must speak in more absolute terms because upon you much depends. Some of you may be shocked by what we say but be sure that it is all necessary for your own success.

We're going to brush aside comfortable concepts that lull us into a present dream state until we are ready and awake and not plunge into a flow of seemingly incurable conflicts. This seminar will be unique to many of you if you are a healing practitioner seeking advanced techniques or if you feel an inner calling to be a transparency for the light. I believe this seminar will and can play a vital role in your journey to higher realms of consciousness.

The power and scope of spiritual healing are virtually unknown in our mental and material world. Most people know it only by name and usually by hearsay. Exactly what is spiritual healing? What makes it so different? Why is it totally unlike any other type of healing known to the world? How can society learn to depend on spiritual healing to lift itself above world problems that no man or nation has been able to solve? We will find all the answers I hope in these tapes that are to follow.

One feature above all distinguishes spiritual healing apart from every type of healing on earth. That pearl of great price, that unique feature which is the very substance of all Christ healing and which can govern every student who seeks the invisibility and invincibility and the dominion of divine omnipotence, that feature was revealed on earth when the Son of Man declared,

"I am the resurrection and the life. He that believeth in me thou he were dead, yet shall he live and whosoever liveth and believeth in me shall never die."

And that's one eternal truth proclaimed by the Master of Masters, you will find the termination of all disease, the end of every war, the triumph of man over every human problem. The path to life eternal, without an aging process, without disability, without deterioration and without human limitations. Whoever contacts the power of resurrection will radiate Christ healing to the world and will walk in the kingdom of eternal life lifting his brothers on earth. That is what we are here to learn how to do. Spiritual healing is the gift of God to his eternal son. These Christ words make every man a spiritual healer, who hears them within. They are the words of power direct from divine source. They are the substance of divine life and they are backed by the unlimited resources of infinite spirit. These words tell us another secret that no man is a healer only Christ power released through man, through his immortal soul can perform the greater works. And finally these words reveal one of the most exciting truths that is destined to change our world. A truth so unsuspected that our realization of it in fullness will make all these baffling horrifying evils on earth dissolve into total nothingness. That truth awaiting your recognition is simply this, please jot it down in your book of things to know forever,

NOTHING, ABSOLUTELY NOTHING IN GODS CREATION NEEDS HEALING.

Nothing in Gods creation needs healing. When you truly believe that, know that and are true to the truth of that you will be one of the worlds great spiritual healers because that is your number one healing truth. And know that when you learn it well that the world will beat a path to your door. If you cannot be persuaded that anything or anyone created by God needs healing, correction or improvement you will experience the healing power of Christ. On the other hand if you can be persuaded that something in Gods creation needs healing I can tell you now your patients will not receive divine help because you will be separated from Gods universe in that belief. You will separate yourself. If you believe in a God who is imperfect you are believing in what does not exist. There is no such God and your divided consciousness will deceive you into a false relationship with the God who does exist. Today we must move out of your divided consciousness. We must open your eyes to the healing Christ within, today. We must restore the conviction that divine love, divine wisdom, divine power have no opposition and no opposite. That they are always maintaining Gods perfect creation, everywhere in the universe including where you stand.

So now with your inner ear listen carefully not for sounds but for meaning until your whole being is receptive to a presence within you. A presence with a message from the kingdom to your soul. A message saying to you with total truth that only your enlightened soul can hear.

"I, I am the resurrection and the life. I am come that ye may have life and have it more abundantly."

Where the Christ within presents through you this message. The illusions of error will be released in your patient revealing God's perfect and eternal idea where suffering has fooled the world mind. Christ entering your consciousness is the healer, the miracle worker, the resurrection from the grave of illusion and this inner revelation of the perfect spiritual reality is the true spiritual healing as contrasted to medical, mental, metaphysical, holistic and other types of healing. It is a matter of degree. If we see improvements to make life more bearable in our material consciousness or mental consciousness we overlook the whole self. Physical healing, financial stability, emotional balance can tell us to the most direct route to fulfill these needs to establish peace as quickly as possible. And in our anxiety to restore a relative degree of comfort we seek immediate relief from pain or stress while overlooking a long range recovery needed on higher levels. Without realizing the total possibilities available we fall into a strange trap, we do not expect the maximum from our healers. We seek temporary repairs for human bodies and that is precisely what we get rarely more. Our patch-up job, it may work for a while but later when it fails, if it fails we seek more temporary relief. Psychically, mentally, medically, psychologically, economically never realizing that all our human healings are in the dream, the dream mind, the dream body, the dream life that imitates the true creation of God. So healings are temporary, fragmentary because they are not backed by God power or God substance. The simple fact is that these healings are performed by mortals for mortals in time that God did not create.

And there is still another side to this picture that has never truly been presented to the public. When the patient dies on the operating table where is God power? Does God heal one patient and not another? When a condition is arrested but returned did God change Gods mind? Or was God ever in the picture in the first place? The truth is that the limitations of matter and mind are the limitations of material, mental healing, they are inevitable.

World mind is the very substance of mortality and all mortals are bound by the same limitation through time, space and matter. Mortality worships two powers, good power, evil power. All mortals stumble into this same bottomless pit worshipping a make-believe God who creates good and evil and then impotently stands by while evil powers kill terrorize or violate helpless powers of good.

So you see mortals have a very superficial concept of life. It begins with birth, it ends with death and within this fragmentary framework all so called healings are very shallow, very partial and very temporary just like mortality itself. The function of the spiritual healer is to bypass material law with its belief in two powers, not to deal with human limitations or human bodies. The kingdom of the spiritual healer is not of this world. He never prays to God outside his own being. He never makes a mistake of treating the symptom of a disease or even of treating the disease itself. This is very important.

When you can learn to dissolve karma, you can transcend pain, you can reveal celestial harmony, boundless peace, wholeness where the human eyes sees disease, disability, even death. All spiritual healing secrets can be learned. We call them esoteric because they are performed by invisible mystical techniques beyond the cognition of the senses of man. Beyond the perimeter of the human brain. They defy understanding but they work when your consciousness is awakened to the invisible spiritual reality around you. And when these mystical principles work for you, when they happen, when they manifest they prove beyond a shadow of doubt that the power of God is available and ever ready to reveal the divinity of all men. Your soul, your spirit, your life are now immortal. The spiritual healer accepts your immortality and contacts the divine life source and lets the resurrecting Christ reveal its perfection, its perfect presence where you stand.

Forsaking all human concepts of health and of life the spiritual healer is one with the truth of God. Voiced in scripture or within his soul. He is never interested in human authorities who are misled by world beliefs. The one, the only authority he obeys is his heavenly father the perfect creator of reality. He is also the father of all spiritual immortals. The garment of spirit is substituted for the garment of skin. The spiritual healer knows his patient is spirit the Son of God. And that his father has laid down the flawless rules of spiritual healing no man can improve them. By obeying these rules, these divine principles invites infinite Christ power to break the hypnosis of the dream, to reveal the pure creation. Without evil, without darkness, to dissolve all karma, to replace the illusion of defective deteriorating mortal bodies and mortal limitations with the original divine blessing of harmony and eternal perfection.

When you experience the change over from human mind to Christ mind which is the renewal of mind spoken of by Paul all things become possible as a spiritual healer living in the spiritual consciousness of life you are God led, God fed, God directed, God sustained. Linked to Christ within you build receptivity to God power. As Christ love pours through you the walls of fear and distrust between people and nations come tumbling down. Water flows over parched land. Divine Joy fills the soul of man with new hope, new understanding, new life.

I found on page 81 in Joel's book "The Thunder of Silence" this statement.

"People of any nation can be saved, of any race, of any family if they have learned to pray and to open themselves so that the voice can speak within them, direct them, lead them, guide them, feed them, clothe them, house them."

Be now in stillness contemplate these words. All nations can be saved, all people can be saved by the resurrecting Christ within you. Within you is the potential for a better world. Release that resurrecting Christ within you and let Christ do the work. This is the task at hand.

Right now God is ISing. You do not have to ask God to be or to do anything at all. You stand in the infinite silence awaiting his living WORD. Don't push that WORD away.

"Father I await your words, your WORD, your grace, I am ready to serve. I am ready to know your truth and to follow it. I am ready to live it daily. I am ready to lay down my life that your life in me may live for I know that your life is my life and I have no other. I am immortal life now. All sense of mortality has been my dream. All sense of a life separate and apart from the father within has been my dream I cannot have such a life that is a world dream and I no longer subscribe to it."

Now let us plant within ourselves new healing principles based on the knowledge that nothing in God's creation needs healing. Let us open the door of consciousness to infinite God power by trying to understand who and what God really is. Is God a man or is God the creative principle of life? Is God a separate individual or is God my Self and the Self of all? Is God finite or infinite? Does God the creative principle of life, say "It is my good pleasure to give me the kingdom?" Do I trust that? Do you trust that? Does the world trust that? If God is infinite intelligence what can any man tell infinite intelligence that God does not already know? Is God love infinite? Is it available to Saint and to sinner? Then what is hate but a concept. What is stupidity but a concept. If God is infinite intelligence, love and power what is a problem? Is there a God of good and a God of evil? Does God love helping young people and not old people? Did God say, "My grace is thy sufficiency in all things," to young people as well as to old people? Are God's children under-privileged? Do you see divine truth reveals that God's grace is infinite. God's love, intelligence and power are infinite. God's abundance is infinite.

Then what is wrong in the human picture? We do not believe God. That's the truth. We shorten his kingdom. We believe God is for some not others. We believe there is a power that can keep God's love away from one group, from one race, from one color. We believe there is a power that can cripple, hurt or kill us. We believe that God is not the only power and we accept these anti- Christ powers because we have seen them operate among us. But now we face the real cause of our problem. We have accepted these problems with our human mind. We have not accepted these problems with our Christ mind. Think on that. The same human mind has also accepted you as a human being. That is not the way for a spiritual healer. Now correction must be made.

[silence]

Let us be still a moment longer as we contemplate how we are going to make that correction.

∞∞∞∞∞∞∞∞∞∞∞∞ End of Side One ∞∞∞∞∞∞∞∞∞∞∞∞

Accept God as your Father. If you do then you must also accept the Word of God. Now God said, "I will never leave you or forsake you." So if you believe on one hand that God will never leave you or forsake you can you on the other hand say, "I have a problem. I am going blind. I am losing my job. My husband is leaving me. My child is deathly ill."

In the presence of God your Father all things are provided. His grace is always your sufficiency in all things. His intelligence always knows your needs and his power always provides these needs. Then what is your real problem? You do not believe that God is your Father and so you cannot believe that God is fulfilling his promise never to leave or forsake thee or to provide a sufficiency of everything you need. And why do you fear? Why do you doubt? Because you are making decisions with a human mind. And that human mind must separate you from God even while God declares that he is inseparable from you. The human mind can never know God. It doesn't matter how honest you want to be, how God fearing you want to be, a human mind can never accept the kingdom which God has already given you. As a spiritual healer you will learn how to use your Christ mind which lives in God's truth. Which knows that God's perfection is your perfection and which refuses to abandon you to mortal appearances, mortal limitations, mortal beliefs.

Let's establish a principle now. We'll call it, ***The first principle of your spiritual healing consciousness.***

1. Perfection is the infinite law of God.

Whether you're a blind man, a cripple or a thief your Christ mind knows that perfection is always present because God is always present. And when you doubt that perfection is present you are not in your Christ mind.

Now let's establish a second principle.

2. Your patient has one Father, God.

And everything God promised you he also promised your patient. That includes love, power, intelligence, abundance, grace in all things. Therefore whatever appearance denies the WORD of God must be a lie, must be a false image without law, without power, without substance. Those are two very simple principles. So let's go on. Only God's perfect child stands before you. Now you know that is true in your Christ mind misperceived by the human mind. Call no man your Father upon the earth. And so the Father of your patient is always God. The one infinite Father of all and God is always maintaining infinite eternal perfection. And if you don't revert to a human mind you will know that is true. When you accept the appearance you're out of Christ mind into human mind and you're no longer a spiritual healer. Christ mind accepts the WORD of God with total faith.

Now these are your two principles which form the foundation, before you even learn techniques. These are the foundations of spiritual consciousness. Everyone coming to you is God's child. Perfect as his heavenly Father. Your spiritual treatment of that patient cannot begin until you are honoring the principle that this is the child of God before me, made of spirit not matter, perfect as the Father.

And so in your human mind you may find persons objectionable, distasteful or what you call bad character even repulsive. That's not the way of the spiritual healer because it's not the way of truth, its accepting the human mind as a judge. So you cannot be lifted into a rage or resentment and also be a transparency for the light. That is what we call malpractice. Mal-practicing your patient and betraying the reality of your own identity.

Now when Jesus teaches resist not evil, judge not after the appearance he is emphasizing that any reaction to any imperfection is a lie and shuts you off from the power of a perfect God. You must go beneath the surface of that and see to that your non-resistance must also go beneath the surface. Deep hates, superstitions, resentments, feelings from one generation passed on to the next. These must be uprooted so that you can face every individual, every circumstance with equanimity. And when your consciousness even tries to accept every inhabitant of earth as spirit made in the image and likeness of God you will understand why all things that are possible to God are possible to you. And the power of God will begin to pour through you in increased measure. These two monumental principles must become bone of your bone. So please accept this assignment.

Daily develop an automatic acceptance of the divine presence by accepting the divinity of everyone you meet. Deny divinity to anyone, ANYONE! And you remove yourself from divine grace. There is no escape. Each one you see is the invisible divine self. Don't be fooled by the human mask, don't be fooled by disabled bodies. To human eyes divine life is not visible. It may appear to you in a disabled form because mortal vision cannot form an infinite image. Every human error, sin, sickness, evil presents a false sense image about the perfect infinite divine life or what appears to us as persons. You must know the truth, believe the truth, act upon the truth. Only divine life is present. Only the child of God is present, not the visible form. Forgive everyone their seeming indiscretions. See no thief where a thief appears, no adulteress where an adulteress appears. No person where an individual appears. And the light of Christ will bless you with healing power.

Practice 15 minutes daily. More if possible, never less, until you know the life of every patient is divine. And all God has is his. When you have a perfect universe and a perfect patient, not before, you are qualified to perform the functions of a spiritual healer. A transparency for the immaculate divine creation. You are above human judgments, above the divided consciousness that lives in two worlds, one good and one evil.

Now, now you're ready to learn practical techniques to part the Red sea, to move the mountain, to command Lazarus to come forth. The human race would never deteriorate, mothers would never die in childbirth, breast cancer would never be the disease that women fear most. Truth and the discipline to apply that truth can make you an effective servant of God. But you know great healers have even something greater than this, something more that can't be memorized or simulated they possess that intangible essence called Divine Love. This love coupled with the knowledge and instinct for divine law releases the power of God on earth. If love moves through you animating the healing principles that you learn, nothing is impossible for the power of divine love in the midst of you is infinite without limitation. So with reverence for the divine works we will witness the deepest devotion to the responsibility we are about to share.

Let us now stand in the body temple not made with hands. Meek unto the infinite light, ready to inherit the kingdom of reality.

"Speak Father thy servant heareth."

These are your healing techniques. Healing revolves around the mystical truth that God is one. Without this sacred truth you are deceived before you start. God is immortal spirit, God is one immortal spirit and there is no other one. There is no God and you. No God and mortality. No God and a patient. No God and a man, woman or child, just God. It may take you a year or even ten years to prove that principle to yourself. But when you practice it faithfully and observe how the truth changes the conditions around you, the appearances and the freedom of your patients, you will know that you have discovered one of the great healing principles that is Christ consciousness. As different from mortal and material consciousness as anything can be. Mortal material consciousness judges. But ask yourself how can you be sick if God is well? Christ consciousness judges no man. It says, "God is not sick so you are not sick because you and the Father are one."

Remember this important principle, it is called impersonalization. Understand it and your healing practice will be bountiful. Fail to understand it and your ignorance will make healing very difficult perhaps impossible. There is no room for quibbling here. Impersonalize means there are no persons. "Only spirit," Paul said, "There is neither male nor female, Greek nor Jew," and here is another tip; Don't waste your breath trying to explain this principle to anyone. They will not understand. Now let's sharpen our understanding of the full meaning and application of the great principle of impersonalization. Later you'll learn how to impersonalize yourself but we'll save that principle until we have established a few other thoughts.

The second principle is nothingness. As you know nothing needs repairs in God's creation because God is a perfect creator. Whatever God created is forever perfect. The Son of God is the spiritual substance of God. The Self of everyone is the spirit of God, perfect forever. Your mind and your senses personalize the spirit of God so that you do not see or experience spirit. You are hypnotized by mortal mind called devil or Satan in the bible into personalizing spirit. Just as you imagine persons where God's spirit is, you imagine conditions in and on these persons. And because the persons are not there, but spirit is, can there be conditions on the person who is not there. When you impersonalize a patient, you realize his reality is invisible spirit. Now you nothingize his condition. Spirit has no conditions. Therefore his condition is as imaginary as anything else that God did not create. The condition does not exist in God's spiritual substance and your patient is God's spiritual substance. Therefore his so-called condition is not his reality. His perfect spirit is maintained in perfection by God. The material forms that we have accepted is not even a person but a world mind image projected subliminally, seen within ourselves, and imagined through our five senses as an external person.

All persons are the illusion we entertain about spirit. Similarly defects that we seem to see in persons are also illusions as we entertain about people who are not there. Cancer appears in the colon of a person but spirit is the reality of the person. Is cancer in the spirit? No, then where is the cancer. The answer is breathtaking. We have an imperfect concept of God's perfect creation and the cancer is in our imperfect concept. Automatically now we substitute persons for spirit without thinking about it, physical bodies for the one spiritual body without thinking about it and subliminally we give physical conditions to the bodies we have imagined without thinking about it and in this imperfect concept of God's perfect creation we try to live healthy, happy, harmonious, fulfilled lives in peaceful co-existence with our neighbors. And when conflicts arise in the dream we blame it on human greed and lust for power, never suspecting that the fabric of all human lives is a synthetic mental substance that must disintegrate in the illusion of time.

Tape 1: New Dimensions In Spiritual Healing

Before healing ourselves and others of human conditions, listen to several important statements from one of the worlds most successful spiritual healers, Joel Goldsmith. And if the words sound familiar it's because you have read them many times. These quotations come from chapter 9 of Joel's book "Thunder of Silence." Quote;

"What we see as body, is not body, it is a mental image within our own thought, a universal mental concept. Individualized within us. There is no such thing as a material body. There is only a material concept of body. There is no such thing as a material universe. There is only a material concept of the one spiritual universe. As long as we accept a material concept of universe we are under the law of matter. But we are free as soon as we begin to understand that we live and move and have our being in the first chapter of Genesis where man is made in the image and the likeness of God, Spirit. And that the soul of God is the soul of man, the life of God is the life of man, the mind of God is the mind of man, the body of God is the body of man."

I might add if you have not read chapter 9 recently in "Beyond Words and Thoughts," give yourself another treat and a treatment. Read it again and you'd be surprised how much you've learned since the last time you read it.

When you impersonalize your patients and nothingize their problems you are following in the footsteps of Christ, then you will notice a change in yourself, a lightness, a strange freedom of detachment because in freeing them from the body concept, you really free yourself and you feel it. You begin to experience your own spiritual body as the temple of the Holy Ghost, the invisible substance of all forms on earth, is God. And to the degree that this truth is realized by your soul the cripple will walk again, the blind man will see again, the nations of the world will lay down their arms and bathe in the pool of infinite love.

Impersonalizing, removing the belief in persons, also means removing criticism of persons. So if you're still judging the sins of an individual you're not an instrument for his healing. As long as you accept persons, personal evil, personal error, personal sin, disease you need as much help as your patient. God is the only creator and God is not the creator of evil. Spirit is the only substance and the spirit contains no evil. There is no person, only spirit. Therefore evil can never be in a person. Evil has no creator. Evil has only the fabric of illusion in which to appear. The illumined realize that all evil is a projection from world mind, which is not a mind and that evil has no person in which it can be. The cancer that frightens us is not in the Spirit of the patient but in the false or illusory world mind which projects the false image of matter into the I of the beholder.

Nothingize is the principle which is the realization that the spiritual creation is infinite without a material opposite and contains nothing, no disease, disability, deterioration, evil, darkness, sin or iniquity for spirit is pure unconditioned, perfect forever. It is wise in advance without waiting for a patient to nothingize all evil conditions. The dedicated healer begins his day everyday by impersonalizing the human race. Eliminating material mortality from his consciousness and then nothingizing all evil.

This is how Joel actually spent his early mornings. Usually from 3:30 A.M. until the click told him that he was invulnerable to persons and conditions. Jesus himself never faced a sick man or an evil condition. His consciousness was trained to remain above universal hypnotism. "Who convinceth me of sin," he said. Is not the thief on the cross the perfect child of God? Did God create an adulteress or is the adulteress, man's misperception of spirit? Who created the girl in the coma. Which is real God or evil? Is God the only power or does evil have power to change Gods spiritual creation? Can the life of God be sick or die? Always the spiritual healer is faced with a paradox. The lie he sees and the truth he knows. If he fights the lie he loses and his patient's condition continues. If he sees through the illusion of the condition and calmly puts up his sword with confidence that divine perfection is maintaining itself. God's law is working in spite of appearances. Then he stands fast in the face of universal beliefs and his fidelity to spirit will prevail.

We have another healing principle. Because the qualities of spirit are infinite there's no place where there are opposite qualities. Where the life of spirit is, death cannot be. Where the infinite self of God is, no other self can be. So therefore your third principle is a universal truth and that is where you must rivet your consciousness. Principle 3;

3. You are Divine Being Now. Your Neighbor is Divine Being Now.

And you must expand this truth by accepting that because everyone is divine being, God is the only self in God's creation. Now look beneath the surface of these precious words from the infinite one comes the words;

"All that I have is thine."

God is the only one, all that God has is thine, so who are you? If you have all that God has and God is the only one, can you handle this truth? Is it too big for you? Are you afraid to know that if you have all that God has, you must be God. And that what you appear to be must be a false graven image. Can you rise to the same pure realization that compelled Christ Jesus to say,

"I and the Father are one."

Impersonalize every patient. Nothingize every condition. Stand in the shocking truth;

I am the only Self.

Three indomitable principles for the spiritual healer. One I, Where the patient stands, One I, Where I stand, this is Christ Power.

TAPE 2
Breaking the Illusion of Power

Herb: From the island of Kauai. It's a joy to send you greetings of love in the spirit of oneness.

Every true spiritual healer knows that he has no personal power. His only function is to learn how to be a pure channel for the grace of God which has divine dominion over all things, which is now functioning everywhere in the infinite invisible, and which is the very substance of all that exists in the kingdom of God – the true creation of the Father. This divine substance is flowing freely as the uninterrupted consciousness of God and of the I Am of every man. And this, this uninterrupted consciousness of the I Am is the miracle worker that lifts the veil of illusion from the human eyes and reveals the perfect harmony that underlies this visible world.

God consciousness as the I Am of you realized maintains God's perfect will in you. Without this miracle substance the spiritual healer is helpless. Truth is adulterated. The seesaw of good and evil takes total control. False powers present false claims. God's perfect creation is clouded by false opposites. And a world of suffering humanity struggles with problems that claim our total attention and refuse to disappear. Quickly the spiritual leader learns that his only hope for bringing order to this chaos is to contact the miracle worker, the I Am in the kingdom of God within himself. And this vital contact demands an ability to walk the middle path between good and evil.

That discipline of the sense mind is emphasized by Joel on page 43 of his *The Art of Spiritual Healing*. Please remember these words. Please practice these words because it is essential to successful healing. I quote:

"When you can sit beside a very sick person with no trace of fear because something inside of you is singing, 'This is my beloved Son. I in the midst of

you am mighty. I will never leave you nor forsake you.' Then you are a spiritual healer."

Christ Jesus gave us one of the major secrets of spiritual healing when he said:

"Resist not evil."

As you and I know, there is more to non-resistance than mere willpower. One of the great obstacles to non-resistance is the human ego and I mean ego in its broader sense. When you find a strong ego you will not find a spiritual healer. The human ego is dedicated first to its own personal identity. And that identity refuses to accept the allness of God. It is committed to God and me. The ego also refuses to die daily. It is too interested in winning applause, getting ahead, proving its superiority. The ego feeds on the attention of others. It is committed to duality. It always sees God and. It separates itself and man from God; prevents wholeness, harmony, peace. It gives power to illusions. To everyone it says, "You are not the beloved Son of God. You are inferior to me." The superiority complex of the human ego shuts down the pipeline between God and man, and it keeps man out of the very kingdom he seeks.

The spiritual healer must overcome the illusion of a personal identity. That is ego in its broad sense – personal identity, much more than vanity. There is no choice in this matter. Human ego always reacts to the good and to the evil of this world. It sees error, it fears power, it tries to correct error. It changes bad to good if it can. It changes wrong to right. Human ego judges every man. Now spiritual healing is none of this. The indwelling Christ judges no man. One with source is the theme of Christhood. Actually Christ sees human life and human death as the same dream. Christ has no personal identity.

"Thou seest me, thou seest the Father."

Christ gives no power to illusion. Christ knows no man after the flesh. Ego sees the drunk. Ego sees the dying. Ego sees the human race. Christ sees God appearing as individual man. And Christ says to all who appear as mortal:

"Thou art my beloved Son in whom I am well pleased."

The ego never gets out of the way. Christ within acknowledges only the spiritual identity of the so-called patient – the ever-presence of God without opposite and the non-reality of any appearance of imperfection in the creation of God. Oh yes, the ego is so conditioned to bare false witness. Christ within and only Christ within bares true witness to the perfect invisible universe of divine spirit. Always the spiritual healer who is a transparency for Christ knows that all mortality is a dream, that both virtue and sin are part of the dream, that only spiritual reality exists and in it there are no sinners, no sick people, no dying people, no diseases, no good health, no bad health, no man, no woman, no one here to change correct or improve. The spiritual healer lives and knows the truth that God is the one and the only inhabitant of the spiritual universe. And this sets the healer and the patient free of the claim, free of the appearance of imperfection.

Have you accepted the spiritual reality of mankind? If not it's time we do. And I think right now is that time. In our meditation let us accept one infinite Father and let us see something you may never have thought of, something that is going to prove vital in your healing work. Because there is one infinite spirit – listen carefully – you will never receive more than one patient. Oh each patient will come to you with a new face or a new claim but don't be fooled; there are not many separate patients, it is always the one spirit appearing to you as a separate patient but it is always the same one with a new material face. Oh yesterday a baby needed help. Last night someone else needed help. This morning a woman with a problem needed help. And you're thinking in terms of baby, another person and a woman, but that's the disguise. It's the same patient always – always reporting a new claim, a new body, a new age, and there are no such things. The spiritual healer has one patient and he knows it. He doesn't have to heal that one patient again and again and again and again. Did you know that secret? You know it now because you are learning how to handle every claim that comes your way. Human life is an endless succession of sense illusions beginning with the illusion of human birth, stopping temporarily with the illusion of human death. Our human view of the entire world is illusion and believe it or not, it has a purpose, it has one magnificent purpose; to train you, to prepare you, to teach you, to convince you, to surrender your dependency on personal resources; to relinquish your belief in your human capacities to solve the conflicts of the mortal world and to raise you to that level called illumination where you realize that only your total faith in the Presence and its perfect power and its infinite wisdom can lift you to higher realms of consciousness. Christ demonstrates this faith repeatedly starting with the wilderness experience and ending with the complete faith in his Father by accepting crucifixion. And always the message was:

"Go thou and do likewise."

As you lose all fear of so-called world powers through your knowledge of indivisible oneness with God, through your confidence in the truth that there is only one infinite self, you will notice more healings are taking through you, for fear separates us from God, whereas faith unites with God and all that is.

And another strange illusion that you should be alerted to, one that you are not apt not to think about too often but I'd like you to think about it now. The illusion of space is a very important consideration and it can take you out of many a problem. Now we have a person calling upon you and asking you to meet a claim. This is your patient appearing to you externally, that is, outside your body is your patient, outside your home and probably outside the city. The patient is there, you are here, so it seems anyway because at first glance there is space between you and the patient. The patient is there; you are here. But wait a minute. Wait a minute. In spiritual healing the concept of space is entirely false. Oh yes, there are two forms – you and the patient – but there is only one I, there is only one Self. How can there be space between one Self? Which is the illusion? The space or the two selves? If one Self is the truth, the space is the illusion. The other way round isn't it? Ah, now go further. The I Christ of you is the I-Christ of your patient. The I-Christ of you cannot be well and the same I-Christ of your patient be sick. In human life we buy into that ridiculous dream, the dream of two-ness – living in different spaces and different bodies, separated, individuals.

But spiritual discernment does not look at superficial surfaces. Spiritual discernment convinces you in your heart soul and consciousness that God is one. That one is universal, unseparated, the body of Christ; the one infinite perfect invisible spirit. Yes, the divine infinite son that your patient is now is always the perfect image and likeness of God and always will be. Never can be a single, separated individual. And with that enlightened consciousness you are impersonalizing your patient. One of the first things we learned in our last tape, impersonalize, now you're doing it. You learn to impersonalize the entire human race. And to identify the invisible divine son in all, and don't forget to include yourself.

Briefly in the silence let us go now to the infinite kingdom of God within and rest there joyously, for you are standing in the only reality. That infinite kingdom within you is the infinite creation of God everywhere. Accept the infinite I which can never leave you; the inseparable I of spiritual man everywhere. And know this truth. The infinite I, Father, Son within you, can never live in anyone finite or anything finite. In this realization you are blessing the world. As you step out of the changing material dream of separate forms your soul rises above the conflicts and visions of all human thought. The suffering of your patient must vanish as your Christ mind, free of world thought, sheds divine light where the human mind had seen error, darkness and disability in a mentally conditioned universe. I-Christ realized in you is I-Christ in your patient. This activates and awakens your patient from the dream of imperfection and restores the awareness of harmony. This is spiritual healing – Christ healing – and it will lift you into new dimensions of healing that break the illusion of power, illusions that currently hold our world in bondage, and it will reveal the living God to all men and in all men. Thank you Father.

You are living the Infinite Way. That means you are accepting the spiritual identity of the universe and all its inhabitants. There are no human spirits. If a spiritual healer accepts people materially and acknowledges material differences between people he will not succeed. Spirit is neither healthy nor unhealthy, rich nor poor, Greek nor Jew, male nor female; spirit never changes identity; spirit is always spirit neither more nor less. The spiritual healer acknowledges only the spiritual identity of everyone without judgment, without criticism, without resentment. The function of the spiritual healer is to be an impartial instrument for the revelation of God's harmony, God's perfect spiritual creation, God's perfect power. He cannot be trapped into mind identifications, mind consciousness which believe in both good and evil. He can never conceive or acknowledge a conditioned universe which needs correction, nor can he acknowledge the presence of human material bodies. He has no personal likes or dislikes. He walks in a spiritual universe which never needs healing. He loves unconditionally. He forgives because there is nothing to forgive. He accepts spiritual wholeness where human perception sees separate physical forms. He does not stray outside the single eye of soul which knows invisible angels where man sees visible mortals.

Listen carefully again please. You must know that in this Christ consciousness the spiritual healer reveals there is no blind man, there is no adulteress, there is no dead Lazarus. He walks on the Holy grounds of spirit in the omnipresent one Self. Spirit of God is his neighbor, his sole companion – the only inhabitant of the earth.

This spirit of which we speak is a dedicated Infinite Way student now appearing on earth as you. In this consciousness you are about God's business and you are governed by perfect divine life. You are led by perfect divine will. You are nurtured and protected by the glory of divine love, for this is the miracle worker, the undivided consciousness of the Son of God which inherits eternal life. This nonjudgmental Christ in you, as you, knows neither birth nor death and is always complete serving truth and living in celestial harmony. This consciousness calls no man Father upon the earth. The one divine source is his Father which art in heaven. This consciousness says, "I and the eternal, infinite Father are one, spirit unseparated throughout eternity." And it is speaking of your identity now. This consciousness says, "In me there can be no error," because error denies the infinity of God. And so in you error must be a false appearance. Your oneness with God precludes the possibility of error in you. When it appears know that it must be illusion. In this fourth principle you rest with the confidence that you have impersonalized your patient, have nothingized his condition, and now in the spiritual identity of one Self you rest one with the perfect creator, unseparated from the eternal, unseparated from the infinite, unseparated from the creative substance of the universe in which error cannot take form. When you meet daily problems with these healing principles, the life of God lives and expresses as your life.

Walking in the middle path is the way to non-resistance, unswayed by good or evil, anchored in spiritual reality. Spiritual healers have learned, however, that human thought is too easily provoked into reaction. Human thought reacts, retaliates, interprets, but more than making judgment, human thought builds the mental images that take form in the external world of matter which is not the kingdom of God. Human thought recreates reality into material images which man thinks he lives in. Human thought invents good and evil where God's perfect creation is and then becomes a slave to its own believed created images. Human thought invents strong hearts and weak hearts, healthy bodies and sick bodies, good weather and bad weather. Every problem in our re-created world of images is composed of the synthetic substance which Christ pinpointed in one revealing sentence:

"Take no thought for your life."

For we are not dealing with disease, disaster and destruction, nor are we dealing with death, nor are we dealing with human conditions. We are dealing with human thought which is a counterfeit of divine thought. And it is these projected shadows of human thought without divine substance that present counterfeit persons, places and things to fill our make-believe world.

Come now, which horse do you ride? The white horse of truth of spirit or the many colored horses of the mind, the emotions, human thoughts. Let us ride the horse of spirit, the white horse. Let us in the deep silence build a vacuum, a vacuum of no-thought – no-thought which does not admit into consciousness world thought. No-thought which honors the allness of God, the allness of divine thought, the intelligence of the infinite source. In no-thought we rest with the confidence that our Father knoweth our needs and is filling every need with divine grace.

[silence]

And as we rest here we are building an impregnable fortress so that when world thought knocks at the door of our mind, it finds that only the Christ mind is at home with a clear vision of God's perfect universe always under divine government. In no-thought you break the world illusion of power and you open the door to the omnipotence of divine thought which has behind it the fullness of infinity to enforce, maintain and sustain all life in the image and likeness of God.

Let's have a short rest and see then what the Father has prepared for us.

∞∞∞∞∞∞∞∞∞∞∞∞ End of Side One ∞∞∞∞∞∞∞∞∞∞∞∞

Our spiritual healing is that sin, disease, death have no external reality. They exist only as an illusory world belief, a concept. Our concept of this world will keep changing but the reality and the perfection of the spiritual universe which is all that is here will never change. This perfect creation made of self-perpetuating, self-maintaining spirit is the finished kingdom of God, in which no war has ever been fought, no disease has ever

Tape 2: Breaking the Illusion of Power

appeared, no soul has ever died. The function of your human mind is not to create but to realize that the whole creation of God is already complete. Nothing can be added, nothing can be taken away. The function of your mind is to be an instrument for your soul which expresses divine mind, divine law and divine wisdom. All the infinite qualities of God function through your soul and when your mind is receptive to your soul these perfect qualities come through your soul pure, unadulterated by finite human thought and manifest as the harmony and productivity of your life. The moment your thinking mind makes finite human decisions you shut God out of your life and you remain in the mortal dream of opposites – good health and then bad health, substance and perhaps lack, peace and inevitably war, harmony and discord.

All thought is the great illusion of life but when you stand in the vacuum of no-thought which is the secret place of the most high God makes your decisions. God handles your problems. Source, which knows all, releases truth through your soul, directs your mind perfectly and frees you from the tyranny of false sense perception.

Realization is not visualization. The Infinite Way teaches that your realization of spiritual truth is the miracle healer. Visualization is mental, not spiritual. There is a border line when we try to manipulate matter with our thought, with our will power, and the problem is that we are trying to change bad matter to good matter all in the same material dream. But when you transcend the belief in matter and transcend the finite, distorting human mind, you are above mental visualization in the realm of soul realization where illusions of matter melt. The world of the senses loses its false power and spiritual consciousness reveals the grace of the infinite maintaining a sufficiency for all your needs. Remember the difference between realization and visualization.

In the spiritual realm there is no laying on of hands. The healer never touches the patient. All physical contact between patient and healer is obsolete. Human words are obsolete; surgery and medicine are obsolete; acupuncture and chiropractic are obsolete; every form of physical and mental treatment is obsolete. Soul realization expressing the perfect government of God overflows into the visible world as a divine blessing. The wind of the hurricane finds no one to hurt, the bullet of the assassin finds no one to kill, the poison of the virus is revealed as a shadow of mortal thought and finds no one to infect. Divine substance realized in your soul dehypnotizes your mind and spiritual man walks freely on the earth.

The human mind has no capacity to demonstrate the power and the presence of God. Only your soul reaches into the kingdom of God, and in many the Bible has been telling you just that, that mind hypnosis is normal to all mortals because the natural man lives in slavery to the world mind. You must develop your spiritual center to remove the mask from all material appearances or you may be as hypnotized as your patient.

The fifth chapter of Matthew teaches us to train our focus from looking out with the mind to looking within, within your soul. Outside you see a cripple, a man with the withered arm, a girl in a coma. This is the external world viewed with mind vision. But now let's look at Matthew 5:25 in the Moffitt translation and we read this mystical advice from Christ:

"Be quick and make terms with your opponent, so long as you and he are on the way to court, in case he hand you over to the judge and the judge to the jailer and you are thrown into prison; truly I tell you, you will never get out till you pay the last half-penny of your debt."

Quite different from the King James version but basically identical. So whether you read the Moffitt translation or the King James version, you're being taught by God that your mind is always a victim of world appearances. Your five senses surround your mind, they project sense images of a cripple, a withered arm, and a comatose girl. Where do these images come from? To the world they're real and we want to help them. We want to help the cripple to walk, we want to see that withered arm stretch out, we want to see that comatose girl wake up. But I have a question for you: How can you do what God has not done? Now look again at the words of Christ Jesus, and you will find your answer right there:

"Be quick and make terms with your opponent."

For two thousand years man has ignored these inspired words direct from infinite divine intelligence. What they're saying is, instead of looking outside with your mind, go within, look inside your soul, do it instantly. That instant focus within instead of without is how you come to terms with your opponent. Who is your opponent? World mind. The cosmic liar who adulterates human perception with images not made by God. This is your adversary, your opponent. These cosmic mind projections of world thought appearing as the disabilities of our world are very convincing. They're especially persuasive when they work on your emotions. And this is the meaning *on the way to court*. If you're not careful a series of mental traps will trick you, your opponent will turn the case over to the judge, meaning your mind will pronounce judgment. It will positively identify the physical problem as a reality. It will be swayed by the appearances. And this verdict of your mind turns you over to the jailer and the door is locked behind you. You have let beliefs in the reality of a cripple. a withered arm, and a girl in a coma into your mind. Now there's no way to get them out. Your karmic debt is the conviction that material defects exist in God's creation. And you're going to pay for this belief with your own material, mortal sense of life. This is your last half-penny – or in the King James version, your uttermost farthing that you will pay.

Now then, what does the next mention of consciousness tell us? You are close to it but you must be willing to work for it. It doesn't come like a sudden bolt of lightning. It's an inner movement and it begins with your yearning for God's pure truth, plus your understanding that your senses can never transmit truth, it can only make the God contact through the silence of your senses, for in that silence your mind will not react to the appearances of matter, of material images of cripples, withered arms, comatose girls, dying people. And as you maintain that inner vacuum of no sense reaction to outer stimuli, while the images that appear in your eye do not move you, you are indifferent to the nature of them and the contents of those images as they pass before you. You do not identify or respond to the images, you do not judge the images; the movement or quality of the images does not affect you. You accept all images as mere mental shadows without substance, without reality, without divine ordination, without power. And as you behold your patient in this vacuum of sense thought, unmoved by what you see, holding your five senses in a state of no resistance, no judgment, you are making it impossible for the world mind to turn you over to the judge. You are breaking the illusion of power which convinces mankind that mortal forms are real and can suffer from heart ailments which deny and defy the all-power of God. In that discipline of standing fast in no-thought, you are confirming your faith in God as the only creative principle, the only source, the maintaining, sustaining power of the universe which makes all appearances of the power of evil false and impossible.

This way of life repeated seventy times seven and seventy times seven again and again and again until it is your nature to remain unaffected by material images removes the beam of hypnosis from your eyes and releases the pure light of your soul; opens the door to your kingdom within and takes you to the throne of I Am which is the perfect will of God in action.

By your willingness to discipline yourself, to discipline your sense reaction to matter, you have upheld the divinity of your patient. You have accepted their spiritual identity as the perfect image and likeness of God, their Father. You have refused to believe that spirit can be crippled or disabled or comatose. You have not seen them as persons but perfect spiritual children of God. You have impersonalized your patient. You have nothingized your patient's material condition because spirit has no material condition. You are being true to the one great mystical secret which every spiritual healer knows and practices everyday. This is it:

Only God is happening.

Only God is happening. Never waste a single moment analyzing the problem you've been called upon to heal. That's your first major temptation. Instead freeze your sense reaction instantly, in one motion take no thought and in that moment go straight to God in your soul. Practice, practice, practice. You have refused to recognize the problem. You have not accepted the false appearance of person. You have not violated a single divine law. Now you have passed through the false powers of world mind, unwavering, not denying your heavenly Father as the one life of all. The dream of mortality is almost gone. Is there a God and a patient? Of course not. There is one and that one is the only one – one undivided infinite spirit where you are and where the patient appears, one. One divine life where you are and where your patient appears. One omnipresent divine power where you are and your patient appears. Can spirit be less than perfect? What else is present beside spirit? Is a claim of error real or imagined? Now we rest above the senses, above the mind, above the beliefs of the mind, letting human thought float by, knowing God is, ising throughout infinity. There is no patient. My patient and I are the one spirit of God, unconditioned, unseparated, perfect and undefiled. You are seeing through the illusion. God's perfection is our perfection. Everywhere "I am" is running a perfect universe. In this we continue resting in the word, confident. Then truth in consciousness will reveal itself visibly as the absence of error.

Now then, when the Bible reports that a cripple walked, a withered was straightened, a twelve-year-old girl awakened from a coma, Christ Jesus is teaching that there is no God and man. God manifests as individual being without man, without separation, but only when you are one with source will this wholeness, this harmony and peace become visible. When you realize that every patient is not a human being but God appearing as individual being then your patient will manifest the qualities of divine life and so will you. As you witness Christ behind the eyes of every individual, your own soul faculties will awaken to the joys and harmonies that invisibly surround you. Disease and death will cease to have an external reality when you feel the power of silent grace.

We are now moving into a new age of spiritual healing. Man will discover that God is here, that God's creation is here as invisible spiritual man, universe and body; that the visible is unreal, including sin, sickness, habits and even persons. The knowledge that through physical senses we behold mirages will soon make more spiritually conscious souls discern reality. And that special extra something that adds new dimensions of life to your experience will reveal the magic of your environment like an unseen source with a new fragrant bringing enchantment from heaven and transforming the earth. We see this all around you these days. The transition is taking place. The awareness is taking root. Eyes are opened. You can make them open faster. You can release thoughts to their reality.

I leave one parting thought with you – a thought which I hope can hasten the transformation in our universe. The whole of next week take this idea with you; it can make a very big difference in your living and in your healing work. Become aware that only God can happen because only God is. You've had thousands of years of false thought to transcend, but much has already been transcended and much invisible help is being given. You can be sure that the consciousness of those who have walked before us is always with us, to help us become aware of the invisible presence of God as the only reality.

So I recommend that you take thirty seconds right now to remind yourself that God is happening and only God. Regardless of what your senses may have read in the morning newspaper or heard on the morning TV or what accumulation of beliefs have welled up within you through the years, the truth is that God is happening now and only God. Hold that in your consciousness. Start with 30 seconds during the day. You'll find that the accumulation of this truth will do something for you that very little else can do. It will give you an unexpected confidence. It will release many of the fears that accumulate beneath the surface, fears that you don't even know you have, little fears.

"My daughter went to school today. She forgot something. Will she be well? Did she get a ride? Will the children there be kind to her? She was sick when she left, how is she?"

Things that weigh on your mind. And, oh, if you can take an inventory of those things they're so numerous. Your entire inner self is flooded with these aggressive thoughts. Only God is happening today. Have you accepted that? Do you know at this instant your realization of that can prevent the fears that you're worrying about? Do you know the power in that truth? When that truth becomes your living consciousness, "Behold, the world is new."

But now comes the application of that truth. You receive a call for help for a problem or an unwanted condition, now how will you start to meet that request? Here's a suggestion, perhaps a way you may not have thought of. To begin, instantly meet the claim by knowing that only God is happening. Good start, isn't it, whatever the claim? Oh, they told you about a lot of conditions that were wrong didn't they, but is that the real claim? No. The claim is that God is not happening. That's the claim. Whoever called you said, no matter what they said, they were saying, "God is not happening." But you know that only God is happening, so every condition, every problem must be a claim that God is asleep. Now take the claim and reverse it instantly, silently; don't tell the patient about it, silently in your consciousness. You heard the patient say, "My arm is broken." Right then, right then, you are saying silently within yourself – not to the patient – within yourself you are saying, "Only God is happening and there are no broken arms in God." Now get steady with yourself, rest there a moment. Forget the broken arm, forget the claim whatever it was.

Rest inside secure in the truth that God is happening and only God, that God is the life of the patient, that God is the spiritual body of the patient. And every time the thought of a broken arm tries to enter your mind meet it with the quiet knowledge that infinite God life is all that is present, contains no broken arms, no cancer, no tumor, no this, no that, and then let God in you do the healing. Do you trust that? Can you do that? Let God in you after you know the truth, can you let God do the healing by maintaining no-thought about the problem? Christ did, some of us learn to do it and it works...

TAPE 3
Hard Sayings

Herb: From soul to soul, spirit to spirit. Greetings of love from the garden island of Kauai.

This tape series in preparation for the Chicago healing seminar next Easter is called "New Dimensions in Healing." And today I believe you will hear about healing truths which rarely are taught to students anywhere in the world. For one thing spiritual healing never can be taught to a material consciousness, only spiritual students are prepared to understand fourth dimensional healing truth. But even spiritual students will find the hard sayings of esoteric truths are difficult to digest and to apply. And yet there must be a place on this earth where the healing grace of God is taught in its absolute form; without fear of shocking anyone or of alienating the timid or the traditional healers who cling to methods that cannot produce the greater works. Christ healing is revolutionary and to fulfill our responsibility as servants of the Most High, we are compelled to follow the Master; we are bringing these hard sayings into our daily healing work. And so today perhaps we should first heal the healers, to prepare them for every challenge that will be called upon in each of us to face problems that the world needs to solve.

As you know any attempt on your part to explain these hard truths to a material mind will be rather difficult and will surely meet with instant disapproval as you may soon discover for yourself. One key truth that mankind has managed to overlook for over five-thousand years is that **God is all**. And to that we must now add a second truth. And that is the important truth we wish to discuss.

God is Immortal.

Now where does that leave you? It leads to another amazing truth because God is immortal and God is all;

Tape 3: Hard Sayings

There are no mortals on this earth.

The application of this one truth can magnify the power of your healing work. A Bible student can get by without surrendering his mortality, but truly it is foolhardy to believe that a spiritual healer can live in a mortal body of matter and can be a channel for spiritual healing. Mortals who try to heal other mortals can be effective, through mental healing and a variety of other good methods. But they will also have many weaknesses and many failures. If you have not known before, realize now that the extraordinary healing miracles of Jesus were only possible because he had learned how to unlock the infinite power of the immortal Christ of his own eternal being. This immortal Christ in you can heal the universe and you can learn how to release this same Christ and all its power to the world when you learn to follow the hard sayings of the Master. And that will take all your courage, all your vision, all your pioneering spirit, all your determination plus divine inspiration to release you from the fetters of false boundaries. *"Sell all thou hast."*

Ahh. What did the Master mean by that statement? Was he advocating that we walk around in sackcloth? Did he want us to sell our homes and our investments? Turn it all over to charity? His very close friend Lazarus was a wealthy man and what did Lazarus sell before he walked out of a tomb in a new spiritual body? Lazarus did what every disciple of the Master learned to do. He sold his mortality. He surrendered his concept of mortal flesh. He accepted his immortal Self as the only self that he was.

"Lay down your life so that you may pick it up again," said the Master.

And Lazarus did just that. He lay down his mortal concept of self. Picked up his immortal life just as each one of us on the spiritual path is learning to do. Now you must admit that is a hard saying and the pity of it is that because mortals have been afraid of that hard saying, they have gone through the illusion of dying on battlefields, suffering the tortures of the damned, with crippling diseases that have no divine Creator and exist only in the hypnotized mind. The belief that man is mortal is the hypnosis and from this erroneous belief evolves the equally erroneous belief in mortal problems, mortal diseases and disabling mortal sickness; the entire inventory of mortal illusions that culminate in mortal death.

The first shock is over. We have learned, **there are no mortals on this earth.** Immortal God created only immortal man. Mortals do not exist. And this truth is so breathtaking, so essential to your realization of identity, so vital to your healing work, and to the fulfillment of your eternal life, that Spirit commands you to pause right here to reach a higher understanding of who you are, and to look beyond the mortal tomb of flesh that you have naively accepted as your body.

Rest in the quiet for a moment find the incorporeality of your Self. The you without a physical form. Let your spirit rest there as you live in your incorporeal Being.

Your function, and this is not the words of a man, your function is to honor God supremely. We all accept that. It may surprise you however to learn that if you do not accept God as your source, as your Father, you are dishonoring God. The son of God is as immortal as his Father. The belief in your mortality is a denial of your divine Sonship; a denial of your divine identity, a denial of the Fatherhood of God. All mortals are denying Sonship and thereby dishonoring God. Mortals can never be one with an immortal God. Mortality is duality. Only immortality honors God. Only immortality is one with God. Only immortality is the truth that makes you free. And this is one of the greatest secrets taught on earth by Christ Jesus unknown to most of Christendom. He was not resurrected. The purpose of his demonstration is still unrealized; in one of the most remarkable teachings ever given to the human race, He demonstrated the illusion of mortality. He had one body and it was not the body that men saw. He had one life and it was not contained in that mortal body. And when the illusion of a mortal body was removed by crucifixion, the immortal body and the immortal life remained untouched by death, because it was one with God, unseparated from God and that immortal body and that immortal life is the divine body and the divine life that you have now. Rest in that beautiful truth.

The day must come, and the day is now, when you declare your divine Sonship by surrendering your false sense of a mortal body, containing a mortal life, and accept immortal body, immortal life as your real Self, your only Self, your undying Self. Then, then you will honor God supremely. Hold this truth deep and hallowed in your consciousness. Every word has a unique and wonderful meaning for all of us.

"Follow Me."

Oh what a hard saying because "Me" is the immortal Christ saying, "Follow Me," out of your false mortality into your God given immortal life, your God given immortal body. And do it on this earth as I have done it. "Sell all thou hast." Lay down your mortal that you may pick up your immortal life now. As your mortality is surrendered and released, your mortal problems will go with it. Sickness, disease, every appearance of imperfection, is part of the one mortal illusion.

"Be ye perfect as your heavenly Father is perfect."

What does it mean? Be immortal like your Father now. Do you feel the inner rhythm of your immortality? Can you feel the reality of a body that you cannot see, your immortal body? That is God's gift to you: your invisible body of eternal life. The body that was yours before birth, eternal, unconditioned, perfect forever. A body that is everywhere now. Always present, always divinely protected, never born. You have a body of infinite Spirit which lives now in the invisible kingdom of one infinite Self. This immortal body which exists before Abraham, meaning before the appearance of your mortality, before the world illusion, is your eternal life body. And you must know the miracle of your infinite Christ body because it is the one inseparable, immortal body of all who walk this earth.

This is the lesson you will find yourself returning to very frequently. This is the lesson your soul will call to your attention repeatedly. This is the lesson that will make you feel incomplete until you are the living lesson.

And now while you are expanding consciousness to the full depth of your being, let's take a look at your patient the one who will come to you and say, "I have a problem." You have just learned beyond doubt who you are. Now ask yourself this: who is your patient? This is a very crucial question. In spiritual healing you must identify your patient correctly. You must not judge by the appearance of form. Do you think your patient is a white male about thirty years old? If so you have already lost the case. Is she a black female about forty years old? Wrong again. You are still judging with a natural mind. That can never see reality, only its sense of reality.

Now let's look again without judgement. Who is your patient? Is this the Son of God or a human being? Is this the Son of God or a Eurasian male? Who is sitting in the chair in front of you saying, "Help me?" Who is your real patient? Now let's remove the mortality of your patient. No mortal is sitting before you, there are no mortals on earth. This is where you make or break your case. Immortal God is appearing to your mind as a visible mortal male or a mortal female. But the invisible Son of God sits before you, the one immortal Self is appearing to your senses in a material form because you do not have spiritual vision.

Now look once more - not with your eyes, but with your soul. Look at the spiritual reality concealed by your senses. And you will discover who your patient is. Are you ready? All right. Who is your patient? The answer is this; *you are your patient*. Every patient coming to you, is you. I am your patient. The I of you stands before you, the infinite I. There is no problem in I which is God expressing. God is one without opposite. I is God. I and the Father are the inseparable one. I God, the Self of you, am your patient. I am perfect, for I am the Father. I can never be sick, for I am all the perfect qualities of God. I am the immortal body of the universe and your senses are seeing Me through a glass darkly, as an individual mortal, with ailments, but I am the invisible body of all men, the body of eternal life. The same body that remained alive when the illusory material body of Jesus was crucified. I am the Christ body, the Holy one of Israel. And when you have faith that I am the Christ of your patient and of you, one forever, then you will have the secret of spiritual healing; then you will bare witness to the truth of God in every man, and the miracle of Grace will reward thee openly.

Every claim of a problem is a denial of divine identity because the identity of all is I, the perfect self of God. The real identity of your patient needs no healing. But rarely will your patient be aware of his real identity. He will be asleep in a material sense of mind and body. And so your job as the healer, is to lift him to his true Self and to prove that God is the self of all. This is what makes spiritual healing a true delight. You are not healing. You are not healing bones, muscle or tissue. You are restoring your patient to his divine Self. Taking him out of the belief in a mental created image called body. Out of the belief in material flesh. And your secret method, is not the words you speak, but it is your recognition within of his immortal life and his immortal body, which are unseparated from your immortal life and your immortal body.

Take it all the way to that. For God is the I of you and of him, and that I in the midst of you and your patient is the invisible divine substance of him and of you. Your realization of the one indwelling Self of you is the trigger. As you abide in that realization your consciousness will expand and rise and not by might, not by power, Spirit itself, will pull the trigger, with truth, to explode the myth of mortal man, mortal matter, and to dissolve the mirage, and to reveal the underlying perfection that never left your patient. All error, all sickness in our world, is sense hypnotism. We stare at God's spiritual kingdom; infinite, eternal, immortal, perfect Self, and the world mind interprets this infinite spiritual perfection, as a finite imperfect world, with imperfect selves, spinning in make believe time.

Our sense mind completes the mirage, by looking out at the One undivided, infinite, immortal Self and seeing millions of mortals separated and finite; individual mortal bodies, individual lives. And because the illusion cannot sustain itself, it deteriorates; body cells seem to die, organs refuse to work, life seems to ebb away. And new life seems to be born. This imitation of Reality, called human life, denies the perfect power and harmony of God's spiritual creation. It denies the divine Love that maintains the integrity of that creation, and it denies the allness of God. This total hypnosis governs our world and the human race.

But you as a healer and an Infinite Way student of spiritual truth, you must constantly know that anything less than perfection is hypnosis, because imperfection is impossible in spiritual reality. Perfection is the eternal unchanging nature of reality. So as the transparency for Christ you must prove this everyday of your life, until you accept the divine Immortality of everyone you meet, patient or otherwise. You will be proving:

"The earth is the Lord's and the fullness thereof."

And you will be loving your neighbor as yourself, in the true sense of the words. Best of all, you will be fulfilling divine law and the blessings of the Father will pour forth in every aspect of your life.

In the silence let your soul recapitulate who you are, who your patient is and the opportunity you have to prove that everyone coming to you for help is God invisible in a perfect immortal body living a perfect eternal immortal life and then live with that pure truth. The fruits you reap are beyond measure.

Stay with the silence. Let the glory of your own Spirit fill your universe with its magical substance. Feel the pulsing spiritual life that animates all who walks this earth and know that that spiritual life will never depart. We are immortals in an immortal universe and the one immortal that we are is God himself, for I and the Father are one.

You may not hear the second side right away so I would like to tell you about something I intend to put on the second side. It's about time that we started meditating together on world work, and so, probably toward the end of the second side there will be a discussion about what we will do and when, but I want you to know that meditation in world work will be called upon and it will be on I think Saturday night, Saturday 6pm. Every Saturday 6pm. Now that time fits in very well if you go by California time. 6pm California. Some of you will find it a little earlier, some will find it a little later. Here in Kauai for me or whoever it happens to be meditating on the islands, it would be 3 hours earlier. New York it'll be a few hours later and so forth. And abroad: South Africa, Thailand, England, Switzerland, France; you'll have to check California time. 6pm Saturday nights California time, and your assignment will come in the second half, at the end of it.

Let's be still now and remember that every hard saying is a teaching to open your soul to your eternal Reality.

∞∞∞∞∞∞∞∞∞∞∞ End of Side One ∞∞∞∞∞∞∞∞∞∞∞

In this lesson, so far, you have learned new dimensions of healing that you will not find in books. To be sure that these vital principles are included in your healing procedure, it would be wise to review them very carefully right now. Until the hard sayings have done their work in your consciousness. You probably have never really tried to live in your body of life instead of your body of death.

Mortals accept the cycle of life and death so they spend lifespans after lifespans living in mortal bodies that must die. At one time every person on earth lived in the sea. We were water creatures with bodies adapted to living underwater. Before that we were minerals without animation, without bodily organs, but if you reversed the scale of evolution and returned to your source, you would find that in the beginning, you were immortal. What we are learning now is the revolutionary truth that what you were in the beginning is what you are now. The *I* of you has never changed. You are still immortal and you always will be. There isn't a thing you can do to change from being immortal forever. The complete cycle of material evolution from a one celled amoeba, to millions of years of genealogical changes, terminating in twentieth century man, is one continuous time illusion, which has mesmerized the mind of all physical creatures; from the lowest protozoa to the highest primates.

"Before Abraham was I Am."

In one breathtaking sweep Christ revealed that before physical man was, Spirit is. Before mortality was, immortality is. In other words the Christ, spirit of God, is the same yesterday, today and tomorrow. God does not evolve. Spirit is perfect and changeless forever. The entire purpose of the Christ mission on earth is to take man off the tree of physical evolution, in which every man dies, and reincarnates to die again, and to lift him out of a concept of a human body that dies to the spiritual body of life, which is the secret of life eternal. You have a body of life.

Christ Jesus found his body of life, his eternal body and his eternal life. Not by physical evolution, but by awakening from the dream of physical evolution. Do you see that? By moving from the body of illusion, which dies to the body of reality which lives. The I of you, the Christ of you, is the immortal Self, which never, never, never evolves; which is never sick; which never has problems; which never dies; and which therefore, honors God supremely. You will never become that immortal Self. You either accept it as your reality now, or you continue living in a false mortal sense, a false body, until your mortal lifespan runs out.

"Choose ye this day God or mammon."

Mammon is that mortal body of death. God is the immortal body of life eternal.

In the silence let Spirit provide the inspiration and confidence we need for the dawn of a new awakening in consciousness, as our souls open to the inner Christ. Above your mind, above this mental world, in which men live, are three levels of Consciousness. They are called the three heavens. These three heavens are the sum and the substance of who you are. In Chapter 12 of 2nd Corinthians verse 2, Paul says that he saw a man caught up in Christ in the third heaven, that third heaven is your eternal Christ; your eternal Christ life which is your real and only life right now. The second heaven is your immortal Spirit. The first heaven is your immortal soul. These three heavens above this mental world constitute the fullness of your immortality and when you deny your immortality, you deny the existence of your soul, your spirit, and your eternal Christ life. And this, unfortunately, is precisely what keeps mankind from enjoying the fruits of the Kingdom. Like shutting out the sun and then saying, "We have no sunshine." Without the conscious activity of your immortal soul, you're immortal Spirit, and your immortal eternal life, you are the natural man who receiveth not the things of God. So another hard saying is;

"Keep your conversation in heaven."

Mankind has not heeded that hard saying. Our mental world keeps us earth bound, buried in the tomb of mortal flesh. Walking on a treadmill; which makes us labor for material things alone, material things that perish.

Your high levels of healing work will begin when you realize your own immortality. For only then can you realize the immortality of your patient. And this is the essential key to opening the doors of your patient's soul.

"Ye shall know the truth and the truth will make you free."

You are now standing on the threshold between material consciousness, mortal consciousness and immortal consciousness, between humanhood and Sonship, and you must ask yourself, is the Son of God mortal? You know by now that by believing we are mortal we are rejecting Sonship. John helped clarify who we are with this statement;

"Love not the world neither the things that are in the world. If any man love the world the love of the Father is not in him."

Mortals love the world and they seem to die, because this world is our mortal imitation of the Kingdom. Immortals love only the Kingdom. They will not accept an adulterated version of the Kingdom. Know this:

"All that is in the world, [all], the lust of the flesh, the lust of the eye, the pride of life is not of the Father but is of the world."

"And the world passeth away and the lust thereof, but he that doth the will of God abideth forever."

Let's catch a point there. When you cross over from mortality to immortality, without dying, you are doing the divine Will. You are accepting immortal God as your Father., here and now. You are declaring your birth right to live now in God's perfect Kingdom. You are obeying God's Will. And that crossing over, that transformation in consciousness, is your spiritual rebirth. It should be clear from many signs we have received, that your immortality is really the only direction you can go to seek enlightenment. The mission of Christ Jesus pure and simple is to lead mankind away from death to life; from mortality to immortality. And if you do not make that move, now, while you're alive and have the right to choose, it'll be too late when the right to choose is taken away.

"Turn ye and live."

How perfectly clear. Every word of Spirit rings with new meaning. Turn from death to life, from mortality to immortality, from matter that dies, to spirit that lives. Lazarus, a wealthy man, made the transition in consciousness, and walked out of a material tomb in his immortal body. Peter made the same transition, walked out of prison. And there be some among you now, who will never see death, because the immortal Son of God, realized, is your life eternal. Actually, your life work is just beginning. Everything you have learned is to prepare you for rebirth, from the world mind, to your divine soul; from the body of death, to the body of life.

"What fools these mortals be."

When Shakespeare said that through one of his characters, he was chastising us for clinging to dying images. We have prayed to God to help us whenever we suffer. We've failed to realize however, that divine love can never leave us. And in our human conflicts we've overlooked one of the great truths that makes all sense of suffering unnecessary: we are not in a mortal body that suffers. Every physical problem is based on our unconscious rejection of the immortal body in which we truly live and in which our divine Self is living now.

Remember Paul, how he walked the earth unafraid teaching the revolutionary Christ message? Because he had discovered his immortal body was under divine protection. The disciples transcended to their immortal bodies and followed Christ Jesus to the three heavens. And today some of us are ready to embark on that same exciting journey in consciousness. Let us break the hypnotism by awakening from the dream. The dream that God made suffering bodies, that God made bodies that grow old and deteriorate.

Let us love the Father who loves us. I am not separated from God. There is no place where God's immortal body separates and part of it becomes mortal. The life of God flows in God's infinite body. I am that infinite divine body, because no other body exists. I am that infinite divine life, because no other life exists. I am that perfect life, because the Father commands me to, "be ye perfect." And my perfect life is immortal, now, alive forever. I will never die, I am immortal life. The same one infinite immortal life that is the life of Christ, Buddha, Krishna, and all Sons of God; there is no other life.

I have never seen your body and you have never seen mine. We live in one invisible body which never knows pain, suffering or age. We are ageless, eternal life substance permanently alive. We have no place to lay our heads because we are incorporeal, we are Spirit. We do not live inside the illusion of mortal flesh. We have no finite form. We are the invisible temple of God. We are the only body on earth, alive everywhere, simultaneously, and without interruption. We are the one invisible body of the so-called human race that walked in ancient civilizations, the human race that walks today, and the human race that will appear in every tomorrow. We are the eternal body of God. Always perfect, always manifesting the perfect qualities of our perfect Father. All imperfection is impossible. Perfection is always present. Imperfection is always in the dream. God is the immortal substance of the universe and anything that is not immortal is unreal.

During the next month while you secretly and silently practice reminding yourself that you are immortal, something wonderful is going to happen; an opportunity will arise for you to heal another individual. That person may come to you and say, "You are a student of spiritual healing and I am in great pain, will you help me?" When that individual comes to you very much in distress, how are you going to meet this request? What will you try to accomplish? First;

"Fear not."

Fear is a denial of the presence of God. The moment you're in a state of fear you're denying God is there. So if you fear, steady yourself with the knowledge that only God is there; not even you or your patient, and that God can never go away. When you catch that you find a great release. No matter what you see or hear, only God is happening, and only God is present. It's truly a great release. Now this patient is your opportunity to prove that God is all, that the only life in your room is the life of God.

Now comes a big addition a big change in your healing technique. You are immortal. All month you'll be practicing that you are immortal. But now stop! Look at your patient. What do you see? Do you see a physical man, physical woman in distress? Did God create men or women in distress? Do you see another mortal? Did God create mortals? Are you getting the point? Because only God is present. There are no mortals. Just as you are immortal so is your patient. Makes no difference whether your patient is ninety years old or five years old. Stop fearing, stop worrying, stop doubting, know the one truth: The person sitting in your room is immortal. Every person who ever comes to you, is as immortal as you are. When you know this, you will feel a great weight fall from your shoulders. When you accept the person's immortality, it'll be because, you have accepted your immortality.

More healings have failed because mental teachings try to heal mortal patients with mortal practitioners. And the healing of Christ Jesus succeeds, because being immortal he realized the immortality of everyone who approached him for help. No successful spiritual healer has ever had a mortal patient and has never treated a mortal condition, because his so-called patients are all immortal, unconditioned.

You have received this vital information because you are now ready for it. Now apply it. Daily build your consciousness by realizing that only immortal life is here on earth. In your contemplations be alert, for inner wisdom about your own immortal life and the immortal life of the entire human race. We have all been entertaining angels unawares, but it is now your time to crack the shell of mortality; to discover the immortal Kingdom of Spirit in which you really live.

World Work

During the past twenty five years many of us have joined in world work with a great deal of success I think and often a few wonderful surprises. World work is something you do from your living room or wherever you meditate. Groups are invited to join us as we start this work now. Groups and individuals. We would like to begin these world work meetings starting at once. Every Saturday at 6pm California time., let us set aside one hour in which we join around the country and abroad to bring spiritual light to a world which needs all the light we can release.

Today the conflict seems to be bubbling over in China, so perhaps that's where we should start. Let us make, "peace in China," the subject of our meditation. But let's change that to something else to make it possible to attain that peace. Let our theme be, "Immortality in China." And then we can use the new spiritual wisdom that we have received today.

Suppose we run through it briefly together, we may run out of time, but if not, we'll try to cover it as well as we can. Here's our first step;

Look past the headline events in China. Look past the bloodshed, past the tyranny, past the horror of a nation at war against itself. Instead let us look at the reality.

God is happening. Where the world sees genocide, where a brother dies from a brother's hand. We must ask does God create a bloody China? Of course not. We are seeing a world illusion on the screen of the world mind. We are looking at mortals in turmoil, where mortals do not exist. *"Pick up your bed,"* rise in consciousness, there is no mortal. *"The earth is the Lord's and the fullness thereof."* Immortal God everywhere, is the only life, the only body, One immortal Self, at peace forever, standing now behind the image of mortals at war.

In your fidelity to God accept the immortality of every resident of China. Whether he be a student, soldier, or member of the government. Let the names and the forms fade away. The immortality of China, the immortal Son of God, is now today, this moment, the identity of all China, past, present and future. Within you, feel My peace and watch the lie fade away.

"My peace I give unto you, not as the world giveth, give I unto you."

And now one more step; Who is meditating? Are you in your soul? Are you in the peace of your soul, or in your mind? Are you in your Spirit, or in a body of flesh? Are you Immortal, or human? Do you see? When you have accepted that you are Immortal, that you are the immortal I Christ, you will recognize the immortality of the Chinese people.

So now, let us drop the concept of being in a mortal form, governed by mortal law, as the I of you recognizes the I of China, recognizes the One divine life of all nations; recognizes the one immortal Self of all nations, and now you are a channel for the perfect immortal law of God. That realized oneness, translates divine power, into divine peace, harmony and love.

TAPE 4

Are You Still A Body Prisoner?

Herb: From soul to soul, spirit to spirit greetings of the heart in oneness from the island of Kauai. It is such a wonderful feeling to be with you again to share the words of the Father.

You may remember that before the crucifixion of Jesus, Pilate offered the angry multitudes a choice. Among the prisoners was a murderer named Barabas. According to tradition, Pilate could release one prisoner and only one so he cried out, "Which one should I release, this one who committed murder at the insurrection or the King of the Jews?"

Perhaps we should point out the symbolism of this choice. The real choice was not between one man or another man. Mankind was being told that every man has a choice between death and life. You can continue to live in a body that dies, or you can elect to live in a body that is eternal. That choice has never really been offered to mankind clearly but it is there always. Pilate himself was a symbol of "world mind" and its reliance on the authority of physical power.

Now he gave the crowd a second choice they wished to release Barabas, he was uncertain, so he cried again, "Then what should I do to him who ye call the King of the Jews?" And the angry cry came back, "Crucify him!" And so again the symbolism is that eternal life was being rejected and death - human life in a body that dies - was to be released. And I'd like you to remember that broad symbolism.

At that time the eternal Christ body of Jesus which had performed life giving miracles on earth was unknown to the human race. Man spat upon that life. But unaware that they were defiling their own eternal body. They scourged him, they mocked him and in their mockery they did a strange thing. Blinded to life, hypnotized by materialism they were compelled by spirit to clothe the body of Jesus in purple to mock him as a false King of a false kingdom. That was their purpose but spirit had another purpose. Spirit was talking to mankind. It was saying that all men live in the illusion of flesh except this one whom the mocking crowd had clothed in purple. The color purple was the hand of spirit identifying for us the eternal body of the one called Jesus the Christ. Barabas of course is a symbol of human materialism dead to his own immortality, to his own immortal body, to his own eternal life.

Today we are still prisoners in our physical sense of body. Two thousand years in human bodies. When the Holy Ghost breaks that illusion for you, you will experience a strange and wondrous peace, peace that passeth understanding. Ignorance, superstitions of your human mind manifesting as material laws, material concepts will be revealed as mirage. Human will with its many detours will dissolve and God's will express as your living thought. The kingdom of God's creation will no longer be a stranger to you. Your new body will look exactly the same to everyone who sees you. Your children, your friends will see the same body where they see you. But you, you will know that a transformation has taken place. To you good and evil will no longer clearly be defined. Your new consciousness will not see good health and bad health. Impressions will be different. Your goals which once loomed so large and enticing, will seem to be less in the future but more in the present and already standard equipment for your being. You will feel a constant sense of rightness of confidence that something wonderful is living your life in higher dimensions. Something more wonderful than you would have even hoped for but had never realized. You will discover that error, frustration and doubt have all vanished from your life. Something has been added; automation on a large scale and it moves you into projects that you have never quite experienced, in a way that is earth shaking and always with a sense of harmony that defies description. Out of the sense of physical form you live under grace, moving in the rhythm of God, fulfilling the divine plan in you. Perhaps you have already discovered that as your healing consciousness is strengthened and the release of healing power increases in you that there is also a noticeable release from your own sense of physical body. This change will be followed by a larger release from material limitations as you become aware of certain weaknesses you may have accepted and learn to eliminate them. Before we isolate these weaknesses and correct them let's give the universe back to the Father, to the source and let us stand quietly in the secret place of the Most High.

[silence]

This may shock you but have you been trying as a healer to heal human bodies? That is a no no and for many wonderful reasons. Even God cannot heal a human body. You see God never made a human body and God is the only creator. God made all that was made and God did not make five million human bodies with AIDS. God did not make twenty million human bodies with cancer or fifty million human bodies with infections, dysfunctions, defects, defective organs and so forth. Well then who made, who made these billions of imperfect bodies. Do you have a God capable of this insanity. Now here the spiritual healer must turn from the broad way that leads to destruction and follow the narrow path that leads to life, life eternal. This is the place where you leave the concepts of mother, father, child. This is where you become absolute and really you have no choice. You must live in spiritual wholeness with spiritual integrity. You must know that the human body which denies the allness of God and the spirit of God as the only living substance in creation; that human body has no existence. And the best way to nail down your knowledge of the non-existence of human bodies is to begin with one essential truth. Please listen carefully and make this truth the nucleus of your healing consciousness.

I have no physical body. My patient has no physical body.

I have no physical body to heal. I cannot heal a physical body because God never made one. I am spirit. I am a spiritual healer. This patient has called me to heal his concept of a physical body and if I try to do that I will fail. My job is to take this patient out of his body prison, out of his body dream above his sense of physical body and my treatment begins when I avoid the trap of believing in two bodies, his physical body and my physical body and recognize there is one body present, only one. And that is the one infinite spiritual body of God. And that is the Christ body of my patient and that is the Christ body of me and that is the Christ body of mankind. This is spiritual wholeness and this prepares you to be a healer.

Now I must raise my consciousness to contact God. Now I must recognize the spiritual truth of my body and my patient's body in order to release the flow of power into consciousness, to reveal a spiritual harmony that has never changed. The harmony that always is. To reveal the divine identity of the one who requested the help. Above all physical appearances where there is no person to be healed, no body to be healed, no corporeality, no discord only the spirit of God, the image and likeness of God, the temple of the Living God. You see the temptation to improve humanhood is the trap and when you start off on that foot you're moving away from Mecca. When you accept a graven physical image you are the blind leading the blind. You must live above the belief in human substance drawing eternal substance from Christ within seeing perfection through the single eye of Christ Consciousness.

Now let's review the first phase of treatment to reach the inner emanation of God the pure spiritual substance of God. I am that substance. I must be awake and aware that I am not finite matter living in physical space. I am not living for the meat that perisheth. God is my Father. God is the Father of my patient. They are not human. They are not human bodies. We are one imperishable divine substance. We are God substance. We're not prodigal. Above the mirage of form. Above the sense consciousness which sees form through a glass darkly. Above the limitations of human vision we know the truth: God is always right here and God is all that is here. Ah yes you have been tested. Finite matter is the test. Accept finite matter and you deny the allness of God who is infinite. Encompassing all that is real and spiritual. Accept finite form as reality and you are open to the never ending sense flow of imperfect human body images that have fooled man into thinking that men live in human bodies.

The second false belief is that there is life in human bodies. The only life there is, is the life of God. And until *you* are the realized life of God your separation from God remains the separation of your patient. The power of God's life flows through your spiritual body which is the one body and the one life of all men. And when you are willing to accept no less than that one spiritual life and that one spiritual body as your life and your body, the power of that life and that body will raise up your patient.

Your treatment is not yet over. You must know the truth, the whole truth to be free and there is no truth about man. The only truth there is, is the truth about God, for God is all. Do you have a sick patient? If you have you have been tricked into believing that God is not all. Just as your patient has been tricked into believing that he and God are two. To this false belief there is exactly like ten billion others. Mortals who live in a false sense of self a false sense of body and a false sense of life. Your job is not to fall into that trap.

Please remember no matter what claim is presented to you it must be false. Every claim is false. And that false claim exists only because the patient has accepted a life and a body that is not the life and the body of God. This is the source of every infection, every discord, every appearance of a condition, but, because God is all, who are these sick patients? Where are their assorted ailments? Ah, you see the mirage? They are the by-product of a mortal dream projected on a cosmic screen by mortal thought and feared by the same mortal brain that projected them. Now you are called upon to dissolve these mirages. To see them as appearances without substance. Without a law to sustain them. Without power. And as these appearances meet your awakened awareness that you and your patient are the life and body of God, infinite, these appearances will scatter and dissolve and flow back to the nothingness from which they came. Like mighty Goliath crumbling before the sling-shot of little David. Your spiritual fidelity to God's truth in you and as you, in your patient and as your patient will take men out of illusion, out of the sense of imperfection into the perfection of reality.

As the power of your consciousness of truth meets and defeats the lie the peace that comes upon you begins your "real treatment." Up to now you have been preparing the way. Now God within gives the real healing treatment. The sunshine of truth eliminates the shadows. The grace of divine self realized is the miracle worker within. Divine life has no opposite and this knowledge must manifest in a pure consciousness. On earth as in heaven. For thine is the kingdom and the power and the glory forever. The realization of oneness with God for you and your patient gives you the assurance that God is on the scene. And this inner assurance is the living Holy Ghost within you which now becomes the living Holy Ghost within your patient. And this divine Comforter opens the inner eye to inner truth to the kingdom of love, the kingdom of peace, the kingdom of indestructibility. Now we stand in the highest of the high, one, infinite one perfect everywhere and this so-called patient has no existence. There never was a patient. You were healing God unawares. And because God is the only there are not two now. You've come to that Holy place where the divine self is realized and you can say to the Father, "I and the Father are now one - realized." And in that precious moment, that eternal moment we stand now.

"Peace give I unto you, not as the world giveth, give I unto you."
"My peace passeth all understanding."

The glory of the eternal Father will be made manifest in the life of your patient. And in all those who come to you as you are able to reach this pinnacle of realization. That everyone who comes to you is God invisible. That everyone who comes to you is already perfect. That everyone who comes to you is the invisible self of you. And every time you are trapped into believing there are two, that there is a healer and a patient, you will find great difficulty in rising above that false notion. You will be denying the allness of God yourself and your patient will be trapped in your hopeless situation.

We are so fortunate to have these principles of Joel. To have them in books where we can find them again and again and to hear of them and to associate with students who seek only the truth of God. We are blessed. We are blessed because today the color purple is becoming meaningful. Yes they buried Him and before they buried Him they inadvertently clothed Him in purple not knowing that that was a symbol of the eternal body which could never be buried. That symbol is the symbol of your spiritual body which can never be buried. Clothe yourself in purple, weave your purple. Day after day know the purple of eternal life as your body, your only body and refuse, refuse to live in a physical body that must die because you're not living in one now. You're living in a concept. And the truth will set you free. Know that truth and you will be free. I am not in a physical body because God made none. My body is not sitting in a chair. My body does not walk visibly in a room. My body is everywhere of substance that will never die. Dwell with this in your meditations. Bring it to your healing consciousness. Expose your so-called patient to this inner truth of your being and make it his inner truth and the world will remember the healings that come from your knowledge of reality. Peace I give unto you but not a peace that passes, a peace so deep that within you is a well of confidence an inner knowledge of reality, an inner *I* which reveals to you the eternal presence of the kingdom which is your being. You are not separate from the kingdom, you do not walk in the kingdom, you *are* the kingdom. Rest

Tape 4: Are You Still A Body Prisoner?

in the kingdom of your Self, the kingdom of your Soul, the kingdom of God. Rest in your Christ body.

[silence]

This is the fourth tape and when we have completed this fourth tape it is the plan of Spirit that we know that we need not be prisoners of the body. That we can step out of the false prison to which the human mind has surrendered, that the doors of our prison can open as they did for Paul, that we are moving into a new era in consciousness, an enlightened era. When here and there across the creation men stand up and declare their divinity, proudly, unafraid and live their divinity and express their divinity and lift their fellowman to his divinity. Here one, there one and across the universe an army, a divine army, a circle of Christ. Be among that group, stand up show your divinity. Let it illuminate your household and let that light shine.

The Meaning Behind The Color Purple In The Bible

The color purple is a secret symbol used throughout the Bible. Unfortunately the metaphysical dictionary does not mention this symbol and various expository dictionaries dedicated to an explanation of the esoteric meaning of Bible symbols somehow also by-passed this word which is probably the major reason that Bible students throughout the world have been denied the important significance of this very very special symbol.

Purple: means the full measure of Christ Consciousness and more specifically, when the Bible says that an individual is a weaver of purple, or associates an individual with the color purple in any way, it is revealing that this individual has awakened to the truth that he or she is not living in a body of mortal flesh, but is one with the spiritual immortal body of God.

This secret was handled very discreetly by Old Testament Prophets. It's tucked away in the book of Exodus, Numbers, Judges, 2 Chronicles, Ester, Proverbs, Song of Solomon and Ezekiel. The New Testament writers mention a little more openly but not much, Mark, Luke and John all reported purple on Jesus just before the crucifixion and then in Acts 16 when Paul and Silas prayed in prison and the foundations of the prison shake and the doors of the prison open. The writer of Acts gives us a marvelous clue to the deep hidden meaning of that event by placing Lydia a "seller of purple," just before the event and immediately after the event to inform us that Paul was living in his infinite Christ body, the body of God.

And then in the lost books of the Bible there's a spiritual account of the birth of Christ to the virgin Mary. It's written by James the Lesser who is known as the cousin and brother of Jesus. Who was the first Bishop of the Christians in Jerusalem. And this is an authentic account titled "The Pro-Evangeline." In chapter 9 of the Pro-Evangeline it tells us that the High Priests were making a new veil for the temple and so from seven virgins they selected Mary to spin the true purple. Which meant to weave her Christ Consciousness. And while Mary was spinning the true purple she heard the inner voice and it declared that she was full of grace and blessed among women. Mary was realizing her true body was not the flesh. She was being transformed in consciousness to realize her spiritual body, her permanent divine body which was the vehicle for the eternal life of God. And that is what made this an immaculate conception. So the WORD in Mary, became flesh and dwelt among us. For every soul there must be a realization of spiritual identity which homogenizes the female soul and the male spirit and births out of this mystical marriage the androgynous Christ which is the individualization of God or Self realized. From this immaculate self conception your God-self which you always have been replaces the material time illusion which is called mortal and you are now revealed as the temple, the body of the living God.

∞∞∞∞∞∞∞∞∞∞∞∞∞ End of Side One ∞∞∞∞∞∞∞∞∞∞∞∞∞

Enlightenment is the process of discovering your God-self. Faith is the capacity to accept the qualities of your God-self even before realization, as it becomes clear to you that human thought and human vision are cut off from God, from reality. This capacity of inspired faith is lit by the divine flame of God's grace which leads you to itself. The journey from little me to divine *I* is your identity test which trains your soul. As your soul moves through the fourth world of the mind we react to the illusion of separate material selves or we stand fast with our mind stayed on the truth of God's words and deeds expressed through Christ.

The higher journey begins when we intellectually accept the one body of God as the only body in the universe and that is where you are right this moment. And when we refuse to waver from that certainty, when we awaken, something wonderful happens, we are released from the body concept.

I came across a poem recently by an infinite way student which expressed the inner journey in a way that I thought you may find interesting and helpful. It's called:

Awakening

We enter this earth-realm like a Christ butterfly,
emerging from a mortal cocoon, magical, wondrous appearing.
A breath from the one invisible life that envelops this world of love.
Wide-eyed and innocent we love every form and pattern this realm
presents to challenge a young life.
Moving with the gentleness of a butterfly,
we dance and play and glow with each breath.
Heaven is our world, a safe cocoon.
Out of this resplendent cocoon we become youth.
We love and accept with every breath, conditioned
concepts of an earthly realm.
Forgetting for a while how a butterfly, beauty;
looking to externals for life.
Our bodies mature and this life we call adulthood.
Secure in its cocoon of earthly pleasures,
begins its butterfly flight, in search of forgotten love,
questing for meaning, examining this realm of being
and pondering the source of breath.
We reach our autumn years,
and with each breath we take, awaken to an inner life,
glimpsing visions of an invisible realm.
We untangle the cocoon of mortality, embrace God's love.
Soaring in spirit and beauty as a butterfly,
in a swift movement of time,

the butterfly in us hovers on the truth that breath is of the soul,
that God is the love that transforms us to eternal life.
We discard the fleshly body, the cocoon;
and awaken to the glory of a higher realm.
In every heart and life there is a cocoon of love
that gently unfolds as the breath of a butterfly
to dwell in a heavenly realm.

I thank that student for that lovely poem.

On page 112 of the "Art of Spiritual Healing" Joel says,
"My body has neither qualities or quantities of good or of evil. It has neither sickness nor health"

Do you know any human being whose body has neither sickness nor health. Can you accurately make the same statement. Try it. Say the words slowly. See if they feel comfortable. My body has neither qualities nor quantities of good or of evil, it has neither sickness nor health. Did you feel comfortable? Let me remind you that when you know this is true about your body and also about your patient's body and about everybody's body in the world, you will know that this is what

Christ taught. And that Joel could make this statement because he was talking about the Christ body which he realized was the only body that God had given him and you and everyone.

Your changeover from a human sense of body with ailments to a divine body which lives forever is a fulfillment of God's plan that ye be perfect as God.

As you know Joel had several heart attacks but his knowledge that they were not occurring in his divine and only body, weathered the illusion, until in divine order spirit moved his consciousness into the fullness of his next experience.

"My body is neither large nor small," he said

And you can see him he was about 5 foot 2 or 4 maybe 6 but I think maybe 4, well maybe 2 but he was a short man, my body is neither large nor small. Now mind you he walked this earth as other men but he had graduated from the notion that he lived in a physical body. With simple conviction he said;

"My body has neither life nor death."

Now if you saw Joel walk into a classroom you might have assumed that his body was alive. He didn't agree, no, "My body does not have life," he firmly declared. Now he was speaking about the body which already appeared to him in consciousness. Not about the body concept which appeared to his students, the concept body which dies and does not contain life at all. You see real life can never live in a false mental image. And that body which can never be alive can never die. That body which is spirit can never die either. There is one body called human body and it is never alive so it cannot die. There is a body called spirit which is always alive so it can never die. Death is an impossibility. So Joel said, "My body has neither life nor death." Now can we stop a moment can we adjust our consciousness to this great truth.

Science have affirmed that atoms and micro atoms are the substance of your form. Science is wrong, God is the substance of your form. And God is spirit. Atoms are man's concept *about* spirit. You do not have a spiritual body and an atomic body. Your spiritual body is the body of God and will never die. Your atomic body is a sense of body which does not contain God substance or God life. It lives in a false state of being. And living in an atomic sense of body you must experience separation from God which always results in a house divided between pain and pleasure, divided between good and evil, between good health and bad health, a sense of life and a sense of death. Mortality never experiences immortality, mortality must appear to perish because the illusion of life cannot sustain itself. The quicksand of atoms is the burial ground for all who identify as mortals. Fortunately, Infinite Way wisdom teaches that we are even deceived by youth and old age. So Joel says;

"My body is God substance expressed as form, embodying all qualities and quantities which constitute God, the I am, the soul. My body has neither youth or old age."

Every word there is a spiritual lesson. If you are entertaining thoughts about youth or old age you are not living in your real body. God is not young or old and the spirit of God is the substance of your body. So pause a moment, go within, rest in your soul with peace with confidence, be grateful that your heavenly Father, through the Christ of Joel, is leading you to green pastures teaching you how to weave the pure purple; opening the book of life eternal, and inviting you to enter the realm of immortality for each ray of divine light we thank the Father.

As your senses release their grip as the mists of matter reveal their shallow layers of illusion our confidence in the power of truth is renewed and we are ready for new keys, new dimensions leading to the kingdom of reality. Says Joel;

"In my body, my real and only body is neither material darkness, nor mental ignorance, for God is a light unto his Holy Temple which my body is."

With this calm assurance you must answer every call for help. Your patient is always God the invisible substance of every form. In time the illusion of physical form does not fool you. The I of you and the I of your patient stand in oneness while the hypnosis of person and condition go through their little act. Big illusions seem to have more power than little illusions, and as each claim touches your purified consciousness it meets the Christ in you who judges no man. Now listen again please as Joel states truth that you can depend on forever.

"God unfolds, discloses, reveals himself as body temple, place of holiness and peace. God's grace maintains and sustains his body which my body is."

Did you hear that? If you could realize that one truth, and feel it so deeply that you trust it without question, you would experience a major step forward step in consciousness. Nothing in this world would rustle or disturb you. You would know that God's body, the body of everyone in this universe is indestructible and uninfluenced by the changing illusions in the sense world of man. To you God will always be saying;

"My peace I give unto you, not as the world giveth give I unto you."

World Work

I would like to thank everyone of you for joining in our world work this past month. As a group of Infinite Way students around the world we are now meditating in our homes every Saturday at 6pm California time. We'd love you to join us and we think you'll understand as soon as you do.

Tape 4: Are You Still a Body Prisoner?

Starting with this tape our subject will be the body of the universe, the very last sentence in chapter 9 of Joel's' book, "The Art of Spiritual Healing." That will be our subject and I'm going to read it to you, you've just heard it.

"God's grace maintains and sustains his body, which my body is."

Think for a moment of every nation on this planet and think of its inhabitants. The invisible substance of that nation and its inhabitants and of every nation and its inhabitants is the body of God which your body is.

Dwell in your real body now. Are you only in your room? Is the body of God only in your room? Stretch out to your infinite divine body of pure divine spirit. And when you hear or read about a plane crash in Brazil, an earthquake in California, an epidemic in Guatemala; meet that claim easily, confidently with the simple knowledge that God's grace maintains and sustains his body which my body is. You can meet every claim with this incredibly wonderful truth. You will discover that your consciousness of the body of God as your body, is healing unto the nations. Let's do it now. Rivet it into your consciousness.

The phrase we will use for our meditation throughout the world every Saturday at 6pm California time is the last words in chapter 9 of Joel's book "The Art of Spiritual Healing" and those words are;

"Gods grace maintains and sustains his body, which my body is."

We are moving through the invisible now in consciousness feeling the joy of our everywhereness of our eternal body which will always be our eternal body, which will never be sick, never destroyed, never defective, always perfect, always in harmony, always the one body of God is my body. And I have no other body. Dwell in this glorious truth. Let yourself be transported. Find your glorious kingdom of reality.

We're going to stay here in the purity of our soul listening, waiting and listening for that voice which individualizes in each of us, to guide us, to love us, to teach us, to open new doors, new highways, new realms. For this is the age of enlightenment. The age when men discover their souls. And with their souls discover their spirit. And with their souls unite with their spirit to birth the color purple, the Christ Consciousness which gives us single vision and makes us Self-creative. In your true body everything you need you create and as feel the miracle of self-creation you will say, "How fortunate that I was able to go the narrow path to achieve this wondrous spiritual quality."

There will be four more healing tapes before the Chicago seminar and each one will prepare us for new dimensions in healing. Joy to you for sharing today's message with us and may your day reflect the glory that you are.

Blessings from Kauai.

TAPE 5

LIFE BEFORE BIRTH

Herb: Soul to soul. Heart felt greetings from the island of Kauai. Once more we're bringing a message of the Christ to the Christ, which is a very pleasurable message and it is a great joy to be here to see that we have come to another place in consciousness. It is a place of high esteem but it requires a great deal of responsibility.

There was an old gentleman, a man named Melchizedek it was said that he was the Father of eternal salvation. If you look at Melchizedek's life you don't see very much of it. He's a shadow that comes into the Bible and fades out but while he's there Melchizedek does a strange thing, he receives a ten percent tithe from Abraham, the King of the Jews. That's fantastic. Who is this Melchizedek? Why does Abraham give him a tithe?

Listen carefully because you find that Melchizedek is a symbol. He's a symbol of peace, a symbol of righteousness but he is a perfect individual and the reason he is a perfect individual is that he was born without a process, he is without decent. That has a meaning that we all have to find out about. He continued unchanged forever. We are that way. Melchizedek was the forerunner to Christ. He was the Christ figure and all of the things said about him are cloaked in secrecy for a very simple reason. He ushers in an age and the same thing goes for Christ, He ushers in an age and we are the tail end of that age and it is up to us now to fulfill our responsibility. It is up to us to decide now between God and Mammon.

We have come to a place in consciousness where we are meeting people, people are coming to us. We are facing new situations and we cannot give a cold cup of water. We cannot be of a divided consciousness. It's time to wake up. We have been asleep too long. Being awake means knowing who you are. Everything in your experience depends on who you are. You cannot continue in doubt, in two selves, switching from one to the other. Until you have established one identity you have no right to represent yourself as a healer. And if you do know, and you practice it, you represent the kingdom and you will bless those who come to you for help and you will meet situations with spontaneity, confidence and righteousness.

But you must know that the number one truth about you, the truth that opens you to new possibilities, the truth you must express from dawn to sunset, from sunset to dawn is that you are immortal. You are immortal now. Not tomorrow, not twenty years from now, not in the next lifetime, but this moment. You are immortal now because God says you are. There is no truth greater that you will ever hear. There is no truth greater than you will ever see. There is no truth greater that you will ever be. Deny it, doubt it, answer to another name and you are asleep. Treasure it, value it, every waking second, respond to it every waking second and your complete existence will change dramatically. Success or failure, joy or sadness, the quality of life everything depends on your realization that you are an immortal being. There's a big mortal mind right outside, it says that you are not. It says that you are human and you can follow that mortal mind until it spreads an illusion of wonderful things before you. It will run your life for you and if you let it, it will create good forms or bad forms, good health or bad health. It will fill you with the good things of life and then rob you of them when least expected. It will actually rob you of your life. It will rob you of everything wonderful that you create and it will fill you full of false ego that admires its own creation. It will make you watch while it tears down everything that it has built for you. Finally, it will take you to your grave. That is mortality and its destination is death. Its destination is the opposite of life but immortality, immortality, is the true gift of God. The wise man says: *"My brightest dreams go up in smoke. As a mortal my life is temporary, uncertain, at the mercy of wind and tide. I change in spite of myself. The world mind governs my destiny and then it returns me to ashes. This is not Gods way."*

God says: "Choose ye mammon the mortal way or God the immortal way." God says: "If you live in the world, the love of God is not in you." and God says: "Spirit is not born in the womb."

Now that is a very interesting phrase, all around you are the clues about your real identity but instead you have been fooled into reaching for the imitation the substitute, even a substitute life and a substitute life is not going to get you to the kingdom of God. You must make a choice or waste another thousand years reliving a lie, traveling over old travelled roads that you've walked upon many times making the same mistakes over and over, but now the secret can be told, you are immortal because you were not born in your mother's womb. Jesus has been telling you this for centuries but you couldn't hear him; "I am the Way, I am the Truth."

Well, Jesus was not born like ordinary folk. Jesus was not born of woman. Why do you think he told us to be reborn? He could have said, "You've existed before birth so get back to where you were." Instead he told us to be born again. To get back in consciousness, to the same consciousness that we had in the beginning before the illusion of birth occurred. Now this is very important, so listen carefully as he speaks to Nicodemus.

"Except a man be born again he cannot see the Kingdom of God."

Again:

"That which is born of the flesh is flesh. That which is born of the Spirit is spirit,"

and finally:

"Marvel not that I say ye must be born again."

Rebirth is the realization – it's not the traveling back in time - rebirth is a realization that you were never born. You see Jesus had realized this. He had not traveled back in time. He had realized his identity.

"Thou seest me thou seest the Father. Before Abraham was I am. In the beginning was the word."

Do you see that? I am immortal Spirit. I am unchangeable. I am eternal Self. I have not evolved this way I simply realized that is what I am. That what is called birth was not my beginning. Birth was the beginning of a dream. Everything I was before the dream I still am. I too was reborn. I've traveled the same way that I told Nicodemus to travel. Wipe away the mortal mind pictures after birth. Wipe away mortality after birth. Wipe away the temporary self after birth. The illusion begins at birth. Birth is the place where the dream begins and birth is the beginning of your substitute life. When Jesus tells Nicodemus:

"Marvel not that I say ye must be born again."

He is saying return to the eternal life in consciousness which you have never left. God created you immortal, you have never changed.

Pause a minute and think about it. Relax while you know the truth that birth is the beginning of the illusion and immortality is the never changing reality of myself.

[silence]

I am immortal. I have always been immortal. That puts me under a different state of law than mortal law. It brings me under divine law and I will learn how to live with divine law expressing Its will instead of my mortal will. That is the purpose of truth, to stand in the Secret Place knowing that I am immortal and therefore the mortal things that disturb me are not real. There are no mortals out there all is immortality and I will learn how to live with that and I will learn how to be that and it will take me direct to the Kingdom of God.

[silence]

The true translation of the words of Jesus are, your Self always lives in the Kingdom of God. You are immortal. You are before Abraham. The illusion of birth creates the sense of immortal life but the eternal Self which always exists is you and existed before the illusion of birth, still exists and always will exist. Birth is merely the place where man begins the dream. That is where he changes to senses. To a dying self. But I am before Abraham, before physical man, before the birth of the world. Five million years ago the human race was not even human. There were just gorillas. Think of yourself before birth then. You see, you were the same before birth as you are now. You were immortal then and in the dream was a life of a gorilla and it's over. You even had the body of a gorilla and that body was the body of death. While you had the body of a gorilla, and the body of a human, your body of Life was immortal. No matter how many dream lives you had, you shut them out in one moment.

The minute you pause for a second of silence your real Self, your immortal Self springs to life and I am comes forward and the dream is put on hold. Every time you meditate you bring forth your never born Self and your born self goes to rest. "Before the world was" is the instant you pause and maintain the silence; don't worry about time it isn't there. The instant you maintain silence inside and dwell in the secret place with the Father in that instant the world of time vanishes and you are back before birth, before the womb and you are living in the Kingdom of God. Remember that every time you meditate you go to the Kingdom of God. Now let's put this world on hold and give our immortal Self a chance to renew our strength, to renew our spirit.

[silence]

Tape 5: Life Before Birth

Do you feel it? Do you feel the pulse, the rhythm, the harmony, the Spirit. Do you see when the mortal self is still, all that troubles you vanishes. All the little frustrations, all the horrors, all the suffering, it never was, it was always in the dream and you may come back to it, oh yes you'll come back to it but you'll know that all that separates you is a dream. There are no broken bones, there are no bad debts, there are no emotional disturbances. Get hold of your immortality for it alone dwells in the Kingdom of God. Do you see the distinction? The visible world is the birth world. The invisible is a no-birth world, the immortal world but the invisible stays with you. It has been with you for millions and millions of years. It is always with you. I can never leave you. Wherever you go I go, I am the Spirit of God in you, your immortal Spirit. When you claim Me as the truth instead of the world, which is a lie, then you come under a new jurisdiction.

[short silence]

We can see what we have missed before. The rebirth of man from mortality to immortality was the secret that Jesus brought with him. He came into the earth to demonstrate it, to lead the way. His immaculate conception, called a virgin birth, was the prototype for man who was to be reborn from matter to spirit and it is accomplished by a return to a spiritual consciousness that is invisible before the dream of a life when physical time began.

The purpose of Jesus Christ is very clear; He was to lead us out of our illusion, our illusion life. The purpose of the mortal mind is also very clear; it is to lead us into the illusion. We can get out only by returning to our Christ mind, which exists before the illusion of birth, by getting out of the world mind with its endless contradictions, temptations, torments. Oh I know it's a task, requires complete fidelity to the will of the Father, to Christ in you but it's this Christ will which we are forced to follow in order to get out. Which opens the gates of the Kingdom to everyone as we give up our life in this world. The Christ replaces our mortal dream with the divine life - slowly. We take the play away from mortal mind, from finite mind, from limited mind, from material mind and we begin to live in the body of Life. We put substance into everything we do. We do not do transient things. We are joining the Infinite. The infinite body of Spirit.

The mind body, which in the human, stated that we were not from God, we were not living under the laws of God, and so our body had problems. We were operating without Divine instructions. Drifting from person from personal will but now we're in Christ will, we're breaking away from mortality, from mind concepts. We're getting our input from God and slowly we're transforming. God is not the Father of the human because no human exists. While we were living in a body that was born we were outside the law of God living in separation, in separate selves each with a separate will and the result was that humans always were in conflict. They were at war with one another. One nation wanted another's land or its access to a river or its raw materials, vast armies grew to back their will. Each nation was committed to its own concepts and to concepts that support those concepts and on and on. One substitute for another substitute and always away from Divine will. That's how we lived in a human body, in a dream body, in a body separated from God.

Now we're coming under another consciousness. A new dispensation has arisen, a voice within ourselves is speaking. We're beginning to hear that Voice and what It says. When It says, "We are perfect," we listen. "Be perfect." While our heart is fluttering and our breath is short, go back in yourself before birth, you were perfect then and you are perfect now.

How can I be the Son of God when I am deeply in debt, when I am unemployed? Go back before birth and realize that everything after that was a total illusion. You never owed a cent, there was no money to owe. Your debts are as fictitious as is a person to whom you think you owe them. In the realization that you are spirit you will find gold in a fishes' mouth or some equivalent and your debts will be redeemed. Spiritual realization always brings release in one way or another.

[silence]

We are approaching a new level of ourselves. We have learned many things. We have learned to rise in consciousness. We have learned to meditate well, to know the truth, to know the non-power of material objects, but always we have found that somehow or other we could not protect ourselves from illness, we are always getting ill, and then we say, "Oh I forgot to do this or I forgot to do that." But that wasn't the case it wasn't that we forgot something we were going against the odds. We were living that divided consciousness and I know it and you know it. When we embark on a single divine consciousness you're going to go through sacrifices it is not an easy way. But I think you realize that it hasn't been an easy way with a divided consciousness either. And besides, if you're tired of the energy you put out on negation, on denying that you have this and denying that you have that, if you're tired of problems, if you have had your share and are still having them it's time to put all your eggs in one basket. And that basket is Christ. Who is Christ but the unborn self? Who is Christ? Is Christ a yesterday? Something that we learned about and then forget about. If you forget about Christ you forget about yourself. You are Christ and you are the immortal Christ. Christ who says to you:

"Thou seest me thou seest the Father."

Christ who says to you:

"I am with you always. I'll be with you until the end of the world."

Get wise. That's not another person, it's not another spirit, it's yourself. Into the illusion comes the Christ and He appears like an illusion and He acts like other people except that there's a distinction, every healing, every healing brought about by the Christ was brought about by His immortal self. Every healing you do will be permanent only if you do it with your immortal Self. That's what it takes to do what is called a miracle. Your immortal Self.

As we dwell in the immortal self now, here we get a chance to put aside our toys, our many yesterdays, we live in time no more. We do not live in space, we do not live in matter, we live in our immortal Self and It is infinite. You start out with an immortal Self and you think of it as something in your body, but you come above that and then you come to your eternal infinite immortal Self. I stand in my eternal infinite immortal Self and it will do for me, for itself, all the things that Christ did during his lifetime. Jesus Christ graduated and He left an important message;

"Follow me."

Follow me to that great land where all is perfect. I know you see imperfection, it is illusion. All imperfection is illusion because only God created the universe, and God created a perfect universe. All that is not God is not. And only your immortal self will tell this to you. Dwell out of the land of illusion, dwell in the land of reality.

[silence]

We are joining Melchizedek the Prince of Peace, the prince of divine righteousness, born without process. The author of salvation. And as we stand in the Holy place we can feel the depth of our own immortal Self and it will call to us...

∞∞∞∞∞∞∞∞∞∞∞∞ End of Side One ∞∞∞∞∞∞∞∞∞∞∞∞

I'm going to ask you now to list five qualities. You can take a pencil and write them down or you can leave them right on your tape and take them off the tape later. I'll wait a second so that you can grab a pencil and paper if you want to and we're going to list these five qualities so that you can have them for use in the future. I'm talking now so that people who want to get a pencil can get it and we'll wait a minute so that you can feel that you're going right along with it. We're going to use these five points in the talk here today and maybe it would be wise if you could jot them down. Well anyway I'm ready to start and I hope all of you have your pencils, and the first one is;

1. **My Christ Self, my before birth Self is present.**
2. **All bodies are sense images.**
3. **Nothing I see today is real.**
4. **Improve no sense images.**
5. **Sense images have no power.**

Now Jesus Christ has appeared on earth to show us the I am the way and He has said;
"Follow Me."
Before we were born He appeared on earth to show us that He was born of the Spirit, immaculately conceived. You remember at two years of age he lived in a spiritual body that was protected against death and destruction. You will remember that at twelve years of age he was about his Fathers business. He was living under the protection of spirit in his spiritual body before physical birth, and that's what protected his two year old body against the High Priest, and that's why he was about his Fathers business not his human Father. He was calling this to our attention. Just as at the wedding of Cana he addressed his mother as:

Tape 5: Life Before Birth

"Woman what have I to do with thee?"

The term that he used by the way was called Juval, that's a term used for a stranger, it was used intentionally of course. An impersonal term. The same term he had used for the woman of Samaria. A woman who could not give birth to spirit. That was the meaning of Juval. He was emphasizing that the living in a body that was before birth. He was living in a body that was before birth.

"Before Abraham was I am."

In short, I am - immortal. He was always telling us that he was immortal.

"Thou seest me thou seest the Father who sent me."

For three solid years he kept teaching that there is only one way to the Kingdom, that way is narrow. So narrow that few there be who walk that way. For three years he was doing marvelous things and healing everybody and the people in the world did not understand. He was living in the immortal body of spirit. And He knew - understand this please - He knew that the people He was healing were also living in the immortal body of Spirit. Do you see that? He wasn't healing their imperfections He was revealing their perfection. He was revealing that they are immortal.

"Spirit is the first born of every creature."

You'll find that in Colossians 1:15.

"Ye are Gods little children and have overcome them because greater is he that is in you than he that is in the world." John 4:4

"I am in the Father, ye in me and I in thee." John 14:20

All attest to the living spirit of God in you that you walk away from everyday led by the mortal mind and believe that you were born. Oh no time to face the reality. When an individual is born in the womb he can't be the child of God. Birth in the womb is not the child of God. You can't be one with God and be mortal. He's a mind image. Only immortal Christ is one with God and Christ is not born in a womb. Paul caught this, he caught the fine distinction and he walked in the spirit.

"He knew me before the foundations of the world."

Meaning, I was divine and complete before the foundations of the world. With this knowledge Paul lived in the consciousness of midnight; that's the consciousness before human hood, before the false dawn. Paul was never born and in that midnight consciousness he couldn't be held in a prison because he had no physical body. He was immortal. He was in the midnight consciousness, the consciousness before birth. Now we want to get to that midnight consciousness and we can. Your acceptance of spiritual truth, not lip service, but of spiritual absolute truth and no opposite, that is the essential ingredient. It is important to obey these truths that you first established that you are immortal and therefore you have no physical body. Let's try that now.

I accept immortality as my only consciousness. Everything born of the flesh in the flesh dies, that's a fact. I am Spirit not born of flesh. My life began before birth. What I was before birth was Spirit and I have continued to be Spirit, immortal Spirit. Everything after birth in the womb dies. Birth in the womb can't be Christ that is the basic Christ demonstration. Only Christ, only Christ is one with God. I must be that immortal one. To be one I must be Christ. I must be immortal. I cannot be human and divine.

[silence]

Now I am ready, I'm ready to learn the basic points. These points are necessary to the midnight consciousness:

"Because I am immortal my immortal Self is present."

That's your first principle. I am not living a human life. I cannot be sick or have pain. Mortal mind feels sick, feels pain, I never do. Material sense feels pain. I must say no to material sense, to form, to physical body. The body is a mortal mind image. Because of my immortal mind I cannot accept the forms of a mind.

Now your second basic principle is this: "All bodies are sense images."

Just as I must accept that I am not in a body, no one else is in a body either. Look about you, there is not one body. There is not another body and a third body and a fourth body and five million bodies. We are all immortal and we live in one immortal body. I live in a immortal body my neighbor lives in an immortal body. There is only one body. All bodies are sense images. This will seem difficult but immediately we will notice a new sense of harmony. It is impossible for one body to be belligerent, sullen, uncooperative and the same body loving, cheering, cheerful, anxious, to please. There are no separate bodies in Spirit, all are one and one has no limitation, no boundaries, no finitude. Your spiritual body will not be anchored to a place. It is never separated from God by birth or death. So now we dwell incorporeally in a spiritual body.

Your third principle:

"Nothing you see today is real."

Mortal mind is ever busy building an imitation world. But God is all. We do not accept death. We are interested in life eternal and that is the only life that exists. We have become aware of God's Consciousness as we've become equally aware of the illusion. We see nothing to resist. We judge not, we resist not, we condemn not and the reason is that we would only be judging our self, but, there is another reason - there is nothing to resist. I sit quiet now my eyes closed. I see all sorts of things. I let the images come directly toward me feeling their weightlessness, feeling their incorporeality, I impersonalize them. I can take about a half hour a day and see that there is no personal life. I impersonalize pain, sorrow, ugliness, uncleanliness, failure and their opposites. I'm learning how to live in no personal self. I'm beginning to dwell in consciousness and spread my actions with substance. I spend a lot of quiet time getting acquainted with my adversary learning his tricks, rehearsing my actions, reactions and above all the world has been reduced to a doll house. Even the big issues in life, job, family, friend I must learn to see their unreality because only Spirit is.

The fourth principle: "Improve no sense images."

This is another severe test. You are given a variety of images and many of them are needful of repair. Your first impulse is to offer your help, do good, to improve them. You must remain faithful to God. Didn't God make a perfect universe? Doesn't God have the power to maintain a perfect universe? Have you been fooled? Have you accepted the belief that something in God's universe is imperfect? Then the master hypnotist has fooled you too. You are trying to improve the imitation, and you are asleep. Spiritual healing is the very opposite. Always recognize the truth the instant you are given the problem. Nothing is wrong. Nothing is wrong. Accept the problem and then forget it and the person who brought it to you as well. Is that heartless? No. It is the truth and the truth will make you free and your patient free. The perfection of the spirit is a fact that never varies. While you forget the patient and the problem give him back his spiritual self and you will free that patient. Our fifth principle will follow in a moment. Maintain the consciousness. Five principles.

"My Christ Self, my never born Self, is always present and it's the only Self I have."

If I act in any other self I'm living in the imitation world. All bodies are sense images. There isn't one body alive that isn't reality. My husband, my wife, my children, my friends, the President of the United States, the Pope, all the nasty people who do terrible things, all the robbers, the murderers, the rapists - the rapists they are no-thing. You must know this about everyone you see. Nothing I see today is real. It is a fact. Four:

"Improve no sense images,"

But maintain the consciousness. Maintain the immortal consciousness. Know that all is perfect and is maintained perfect; and five? - five you do not have yet and that is coming up.

Your fifth principle is that: "Sense images have no power."

Well think of Daniel in the Lion's den, think of the lepers. Think of an army trying to kill a two year old boy and failing. The human mind cannot figure out how it can be that the human hand can never touch the Spirit of God. Sense images are manufactured in the brain and they have power over other sense images because they are also manufactured in the brain but there the power stops. It is within your power to stop manufacturing images. The truth will make you free. That is why you start with your consciousness of immortality.

However difficult it is to begin and go through these five principles until you have mastered them. I call it the painless crucifixion. An attacker comes with a knife, disease reaches inside your body, the rent is due, the children are going hungry. Your immortal self has the answer but where is that immortal Self? It is the same Self that Jesus presented to the multitude. It draws from infinity. It is free of illusion. It has no personal selfhood. It is one with Source. It is a consciousness that exists before the human. It is your Self before the world illusion. It moves above the world mind universe awake not asleep. The visible images all take place after birth. The invisible Truth exists eternally before birth and continues to exist while the illusions of birth follow at the same time. The immortal consciousness sees no images. The attacker disappears, the disease vanishes, the rent is paid by a mysterious stranger, the two children do not go hungry. Why? because you are seeing them as the Christ and you are seeing truth of them because you are the Christ and because they are the Christ. Christ exists before human birth, Christ is your consciousness of immortality, Christ is one with the Father. We are gods little children and have overcome them because:

"Greater is He that is in you than he that is in the world."

"If any man be in Christ he is a new creature, old things are passed away, behold all things are made new."

Do not make the mistake for waiting for things to get better, they are better. Use the equipment you have. The life that was in the beginning, the WORD is still the WORD and dwells within you. Free it! We are children of God and if children then heirs, joint heirs with Christ that we may be glorified together. Your hope of glory is Christ within, immortal Self of every creature. The sooner you start seeing that you are your Self the Christ, the immortal, the sooner Christ will sit upon the throne of your consciousness.

World Work

We have to do a little world work this time and there has been a change in daylight saving time, so check your time against California. We want to this time continue our efforts to learn about Self. Try to understand immortality. After you establish your silence try to dwell in the immortal side. Dwell in the immortal nature of your neighbor. Move across that fence and see that he is immortal too. Do that to the neighbors on the other side, to the neighbors up the street but certainly do that to him, establish his immortality. You'll notice that you feel differently about him and perhaps you'll notice that he feels differently about you. The immortality of your neighbor is going to be the immortality of the world. That is the consciousness that is growing. It is the consciousness that you require to make the voice audible within you. It is the consciousness of Truth.

So this Saturday at 3pm California time our meditation will be the immortality of your neighbor. I expect you to do that, to do it well. And I think we'll practice it for the moment so that we can understand what it is. My neighbor is immortal. I can take him by name or by appearance. Mr Richards is immortal. Mr Richards gets out there and he yells alot and his dog comes over and its not very nice and I dislike alot of things about Mr Richards, he makes noise at night, has his radio going or his TV going too loud. He doesn't know it but he is immortal and I know it.

I know that his immortality is perfect. And there's no other Mr Richards. I'm going to extend this beyond Mr Richards to my other neighbors. I've got this secret of peace on earth, of goodwill toward man and I've got to live in it day in and day out.

[silence]

I can't think ill of anyone while I think he's immortal and if I think ill of anyone I'm disbelieving that he is immortal, I am in a divided consciousness, I will not fare very well because I have lost my God. Oh this cleans things up so much better. We have to think well of everyone. We have to think well of even the rapist, he too is immortal. And pretty soon there is no rapist you see.

Dwell upon these things, let your heart flow with your soul, let your soul flow with your spirit. There is one universe, one immortal universe and we all live in it and those who know it are making the transition to that universe.

Let us be still. [silence]

TAPE 6
THE INFALLIBLE HEALER

Herb: Soul to soul, spirit to spirit, greetings from the island of Kauai.

Today we're going to try an experiment. We always have principles and we will have them today but we're going for a new depth. We're going to try to feel the substance. To be a real healer you've got to have substance. And I hope that today some of us or as many as possible come to a feeling that I have touched something new. We want to find the healer and it's very important to know that you are not the healer.

The healing consciousness depends upon several factors. The first is that you be awake. By that I mean that you be aware of the spirit. That you be immersed in the spirit and that the spirit of God is the healer. Whenever you're without the spirit you're without a healing.

One of the important factors in the spirit of God is that there is one immortal life and you can feel that life, you can be plugged into it, you can be it and you can share your immortal life with everyone in the world. You can give God to everyone who comes to you. They come to you with a hope and yet they're not reaching to you, they're reaching to God, and they're only reaching outside to God because they haven't find God inside. And you are to help them find the God of their own being which will heal them. That is the principle upon which we work. The immortal life, immortal life is the thing, the quality, the substance that we are trying to raise in man. We must lift him to the place where he feels his immortal life and to do that we must be living that immortal life ourselves.

The one false mind prevents you from living the one immortal life. The false mind which tells you, you have a body, there's a world, last month there was an earthquake, San Francisco famous streets were filled with confusion, Oakland's famous streets were filled with confusion too and all around the Bay area people were wondering what has happened. Man was asleep. Man was not thinking of the one immortal life and he needed it desperately. We must never lose sight of the life that we share with everyone on this planet. It is a one life. It is God's life and when you stand in the one life there will be no accidents, there will be no pain, there will be no death. You are under the protection of the almighty. And if you never do another thing you must train yourself and immerse yourself to always be in the one immortal life. It is the protection against everything you can dream of. You simply have to walk into a crowded room and there's confusion there, there's hate and jealousy and all kinds of feelings that people have amongst themselves. And when you walk in, you must instantly be in the one life and that will change the complexion of the room, the complexion of the people, the attitudes. The one life sets the tone and when you're not in the one you're in the many you're in the confusion, you're in the hubbub.

Let's see now what it feels like to know the one life. It never has any pain. It never has problems. It never feels an ache. It never feels that the stock market will go up or down, it's not concerned about weather. The one life is in a state of total harmony and when you feel this harmony, when you get into it you know it. You can be meditating and not feeling anything at all and suddenly you're aware of something new. Something in you has stopped ticking, something in you that you don't recognize. It's a newness, a peace and now you're in that peace, as you feel the deep satisfying presence as you touch Christ. The peace that descends upon you is unlike your normal consciousness. Oh, you feel peace sometimes but this is a new peace it passes all understanding. It is as if you can't think. Something takes hold of you. Something releases you. And in this peace you stand silent, wondrous, feeling like a child again without care. Nothing can touch you and better still nothing can touch anyone in your consciousness, and you don't even have to think about them. The peace descends upon you, it lulls you, it takes care of everything that is in the world mind. I feel no worry about the future. I feel no need to check my financial statement this month. I feel the need to have bread. The bread that feeds the soul that tells me that God is on the scene and now infinity is mine. The whole world will be still.

I am not in humanhood, humanhood never was here, it is not here now. What tells me this? I am not in a human mind. The mind I have now is the mind I had in the beginning and the mind I had in the beginning was before the world was. The Christ mind. The mind that has ever been on earth is my mind, your mind. The mind that is with you now is the mind of God. It is more than a billion years old, it is timeless, it is eternal. When you feel this mind, feel the miracle of it because it is awake, it knows all things and it is accessible to you. The one immortal life which will never end, there will never be a pain or a problem in the one immortal life.

We are getting rid of the world mind, the mind that always stirs things up. The mind that has brilliant ideas and always sees those brilliant ideas through a glass darkly. For the natural mind is not the mind of God. If you have a mind that is smarter than someone else, that is not the mind of God. If you have a mind that is worrisome, that is not the mind of God. You see that? We have a million minds, we have nothing. Oh, we can build skyscrapers and a war can take them away. We can build all kinds of phenomenal things, they won't last, they won't fulfill us. But the Christ mind, the Christ mind brings to your doorstep the very thing that you need. You need a job go to the Christ mind. Is your marriage failing go to the Christ mind. Whatever you need the Christ mind is the answer.

"For he knoweth your needs and it is his pleasure to give you the Kingdom."

What are you worried about? Give him the problem. He isn't worried about you. He knows who you are. Where is your understanding? What has taken your faith from you? You are asleep. You are doubting Thomas. You are wondering what today will bring, what tomorrow will bring. It will only bring you the Christ if you will let it and the Christ lives your life. One, immortal, life. When you accept immortality the words are not the acceptance. The way you live in immortality you do not sit around and wonder, you do not have a life to lose, you do not have anything that you can gain, you have everything. Nothing can be taken away and so you rejoice and you say to that pain that you have, "I do not know you. You are not my being. You are something that has been added. Nothing can be added. Where did you come from? Oh, oh I see you stole in. You started dreaming and you made me feel that dream. I dreamed I had a sore toe, I dreamed I had cancer, I dreamed many things." And then I acted out the role, because I have cancer this must happen and that must happen. I saw the doctor, I talked to him. He said, "This situation is very serious." And I listened, I believed him. I cannot have cancer. I'm talking about me. Me has cancer but I, I am the immortal life of God. I am the Christ mind. I look and I see, I see what is there. God never placed cancer upon the earth how can I get it? Only by a dream and that dream is going to pass away for I am going to awaken. I will awaken now in the Kingdom of God where the law is perfection. Oh, but I cannot take my human body with me. Ah, did I think I had a body? Yes, I did I was dreaming. The human body does not exist in the one immortal life. So then, I have to leave my body outside. But, I have nothing to leave. You saw Jesus walk from this earth what did he take with him? He didn't take a body. Did he take a human body? Of course not. And everyone who leaves takes a human body they think and they bury it they think. But I, am coming above the human body. I cannot encase the Christ life in a human body. Oh, that's what Lazarus was doing showing the non-existence of the human body. That's what Jesus was crucified for to show the nonexistence of the human body. And I wish to walk on this earth, in the knowledge that I have transcended the human body. It has no existence. It will be there in appearance tomorrow and the next day and the next day. But I will be working on the fact that I am not in it. I am not a human body. I am not a human life. Dwell with that, it is the truth.

God is one, one. Look all over this world and you will not see one, but that's all that is there, the one invisible, the one Self. And when you have awakened, you will be walking around in the appearance of a human body but you will be aware that you are the one invisible body of God everywhere. And you will see that as you develop this theme in you, the physical problems will fade away, the financial problems will fade away, all of the problems of discord will melt. Because you are inviting the presence of God to live itself as you and you will find that that presence does not share any space with another presence. The presence of God is unique, it is the only presence, it is the one presence, it is infinite. In that your human identity disappears, you are the one presence of God.

Can you feel a glimmer of that? This presence will teach you all things. It will tell you what to say, how to live, it will feed you and dress you and house you. It will do all the things that you need, but it will do something that you don't know you need as well, it will bring you a realization of the one life of the universe. The one life that is your life, that is free, that is never anchored, that is not confined. Are you feeling something within? Are you beginning to generate substance?

Now a woman comes to you, give her any problem, you can pick one of five hundred. But she comes to a confident you, you know who the healer is. You know this substance within you is the healer and you dwell almost instantly in that substance. I'm not going to heal you, my Father in you will teach you the things you must know. He will teach you that you are perfect, P E R F E C T. (spells it out) You have always been perfect and now you are perfect as God. And why do I feel so bad? You don't feel bad, me feels bad, the world mind has persuaded your mind and me feels bad. Does I feel bad? I, who am the very healer that you have come to? I am your Self. You're living in a state of duality, I is you and me is that little fellow you brought along, the one who is always complaining, the one who always needs something. When me is no more I will stand in the field alone and I assure you that I am perfect. I am the life of the universe, the life of all men, the life that never sleeps.

"Abide in me and I in you and you will bare fruit richly."

Now then what are your human problems? The minute you say, "I have a human problem," you're denying your Christhood. You're denying that God is the substance of all form. You're denying that God is here. You're denying that God's law is perfect. There are many ways to deny Christ. There's only one way to know Christ and that's to be Christ. You say, "Why I can't be Christ, heaven look at my ailments, I've got this and that and the other thing. Even if I want to say I don't have them I show them forth." And I say, "Right this moment you are Christ and you've got to find it out someday. It's important that you come out of the world mind, that you shake off the dust of earth. The only thing that you require to feel perfect is the sure knowledge of God's presence. Your destiny is God."

Let's see if we can lift up the Son of man in you, that we can build some substance, some experience that you have had, somewhere that you have experienced God. Do you recall any? Wasn't there a time when something told you that God is here? You couldn't touch him but you could feel his presence. Didn't something happen in your life beyond your capacity, that was handled by some mysterious stranger? We all experience the presence of God at one time or another and then things come into life, we forget, we rush with a mad throng. But that experience is a real experience and it stays right with you. It is always true and it's always saying, "Come unto me, come unto me, for my life is your life." Do you see the point? There is never a moment that the life of God is not your real life. And so on faith, in spite of your problems, you begin to accept that God is here now, loving me, upholding me, waiting for the moment that I surrender. Not my human sense judgment, not my will, not all the things I tell myself that I have and must get rid of, I don't have them, I wipe myself clean of that belief. All that I have is God. All that God has is mine. I and the Father are... do you see a new meaning to one? I am the Father. The Father is me and my name is I, I, I. Remove the web, step out of the concept, release man whose breath is in his nostrils. Well, what will I go to? Stay right where you are. I am spirit not matter. I am essence. My spirit is whole. My spirit is infinite. My spirit lives. Am I really the spirit of God? "Son thou art ever with me and I with thee." Yes, you are the spirit of God, I am the substance of your being, the immortal life of you which never has a lifespan. I am your eternal self which never has a human body, I am in the midst of you. "Come, be my Son." Now, is the time to honor the Son, do you feel yourself letting go of someone who isn't you? There is a presence within every man and woman and child, that presence must be lifted up. You must surrender to that presence, you must give all of you keeping nothing, to that presence.

Jesus overcame the world and he taught his disciples how to overcome the world. He left a record on the earth for everyone to overcome the world.

"Come unto me."

You 'come unto me' by accepting yourself to be Christ. And you live with that name until it becomes more than a name, until it becomes the embodiment of everything you want it to be and more. It is the Son of man and the Son of God, it was never born, it will never die. It is you, you are the Son of man, and when you realize that you will live forever, you realize too that the worst problem you can have no matter what it is, it cannot be real for you are an eternal Self, an immortal Self, living an immortal life. You have never been a baby, you've never grown up. And when you march to a different drummer, out of step with the entire world, it will be because you realize at last that you are God's Self living God's life. And ready to assume your true position as the love of God, as the peace of God, as the harmony of God, as everything that God is because that's who you are.

∞∞∞∞∞∞∞∞∞∞∞ End of Side One ∞∞∞∞∞∞∞∞∞∞∞

Tape 6: The Infallible Healer

Under the karmic law that men suffer from we have many, many problems that we constantly are being faced with. But if we break karmic law then we discover that we're in a special infinite freedom, a sort of wondrous place where you can be what God intended you to be. Karmic law comes at you as a form of limitation.

Now, let's say that you're unemployed we have to see through that karmic law. Before you go out to get your job take the nature of God into your deepest understanding, you'll see how ridiculous it is to be unemployed, whether you've got any skills or not. Who is unemployed? The minute I am unemployed I am not the Son of God. The minute I am looking for work I am not the Son of God. The minute I am lacking something I am not the Son of God. Suppose I turn that around, am I unemployed and someone else employed? You don't believe in oneness if you believe that. There aren't two people, one to be this way and one to be that way. And the very essence of your life, the substance of which you're made is the substance of God. Isn't God God's own employer, um-hmm, isn't God self-employed? No one can employ God. Then how come you're not employed? Because you do not except that you are God. And if you want to go by the name of Christ the Son of God, is Christ unemployed? No. I'm stuck all around. I can't find out my status.

Now, this universe is composed of God the Father and God the Son, and God the Son is sitting right inside you and has no employment problems. So why don't you just take the belief in unemployment, file it and then forget it. Why don't you be about God's business. God is always about God's business. Why don't you take God's advice.

"*In all thy ways acknowledge me and I will acknowledge you.*"

We will be a society of one. Why don't you take God's advice that

"*I and the Father are one.*

Is it beginning to dawn on you what you have done to be unemployed? You have said, "I and the Father are not one. All that the Father has is not mine. The Father is not always with me." And yet you believed in your heart you believed that you are a good person. That you followed God, that you loved God. Do you see how ridiculous that belief was? You have some fence mending to do. You had no substance and you thought that it could be taken away. You thought a job could be deprived, you could be deprived of the opportunity to earn a living. Do you see how little you have believed in the Bible? It's staggering. You're probably going off and claiming ownership of something, maybe a car or a home. You don't own anything. Have you forgotten what you have learned? There is nothing to own on this earth. Matter does not exist. You see you have lived in a false belief of a material world of things to own, jobs to get. It isn't true at all and until you come to grips with it you are outside. You're knocking at the door and knocking and knocking and no one hears you God can't hear you. The only way you can be heard is to be nothing. That's hard for you to do and you don't like to do it but every knee will bend. You must be nothing in order to be all. You can't be something. If you're something you've adulterated, you're riding two horses. You're Gods child but you're also your own and you want a job.

Now the best way to get one is to go to God inside. Touch the Father within, touch the

Christ within that's who the Father is, and put your problem in Christ's hands and say to Christ,

"Whereas I was a fool in thinking I was unemployed I have no need of a job." I have only one job on earth, to be about the Fathers business because I am the Christ all the rest is superfluous." Well you'll never know it until you try it.

"Of mine own self I can do nothing."

I let God do Gods work and I might be unable to stop the fullness, the plentifulness, that comes in the way of one little person who steps out of mortality into immortality into the painless, deathless life and finds that she is infinitely employed.

We have similar problems in marriage. Oh, I tell you that really is a problem isn't it? But you see marriage is based on twoness and twoness is one too many. So if you've got a two marriage you've got a difficult one. There has got to be a place where two come together as one and they come together in their Christ acceptance. When they both know they are Christ they have reached the basis of true understanding.

Marital problems are also based on first two instead of one and then separation from God. Of course, if I'm separated from God I've got all kinds of problems. Sometimes, when you can't find the understanding, when you can't get into oneness, when you're bickering, then the separation may cause the couple to find harmony elsewhere, because the only marriage that gives you full satisfaction and which fulfills the divine will is the mystical marriage. And so God says,

"Loose him and let him go."

Who is my brother? Whoever does the will of God is my brother. Does my husband do the will of God? Does my wife do the will of God? If they don't do the will of God how are they ever going to get together? You see people travel at different speeds. Leave husband and leave wife, leave mother, leave father and never above all depend on anyone for a living. If you're living under spiritual identity you're living under grace and your needs will be provided. Oh, you say you don't see how. Well, it is good that you don't see how because when you see how you will always be working with the sweat of your brow. You'll always be finding you've got to earn a living. Whereas in spirit one doesn't work for a living, one works for joy.

Open your heart a little bit, start to share. Realize that you have all God has you have infinity to share. Depend on no one because God is my sufficiency in all things. Now think it through carefully. You've got to be centered in God that's your number 1 priority. That's all you've got to do at all times be centered in God and everything must come your way it's a law. Spirit draws unto itself. Spirit will employ you because spirit is you but if you're not spirit or if you disclaim being spirit or if you act like a human and not spirit how can spirit serve?

[short silence]

"Abide in me in all thy ways. I will fill your cup. You will bare fruit. You can never be without." Every problem in life is a problem only to the person who is not in oneness with God. That is your infallible healer, the spirit of God in you. When you nothingize yourself, your body, your mortal life, get yourself out of the way, you will discover the amazing truth that God lives your life. So climb up, climb up to that circle of God where all there is is divine substance. You see you've got all the divine substance there is but you're asking for things, you're putting the cart before the horse. There are no things to get. That long list that you prepared, those things don't exist.

There are people going to come to you and they're going to say, "Heal me of this and that." And I'm going to tell you a strange thing, don't heal them and don't be kind to them because tomorrow they'll be back with another thing to heal and they'll need some kindness again and you will be giving always what you don't have. Heal no cases for the simple reason that there are no mortal cases. See the case as immortality refused and see them as immortal life. And when you see them as immortal life, see them as they are in Gods eyes without problems and don't think your work is done then, you can't take a physical ailment and toss it out of the window. But now see if there isn't something in you, something deep, something real, something alive that you can share.

I find another level of healing when you brush past the mortal appearance as a nothingness and you are feeling your spirit as a somethingness. You can go to that person and share your one spirit between you. In fact you can go so far in sharing your spirit that you can have an experience inside which will tell you that you have shared your spirit. When that person to you is spirit, when you are spirit, when there is one body between you, you will find the strange sensation of having your spiritual body and his or her spiritual body in such a perfect state of oneness that it feels as if the two have gone through a process of being blended into one. You can actually feel the blending that's like a transfusion. And the other person says, "I feel better." You have lifted him up spiritually and even though he doesn't quite know it, you have brought him to a state of realization of one body.

Everyone who comes to you is God there isn't any other being on earth. I God, thou God, one God. Thank you Father I behold thy presence where the Christ of my being is. I behold thy harmony, thy love, I behold every need fulfilled. I feel a divine substance in all. Loose him, loose her, let them go. The divine substance animates their being. It needs no help of any kind. This is to be felt within sacredly and secretly and told to no man, not even to the patient. Because, you want to invoke the experience when he or she feels that divine substance that will be healing enough.

The children of God are bound together by one divine substance, and when you deny it for him you have lost it. When you see that your patient is the spirit of God, he has brought you the realization of oneness and you are benefited. Spirit is always working, always unfolding, always bringing you the highest. When you desire something, a thing, you have made an error, you've taken yourself out of the circle of God. You've given your life back to mortality. You must translate your life and everything in it to spirit. It is the only substance and when you step into another substance

Tape 6: The Infallible Healer

you have found something that doesn't exist and you are pouring your life into a substance that does not exist.

Do you have to tell spirit what you need? No. The wise man expects nothing. The wise man is a virgin he takes no thought. He lets the thought of God fill his entire being, he anticipates nothing, he seeks nothing, he expects nothing and he gets everything. Try to let grace live your life. If I were asked to define grace; **I would say it's a place where a person realizes that he is God and does nothing and God moves him.** God moves the whole world in such a way that you find yourself in the Kingdom of God, living your life without fear, without pain, without disturbances. You're living by the Word and the Word is quick, sharp and powerful. You're living with confidence. You're living at peace with your fellow man. And each step of the way spirit leads you higher and higher just filling out what you are. And you take this with you wherever you go. Always knowing the spirit of God is who I am and the spirit of God is the only Self in this universe. Only God is present. It is a great and wondrous truth and as you stand in the knowledge of God's presence as the only, you don't have any past regrets, that would be a denial of God's presence being the only. You don't have any fears for the future that would be a denial that God is always on the scene.

Now then you're a healer and you have no persons to deal with and you've got to remember it and you've got to practice it. God will help. God will not admit false thinking into your consciousness if your consciousness is the Christ consciousness. So you are never dealing with a person and your treatment is always God is always that. And God will do the job of maintaining the principle of love and harmony and joy for everyone that comes into your consciousness as the Christ. You lift one person, you lift two persons, you lift the world and it makes you a whole person.

We're going to have a meditation now and let the spirit take you out of your mortality. Let it make you feel that mortality is a strange word, a word that should have no place in your being.

[silence]

You are coming awake. You have passed the point of sleeping. Truth is in consciousness and it will take dominion, it will bring order, even prosperity all by itself. You have touched the Father within. There is no chance, no luck, no false belief, you are working on principle. And if you haven't noticed it, one of the things that make you joyous now is that you are standing in the Kingdom of God here and now. And your spirit and the spirit of all is mingling in the invisible Kingdom of God. You are touching the substance of life and it is you and it is him and it is her, we are one in the substance. There is no karma. There is grace in action flowing freely to meet every need. We live by grace, by the knowledge that we are the substance of God and that substance provides an overflowing and that substance does not admit any form of discord.

TAPE 7
SPIRITUAL SUPPLY

Herb: From soul to soul, spirit to spirit, greetings and love from the islands of Kauai. Today, I think we're ready for a spiritual supply. The type of supply that is quite different from the human form of supply and I think it would pay us to spend and hour or two, discussing the nature of spiritual supply how it works, where you get it. Plus a few things that may not meet the eye.

We're going to open our spiritual vision beyond personal sense and if we succeed in establishing a spiritual sense of supply that will be a tremendous advance, of course. But it's probable that we'll go beyond that. You can take a statement like;

"The Lord is my shepherd I shall not want."

Then you can interpret it several ways. You can personalize it, that means that you depend on God to keep your bank account well stocked, your health protected, a plentiful supply of everything you need and always you're depending on God to be your shepherd and you shall not want. If you're a businessman, you expect contracts to keep flooding in and if you're a fisherman, the fish will keep biting at your line and so forth. And millions of families believe that this is what will happen when they believe that God is their shepherd. I think some of the millions of families though who have children who are starving and people who are sick, invalids, about nine tenths of the world is not benefiting by "The Lord is my shepherd." and I think it's because they have a human sense of supply but God is not in a human sense of supply. That's shocking to some but nevertheless it's quite evident. As long as we have finite supply we do not have God supply. God supply is infinite and before we learn the infinite way, we have to make several changes in our consciousness of what supply really is.

Now you know it's not money because you have it and then you don't have it. Many rich men have suddenly become poor. So money in a bank will not be your supply, its not potatoes in a barn, its not shares of stock, or dividends. Supply is spirit. Now, you go and measure that into dollars, into dividends, into contracts. Supply is spirit it is not things. If you have the tree you have the fruit and if fruit was your supply and you didn't own the tree you would have to go everyday to get more fruit. But if you have the tree you have fruit, perennial fruit.

How do measure out six pounds of spirit or five hundred shares of spirit or ten yards of spirit? That's the one problem but there's another. It is very surprising and that's why I have to be sure that it gets into your understanding.

Supply is not income. Supply is your outgo.

Now let's consider that. As far as we know Jesus didn't own a thing. He was absolutely penniless. He didn't depend on anyone though, yet he seemed everything that he needed. For three years he was unemployed. I don't think he even accepted tithing from anyone. He had nothing. Where did his supply come from? That's one miracle.

The Bible doesn't mention the disciples of course. They wouldn't have millions either. They spent all day just meditating, studying, listening, for three years no income. Oh maybe they fished a little, did a few things like that, just picked up a few things they needed as they went along,. It wasn't easy but somehow something took care of them. But they were not seeking more things. By worldly standards they were as poor as a church mouse. A church mouse had just as much as they had. By divine standards they had everything that God had because Jesus had taught them the secret of supply. They learned that their supply was not outside of themselves. That made it very difficult to give supply to your neighbor, to give supply to the world, how did you do when you had nothing? And then it dawned on them why Jesus taught them store not in barns. Supply was not physical. Yes, supply was real only within and this was the secret. Supply in the world was what you took in from outside. Here today, gone tomorrow, temporary, sometimes plentiful, sometimes short depending on conditions. If a depression or inflation came along supply fluctuated. A fire or a flood

Tape 7: Spiritual Supply

could remove your supply. They didn't have a stock market but today if it crashes, well that's the end of you if you're buying stock. Now that is only the human picture.

Let's look at Gods way. Of course it's very different. You must open out a way for the imprisoned splendor give something. That doesn't mean when you start to give, you start to get. You must give patience, you must give forgiveness, you must give love, you must give cooperation, not jealousy, resentment, impatience. Your supply is what you give. The bread you cast upon the waters returns to you as supply. So let it flow from you. Don't try to get, give. Giving begets grace, it begets health, companionship, opportunity. All is God appearing. Infinity must flow out. The miracle of good begins with you first and then it will find its way back to you with extra to share. Well let's find out how it works.

This is the first major secret about supply. Everywhere is I now. Everywhere is I now. I is your name. I and the Father are one. Are you cemented in that relationship? Are you constantly aware of it, I and the Father are one. One is everywhere now. You are everywhere now. If you understand the universal nature of I, Now, Everywhere the secret of supply will soon unfold. You depend on no man for supply because I am the I of everyone. I do not seek supply, I am supply. I am infinity. I am infinite supply. I am the infinite invisible. As I acknowledge my infinite I, I touch infinite spirit. I touch it everywhere. I forgive all. I love all. I accept everyone now. That's your network, don't disrupt it. You love everyone. You accept everyone, You forgive everyone and you are everyone. You are everyone. When my love goes out to I infinite, it automatically comes back to me because I am the same I everywhere. Whatever I give to I, comes back to I. If I give forgiveness it bounces right back. By loosing it I receive it. If I let out the substance of supply it circulates right back to me. Everything I need I embody within me. If I want love, the more love I give out the more I get. Do you see that? If I give love here it comes back as friendship, cooperation, a home, transportation, translated by the power of I. You don't get back what you give, it is translated by the power of I, into whatever I need. Do you believe that? It works, it works beautifully.

Let's take Moses he needed manna where could he go to get it. To his spirit, his spirit gave it to him and it came down, translated into what his people needed. Elijah, he needed food, there was none in the visible world, where did he go? Well he didn't actually go, his spirit communed with the spirit of infinity and a Raven baked cakes. Jesus needed food, the multitudes were hungry and there was no place to get food except God, spirit. But he was spirit, he didn't have to tell spirit what he needed, he acknowledged his own identity as spirit everywhere. I am the life. I am the spirit. I am everywhere, that nothing else existed in the universe but I. Ah, not only am I everywhere what else is there? We're talking about the infinite invisible I. Is the picture becoming clear? You acknowledge your I as the substance of the universe and its not a mortal I or a physical I or a finite I, but you must follow these steps and you must abide in I and you mustn't act out of character with I. You can't be I this moment and me the next. Me gets angry, I doesn't. Me is jealous, I isn't. Me is lazy, I isn't. Me criticizes, condemns I doesn't. So you must keep the purity of I always and I know it's difficult, but when you see the rewards the difficulty is nothing.

Only spirit is and I am that spirit. And it was Jesus' capacity to be true to universal spirit without opposite and it manifested to feed the hungry multitudes. Everyone received a piece of fish or a piece of bread that day, received it because Jesus knew him or her to be the I, the Christ. That's asking a lot of you isn't it? But you either do it or you don't and you suffer for it. And because Jesus, the Christ knew it and acknowledged it and realized that everyone of the multitude was I, the Christ, they were fed that day. As you build up your consciousness of I the spirit of God and prove it by letting your love, forgiveness, cooperation flow out, you are loving the spirit of yourself as well as the spirit of your neighbor. You are realizing more and more the infinite nature of I. Until one day no longer do you meditate as I, the individual who wants better health, better job or a buyer for his house, you simply close your eyes, fill your heart and your soul with spirit. Without making a specific request, the infinite I of you stands in the infinite I of the universe knowing, spirit knows the need for which an individual has come to you and spirit has already supplied that need.

Come let the one self rest in the joy of being the one. Experience God within. Close your eyes, I am I, I am everywhere I. That's your magic hold onto it. Always know I am I. I am I everywhere that truly is Aladdin's Lamp. That will be your manna whether it's the desert or in an earthquake or in a flood that fed Rickenbacker out in the ocean, that will always feed you. I am I everywhere. The God experience within your self becomes the manifestation of manna without. The God experience within became the multiplication of loaves and fishes without, out of nothing but the invisible Grace of God consciousness, I consciousness without taking thought about how God will supply you. Hundreds of multitudes and they all ate, five thousand men and women and they all ate, and he could have fed an infinite number because there were fishes left over, how many? Twelve and that is spirit, spirit's way of saying infinity. All this came from I infinite within, translated into the without. It was done without thought, by God awareness, infinity manifesting. Infinity manifested itself but only because, only because, there was one consciousness which knew itself to be I am. And we must learn to do this, that is your supply. We will succeed to the measure of our consciousness of truth, to the degree in which we practice impersonalization of ourselves and of God.

"Take no thought for your life."

This is a secret revelation that your life is God's life, one life. Never think of yourself as a separate life. Immortal, eternal, infinite, and as you practice daily, the boundaries of thought slowly wear away, until there is no thought and Grace becomes your way of life. God experienced within becomes the manifestation without. All forms become the added things, now you understand why;

"The place thou standest is Holy ground,"

Because that place is where your divine life begins and it extends over the universe and it manifests on that place, when you no longer adulterate human thought into the purity of divine thought. The consciousness of omnipresence, your omnipresence, becomes the form of supply needed.

"Son thou art ever with me and all that I have is thine."

Always the promise is present. Always it requires the awakened consciousness imbued with the spirit of God, knowing omnipresence is here without opposite, to make oneness tangible. Once more, the ingredients, I when I say I, I'm not speaking of me, I'm not speaking of ten, I'm not speaking of a room full of I's, I'm speaking about one spirit the spirit of all. Everyone in the universe combined is I. I'm not leaving anyone out. The spirit of God is not the person, it's the same for everyone, no color, no size, no shape, no human qualities. Nothing can be added, nothing taken away. It has no age, no personality, no personal characteristics, No good qualities, no bad qualities. I am in the midst of everyone and everything. I am the essence of everything now and forever and I in the midst, I am mighty. I am the universal life force. I am the substance of all form. Those are your ingredients, train yourself, tune your consciousness to the invisible, build you identity daily, carefully, of the perfect invisible, the infinite invisible in I. So that all are one in I. I am the perfect, infinite invisible. And let the consciousness flow with your life force, multiplying form as needed. As God is infinite, your supply is infinite. Now, this is your connection. There's one thing missing though, nothing will work without it. Supply becomes evident only when you love your neighbor. You can't fool anyone. You must give out love, forgiveness, cooperation. Otherwise you're not accepting I am everyone. You can't skip one person. Your I ness is sincerely all loving or you divide God's garment and your oneness with infinity falls apart. One final ingredient, seek no return, no reward you must love unconditionally by recognizing only the one spirit where every form appears. The rest is up to you.

∞∞∞∞∞∞∞∞∞∞∞∞ End of Side One ∞∞∞∞∞∞∞∞∞∞∞∞

Everything depends on how much you want this new consciousness of supply. When you looked to Jesus your eyes saw just the form of another man. You had no idea how he could be anything but what you see. You didn't know that he was infinite. Jesus was the infinite I, whatever you presented to him he saw it differently. He never saw fractions. He never saw a sick man. He saw wholeness. He was letting Grace reveal perfection where the human eye saw imperfection.

Now, you are building that consciousness. The world brings impressions to you, ordinarily you accept what you see. Now, with a new infinite consciousness trying to be born it is going to do the work within. It converts all impressions back to spiritual reality automatically, independent of your five senses which presents an imitation world, it preserves the original and it produces from the original within itself outer forms which bring the infinite invisible into your life. The infinite I consciousness does this for you, once it becomes automatic it's heaven. For a long time however it's difficult, but you adapt once you learn how to take no thought, how to put up no barrier, no judgments of the outer images that you see, no opinions, no evaluations, no reasoning and become detached - that's a hard word for some people to get used to - detached from the outer, knowing God is the only inhabitant of this earth. You will give the inner a chance to make the images conform to the divine plan.

We now know that God does not determine our supply it's determined by our belief, by our developed state of consciousness. Our experience of the I am, the spirit revealed by Jesus when he said, "Before Abraham was I am." He was not speaking of a man with a finite limited approach to life, but to him I was infinite. He was not enclosed in a tomb in the Holy land called body, he was spirit, infinite spirit, and he lived in the infinite kingdom of spirit. And you and I are being taught that as we approach that level which is the Christ mind our supply is maintained by Grace. We're also being told that we can attain that consciousness and because our way shower, our teacher is Christ we're being told that it is God's will that we attain Christ consciousness. The source of your being is God, your source is perfect, infinite, eternal and because you cannot be less than your source your realization of true infinity reveals that I and the Father are not two. Whatever the Father has I have in fullness and I must press on, beyond human thought to Christ thought. Christ thought must fill my consciousness. If I and the Father are one not two I cannot have a separate form. I cannot have a separate form. I cannot be in one form and you in another form. If I limit myself to the experience of my form I'm just another mortal, a branch cut off from God. To receive divine thought I must be the tree of life. I cannot even be an individual branch. For I am the life of the tree and life can never be separate from itself. Release man, release your false sense of life in form. Awaken to the one divine life. Never let go of that vital realization, I am the infinite life of God and then trust it to be your sufficiency in all things.

Now will you sit in judgment of your own life? Do you have a separate life? If there is someone, anyone whom God does not embrace in oneness? Who is it? Is it possible for anyone to have another life? As the life is infinite it cannot exist or be imprisoned in a finite form. The form must be as infinite as the life and the substance of the form must be infinite and omnipresent. Another way to phrase it would be, omnipresence is the presence of infinity. Let's hold that thought for a minute in meditation. Omnipresence is the presence of infinity. God is omnipresent. God is spirit. Everywhere is spirit, God and God is all. If God is everywhere present and God is all then every disease on the face of the earth denies this. God and cancer, Spirit and cancer, can they exist in the same place? No, where spirit is cancer is not, but spirit is everywhere. If spirit is there God is not. But spirit is everywhere, go deeper where is the cancer? Well, where is the cancer? We've just decided that God is all and everywhere.

If the phone rings right now and says, "I'm suffering from angina." Are you going to panic? No, say to yourself, "Where is the angina?" There's no place that it can be and your realization that there is no place where it can be will manifest as the healing. Truth in consciousness heals but it must be truth realized not words. You've got to feel it in your depths. There's no place for disease in omnipresence. That consciousness realized was every healing of divine law, every healing of disease by Christ Jesus. There's no place for disability, pick up thy bed and walk. When you face disease or disability in your healing work ask yourself this question, "Where is the disease, where is the disability?" And then relax. Omnipresent spirit has no place where disease or disability can occur. You are looking at an illusion, but 'you' are looking at an illusion. I am looking beyond the illusion. The infinite I of you must do the looking. The infinite I of you must unsee what the human eye sees. You see an image in mind called cancer or disability. You see that in a mortal mind, still divided between the belief in good and evil. You are serving mammon not God. It's not a crime. You must do this again and again and again until you have overcome mortal mind. Until you can see with the inner I, with the soul and you can then know that there is no disease there, there is no cancer there, there is no disability there. Suddenly, the consciousness of the omnipresence of God removes the belief in disease and disability. The belief is gone, you know it isn't there. You can look at an earthquake and the belief will suddenly depart in the midst of the earthquake. There's no earthquake here, there's no epidemic here, aids is not here, flood is not here, fire is not here, I am not here.

When I first heard the voice say, "You are not here." I was shocked completely. I was coming up an elevator and I heard it, "You are not here." I looked around at everybody in the elevator, we got off and I thought maybe I was mishearing, as I got off the elevator I heard it. As I was sitting with friends to dine I heard it again, "You are not here." Yes, it's a very funny feeling. I even looked around to see if anyone knew that I wasn't here. It's very different but it comes with the healing consciousness.

Your big question might be, what if I know the truth, I know it, but the problem continues to appear to haunt me. What if I know the fire isn't, but it burns down my house, or the earthquake can't be, but it crushes my home? All I can say is, it happened to Job and if you get the message from that everything will be revealed to you. In the consciousness of God's presence, in the knowledge of the perfection of God's presence you are assured that there is no disease, no disability, no disaster, you are also assured of continuous supply. God never needs a thing. Christ consciousness maintains itself, every need is met, whatever form is needed will appear.

Now let's look at the omnipresence of infinity. You're walking in infinity all the time because it's omnipresent. At any point of infinity, infinity is still omnipresent. Infinity is infinite from any point you touch it in the spirit. Can God's infinity be limited? No. Can omnipresence be limited? No. Then God cannot be limited. Can God's body be limited.? No. Therefore God cannot be in a limited form." Son all I have is thine." Can your body be limited? Before you answer that, think. God is the substance of all form, why? Because God is infinite and God is all. Your body cannot be limited, therefore where is your body? Stop and think of yourself. You cannot be everywhere and in a body, and you are everywhere. Your hold unfoldment depends on I everywhere and therefore you cannot be in a body, but if you don't know it, it cannot function for you. You should take time to know I am not in a form. I am not in a place. I am omnipresent. I am everywhere. You must know this, you must be conscious of it until it's an automatic thing. If you take a half hour a day to recognize the omnipresence of your I you will be doing yourself a favor.

When omnipresent God offers you everything, how can you be limited? How can anything in you be limited? That knowledge, that I am one with God who is infinite supply and omnipresent, gives you pure truth that you are invisible supply. Wherever your form is you are invisible supply. Because, the you that has infinite supply is the infinite invisible which you acknowledge. Practice that, you'll find it very worthwhile. You acknowledge yourself to be the infinite invisible and it is the substance of everything visible and it remains your infinite supply forever. You don't even have to pray for it. Your awareness of infinity determines its appearance. Knowledge appears as form, spiritual knowledge. If you are living, moving, having your being in the presence of God, like the Prophets, that presence becomes your shelter, your protection, your security, your everything. Just to hold the presence of God in consciousness and to know that I am this presence without opposite, touches the infinite presence itself. And this realization is the power of multiplication, even the raising of the dead.

Now, let us be still, impregnated with the living Word, and miracles happen. No mental power. Do not demonstrate anything. The presence of God will demonstrate itself as form. Now, ten minutes from now, it has to demonstrate itself as form in your life. We want to hold this. We're asking for nothing. We're merely knowing the oneness. The I that is the universe, the I that I am, I cannot be cut off from God, who is spirit and that same spirit I am. It's an incredible truth that God and I are one, of the very same spirit and there's only one spirit which God is, which I am.

Meditation Times & World Work

Well, we have one more talk to go and then we're off to Chicago. The Easter Seminar will take place at the weekend of Easter, starting on a Thursday night ending on a Monday morning. I think it's probably the 16th I don't have it in front of me but I think it's the 16th. And we invite all of Chicago to turn out and the next town and the next town and the next town. We have room for you, we have an infinite conference room and we want to share the healing experience. This has been a preparation, we want to now get into it. And so you can be sure that the last talk will further that preparation.

As far as our Saturday meditation, let us take into consciousness that disease and disability are impossible, in the realized presence of infinite spirit as the omnipresent truth. In the realized presence of spirit, of infinite spirit as the realized omnipresent truth. In fact if you cared to, you can join me every morning at 6:30 am. Hawaii time is 6:30 a.m. The Saturday meditations for example are now at 6 o clock California time and I will join you at 4 o clock which is our time here. But for these morning meditations I'm going to do them at 6:30 a.m. I'm sorry if it's a little later than you can spare. I'm doing them here at 6:30 a.m. in Kauai so you will have to see

Tape 7: Spiritual Supply

what time it is, its 8:30 a.m. in California and you can go from there around the country and abroad. I'm pretty sure that everything you experience will be the fruit of the spirit and I'd like to speed up our meditations, frequency that is, so that we can really from now until Chicago get into the mood of it. Show up there sort of ready for anything. So that will be 6:30 here, 8:30 California everyday, everyday that you can make it.

Even on Christmas morning, we want to make this year end the spring board for a beautiful expression in 1990. Because during the coming year it is our hope that we will see all of you again and hear from you in many ways but mostly, we would like to know that the message has taken root, so that you won't be looking for Christmas once a year but Christmas everyday and by that I mean Christmas, Christ mass everyday. A chance to know the Christ within is not a one day a year, it's a joy every minute and we wish to inculcate the deep need and deep reward of being aware of Christ every single second. Christ wherever you look, so your instant reaction to anything, is not what my eye sees or what I feel. But how does Christ see it? That will become an automatic thing. A thing that we hope will change this world. This is definitely a spiritual age and this is definitely the time when man awakens from the mortal sleep. And we are going to further that day, so that it comes upon you as a much cherished reward for your effort, in remembering that everyday is Christ day. Going to see you soon and I thank you for being with me throughout this year and we're going to share a lot of experiences in the forthcoming year. By the way look for your tape later in January about January 15th. Until we meet soon. Aloha.

TAPE 8

FREEDOM FROM MIND

Herb: Soul to soul, spirit to spirit. Greetings from the island of Kauai.

Just a reminder that March 1st is the cut off date for your reservations to the April Seminar. That gives you about a month and a half to mail in your reservations. We have a very beautiful convention hall with very comfortable and airy rooms and a special pool for your enjoyment, lots of facilities including a modern gymnasium; its all very beautiful and I'm sure you'll be delighted with it.

A problem that you may have felt is that Christ teaches; "*take no thought for your life.*" Again you find in the teaching another statement. At the same time you are asked to take no thought, you are told, I am, the Father and you are one. I and you, I the Father and you the Son are one. "*I in the midst of you am mighty.*" Creation is greater than the human self. Greater is he that is within you than he that is in the world. There are many other truths that you are supposed to remember and I call this to your attention so that when the call comes for help, when you're faced with a child who has leukemia, or an adult stricken with paralysis, there is a tendency to think the truths that you know, which is the exact opposite of take no thought. You may find this very confusing and so it's important to learn how to face the situation with a clear channel.

The answer is really very simple to resolve the apparent contradiction. The solution lies in a matter of sequence. You don't take no thought and try to remember these laws at the same time. And if you can't go right into take no thought you simply remember the situations, remember the phrases, remember all the truth that you know very briefly, your taking thought consciously, but its getting you in the atmosphere of Spirit, it's preparing you to listen to Christ within; to feel that you and God really are one; to know that there is something in me that is greater than everything is this world. And when you do that again and again when you're called about

Tape 8: Freedom From Mind

a child or an adult stricken or in some way needing your help, then these truths are in you, they're known, you deal with them everyday, then, you approach the situation with no thought. But if you have to stop, if you have to reach out and if you have to dwell, abide, saturate your consciousness with the knowledge of God's presence, and no other presence, then do it, and face the situation with total "no thought" after you do it. I hope that clears it up so you're not in a position of feeling, "well how can I take no thought when I don't... I need to take thought to know these things."

That has always bothered the student and I hope you know now that what you do is bring God to the situation and then get quiet and let God do the work. You're going to become a master of taking no thought. This is going to become what you automatically do. In fact you start to take no thought the minute the patient starts to tell you what's wrong.

Joel tells a story of a man who was going with his family on a weekend vacation and he got up early one morning the day of the trip and he started to pray, "Oh Father keep the weather good. Keep those drunken drivers off the road." That sort of thing, and he just went about it very thoroughly for quite a while until he felt real satisfied and the next thing you know the entire family woke up in a hospital! His divine protection was not there and he had taken the trouble to arise before dawn, appeal to God, ask for all the things they needed for comfort on the trip and for safety, what was he doing in a hospital? It seems that the various things he had mentioned were the things that tripped him up. He had no idea that he was violating divine law – no idea! He had prepared the way for the very accident that he had tried to avoid. Now how did he do that?

In his mind every member of his family was separated from God. What he wanted was oneness, but they were all separated, and their will was separated from God, and their bodies were separated from God, and his mind was separated from God. All the alcoholics had a life separated from God, and a body separated from God, and a mind separated from God. He wanted God, the higher power, to overcome and protect him from the lower power, and that sounded exceptionally reasonable to him. But he was living in a world of matter, of images. He had created with a bad power, that he had created, and he experienced exactly what he had believed.

Many trusting souls think God will prevent and protect them from every evil and when it doesn't happen they're confused. Somehow they feel that God let them down. "Why didn't God do these things? I mean I took the trouble to speak to God," but really they let God down. They violated divine law. They acknowledged separation from God and it hit them almost instantly, they acknowledged a God who does not exist. A God who permits alcoholics in his Kingdom. A God who makes good vacation weather and bad vacation weather. And he had immersed himself in an entirely foreign situation; a situation which left him vulnerable.

Now you can see that such a person has not even a vague idea of the Kingdom and who God is. *"Acknowledge Me in all thy ways and I will direct thy path."* Acknowledge that the God you speak of so glibly, is also your life, and that, *"I and my Father are one,"* life. Let's awake that power of our life and let it work by knowing that it is within you. Because the life that we enjoy as humans is our sense of life, but the individual life, the real life, the life that is every man's birthright, acknowledge that eternal life, not only in yourself, but in every man, the life that is Perfection. Everyone in the world embodies that life and everyone in the world must be included - not in your prayer - but in your basic knowledge. Invisible God life governs this world; unchanging, perfect, forever.

Now let's suppose you go to an astrologer or a clairvoyant and you get a reading. And the astrologer tells you that in 8 months there will be a tragedy in your life that will change it completely. That gets into your brain, it haunts you, affects your work, affects the things you do, it invades your thoughts, seven months, six months, five months; what are you going to do about that prediction? This astrologer was not just an ordinary astrologer, he was the same one used by the President, the same one that Nancy went to, this astrologer knows her business and you've got a big bundle of fear. You're losing weight, your work really suffers, and as your problems pyramid you can't get a grip on yourself, because you're three months away from a tragedy. But you see, you're just like the fella who prayed one morning for that vacation; you're not acknowledging that God is your life.

Can there be a tragedy in God's life? Have I been giving power to another power than God? Is my mind denying that God is the only power? I have been violating divine law. Now let's sum it up.

Tape 8: Freedom From Mind

When your mind prays to God for attention, you're not praying to God's mind. When your mind accepts a strange power and strange possibilities, you're preparing for a real tragedy and God hasn't prepared one for you. This is not the mind of God, but there is only one mind, what have you been using to think with? Does the mind of God fear? Does that tell you something about your mind? Is it your real mind? Is that why it fears? Is that why it believes in a life separate, apart from God; a life that can be destroyed and unprotected against evils that do not exist? That's why it believes that patient's can come to you with pains, diseases, conditions, and it is not so. Every patient who comes to you has relief in his false mind. "Relieve me of this problem." Your job is to know two things; they're the most important truths that a healer must know;

1. **Your patient is God.**
2. **Your patient is perfect because God is perfect.**

Now that's your entire healing practice. You have the patient who is always God - invisible. You must look at him/her you must know that this is God, the problem is not there. Now that's simple to say. Later it's simple to do. It's got to become simple to do, because you've got to see the truth. You don't have to heal that patient. You have to sit there. You have to refuse to be hypnotized. That's what you must do; look at every patient and refuse to be hypnotized, but that's not all! Into the belief that he is imperfect, you must inject the idea that God made him perfect, keeps him perfect and all this perfection is invisible. Now how are you going to get that perfection out into the visible? First know it's there, that patient is God.; until you have no fear, absolutely none! The patient is made in the image and likeness of God. He is hypnotized. I shall not be hypnotized by the appearance. I am standing fast in the conviction, not believing my eyes or ears. And when I am no longer hypnotized, neither will the patient be.

Let's hold that. Let's hold that in our consciousness until it is the only thought we have. And even let that thought go now, your trust is total. He came to me, he thought he had this and that and the other thing, I said not a word, but I listened, and I know that he is God. I know he is God. And right here in my consciousness the hypnotism stops. I don't expect him to jump up and do a hundred yard dash, or his bad heart to start being a wonderful heart, he is God, and my function is to restore him to himself, to bring him the 'experience of God'.

Now a girl phones, from Annapolis, she has a kidney infection. She calls back in one month to you and says, "it's better, the kidney seems to be healed." But she has a friend and her friend had something quite similar. Her friend went to a psychologist, and it came back to her friend later with increasing pain. Now this that she's free of in herself, will it come back? And you sit there and you think, "well if she gets back into the stream of thought with the world it certainly can come back," but she doesn't know that.

How can I tell her that there's a difference between spiritual healing and psychological healing? There's a difference in range and a difference in depth. Christ healing activates your soul. Psychological healing works on the mind level. The soul level is God ordained. The mind level has absolutely nothing to do with God. Psychological healing is based upon the premise that a wrong thinking individual, causes his own physical problem and that a right thinking mind can correct a wrong thinking mind, and thus, eliminate the problem. For a time this seems to work, but there's a universal belief in the world and it will eat at the patient, and the patient's belief system will incorporate that universal belief, and subliminally, it will embed itself in that patient, and while a patient thinks he is cured, something will happen inside to return again if that patient is still in the mind.

Spiritual healing does not rely on the human mind. That's one human mind healing another human mind. But every Bible healing there's not one isn't spiritual. Jesus knew that he stood on Holy ground, he dwelt in the secret place of the Most High. He had divine healings because he obeyed perfect divine will and we must do the same. To Jesus every so-called patient was God invisible, therefore perfect. Did Jesus care about the right thinking of an individual? Do you see that? Or the wrong thinking? He knew that no one is apart from God. He knew there is only one Cause. He saw everyone standing on Holy ground. He did not deal with the human. His job, our job if we accept ourselves as healers, is not to change a bad kidney for a good kidney by right thinking, but to bring to everyone the experience of God's Grace. It's the very opposite of correcting the supposed error. Christ healing, true Christ healing is the recognition of

Tape 8: Freedom From Mind

God's perfection. It has none of the artificial trappings that we mistake for technique; there is no laying on of hands, there's no will power, there's no right thinking, there's nothing for the patient to do but recover from what he did not have, and to stop denying his birthright. As the Son of God, Christ went through the Holy land breaking hypnosis and that is what we are striving to do -- to break hypnosis. The only thing we need is the consent of the patient to do it. And then he can be in China. He can be in India. He can be in the hospital. All we need is his consent to break the hypnosis and we can do it from any part of the world. We will bring him the Light which is already in him. We will bring it to the Light.

To pray without ceasing, is the holiest prayer on earth. "Lord, let me be an instrument of thy light. Let me be a bearer of good tidings. Let me see thy light in the darkness; in the darkest corners of the earth. In every heart. In every home. In every soul. Let the Light that is man, shine forth until the earth is transformed to heaven. until your creation shines forth with a power and the glory of thy Self forever."

We have been saying God is all. Then no person has ever died. When you realize that no one is sick or dying, then you really believe that God is all. And you're really abiding in the secret place of the Most High. Your successful work healing people, depends on this truth, not only that, but your own divine immunity depends on this truth: *No one ever dies*. No one can ever die, because God is all. And with that truth you can learn to face every situation with courage, with confidence, and triumph, and survive. When you know that truth, you have broken the prison of the mind. You have discovered that birth and death are the same fiction, of the mind that violates God law; that the beginning and the end represent a false drama, because God is the identity of everyone, every form, and when the image of form vanishes, God is still there! Mortality is gone and the one immortal invisible indestructible Christ is there! That is why, "the place on which you stand is Holy ground."

We can't tell this to the world, to our patient, but when we realize it, and bring the knowledge to our healing work, we are without fear, without division, and the confidence we feel reflects itself in the quality of our work. You complete this truth with all the implications it brings to mind. You will learn much more because truth has a way of revealing more truth, so don't be afraid of truth, it will lead you deeper, deeper, deeper, until you are catching a glimpse of your Kingdom.

∞∞∞∞∞∞∞∞∞∞∞ End of Side One ∞∞∞∞∞∞∞∞∞∞∞

From this view of the nature of God and man, we begin to get an idea of the nature of man. The outer physicality is ever changing, the inner spiritual Self is unchanging. It is the WORD of God, the God self, that teaches the way to the Kingdom. When you are controlled by the mind, your God self is not getting through. You don't give in and you don't live in the rhythm of God. When you still the mind, your God self comes through and then you are taught by God. Is that clear? The WORD teaches you, and gradually you undergo a change. The outer changes, to conform to the inner. Everything you must know is conveyed from within by the WORD, and when the mind is still, and as you continue in the WORD, it gives you new vision, new hearing, new sensitivity, always to fulfill God's will and purpose. And finally, when your lessons are learned direct from God, God teaches you how to be his Son, and the WORD is made flesh. You must submit to the WORD within, the Christ, who has the Father's ear, and by submitting to the WORD you are taught by God.

Remember only the WORD survives. You can call it I. You can call it Christ. You can call it the Son of God in everyone, but be My Son, be the *living* WORD, because unless you are the *living* WORD, when your world disintegrates you will disintegrate with it and everything you value will go up in smoke. You will no longer begin another lifespan, another parenthesis, if you are the WORD. But you will begin once more your divine life, and you will live where there are no opposites, where there are no doubts and no fears, no frustrations, and you will have learned that life goes on and where you walk, your foot will not stumble.

"My Son, forget not my law, but let thy heart feel my commandments."

This is the first verse of Proverbs. One of the greatest problems we have in reading this verse is that we think of the Ten Commandments, but this verse applies also to the Ten Soul Commandments, which are given by Christ and reduced to a number of two, among which, is the greatest commandment that anyone can ever know. "The Son of woman must be transformed into the Son of man. He must be born of the Spirit."

Tape 8: Freedom From Mind

The Old Testament writers hinted at transformation. When Jesus came out of the Essenes and demonstrated transformation, they were shocked, the days of talking about it were over, the days of doing it had just begun. The promise that it could be done, was always present in the Old Testament.

"For length of days and long life and peace they add to thee." And the book of Proverbs goes on.

"Let not mercy and truth forsake thee. Bind them about thy neck. Write them upon the table of thine heart. So shall thou find favor and good understanding in the sight of God and man."

This doesn't tell you much does it, but it's leading you to an important conversion. For the next word is important, so important, that if obeyed it can bring you to a new level of consciousness.

"Trust in the Lord with all thine heart and lean not unto thine own understanding."

These words were spoken on earth and the world had never yet heard of Jesus Christ. They had never heard of the inner Christ, and yet, Christ was speaking these words. Scripture has always been leading you to the inner Christ, to take man from the law to Grace. Always the voice within which spoke within every Prophet was Christ, providing a continuity of Christ purpose; a continuity of purpose that you can trust.

"In all thy ways acknowledge him and he shall direct thy paths. Be not wise in thine own eyes. Fear the Lord and depart from evil. It shall be health to thy name and marrow to thy bones. Honor the Lord with thy substance and with the first fruits of all thine increase."

The discovery of Christ in you, is the beginning of your rebirth. From that moment on you are safe. Your journey is inevitable, and at times you may seem to struggle, but Christ has a firm grip on your infinite life. Your vision may temporary cloud over, but Christ within will keep you on course. Your clear teaching, is that Christ within is your teacher and you slowly are led by the mind of Christ, from your reliance on your human mind, to the Christ mind. This Christ mind guides you in spiritual living. It takes you from mortal thought, mortal beliefs, mortal will, gradually lifts you from mortal limitations where you can realize the full power of God is functioning wherever you are, at all times.

There are many ways the presence of God is called to your attention. *"God is light, in him is no darkness."*

Saul was on the way to Damascus, suddenly a light shined all around him. Later in prison, when the prison doors were opened without a key, a light shined. Where did this light come from? It was the light of the Christ within Saul, shining without; and while you walk this earth, the light shining within is always there.

"And yet a little while is the light with you, so walk with the light less darkness come upon you."

Walk with the light while ye live. Believe in the light lest darkness come upon you. Light is another word for Christ. While you have Christ within you, believe in the light, that you may be children of the light. So let's clarify this.

When Christ is born in you, you are the child of God. That rebirth, that Christing, is the heart of Christianity. After your Christing, there can be no death. So it is said, you cannot follow Christ into death. If you find Christ, then you do not die. If you do not find Christ, you remain in mortality still seeking the very Christ who lives within you. That Christ is within you this very moment – like a tight rosebud. Every divine law that you obey, opens the rosebud a little further.

You may continue for ten thousand years with no release, if you act humanly and if you seek humanly and maintain human goals and beliefs, but when you live spiritually, the unfolding of the rosebud accelerates, releasing more light, more Christ action, until your consciousness catches fire with the realization that, "I am the light." Then you can face the red sea, or the soldiers in the garden of Gethsemane, or even the disintegration of the world with its false suffering, and the light of God remains, you.

We have one important discovery to make now, and we'll do that after we meditate.

[silence]

I want to ask you where the light has been while we were asleep? Knocking at your door. Where were we wile the light was knocking at our door? We were living in time. We were living superficially, in a sense of now. But we were not in communion with God. The god of time is not God. The god of time is a creation of man. Does God get a day older everyday? Does Christ get a year older every year? Time is a human invention and

Tape 8: Freedom From Mind

it lacks one thing; it is never now. It always was, it always will be. Now is past, while you even mention it. It's gone! And every second of time you are dying, like quicksand, each minute passes away, to be followed by another, and another, and another, which always pass away just as quickly as the first. Now how can man live in passing minutes? There's a mistake somewhere isn't there? What a fool man is to call the sum of passing, dying minutes, his life. That is not God's life. Do you know what causes these minutes? Your eyes, which see the sun rise and set. Your ears, which hears the crescendo and decrescendo of the wave. Your touch, which feels the rise and fall of the wind. Sensations, tell you that years have passed; sensations that cannot report the miracle of Christ, who never grows old, and of God, who was never born and never dies, because he is always, always now. As the Son of God is always now, as we are always now.

The transition from the momentary now in this world, to the eternal now in God's Kingdom, of reality, is imperceptible, but only to mortal sense. To you, your patient appears sick, but your patient is God. And why does your patient appear sick, because your patient is in a false now. He's in the fleeting now; the now that is gone the second it arrives. And God is in the now that is so permanent, that the momentary now passes so fast, with your eye and your ear and your senses in the momentary now, that they can never see God, the permanent now, face to face.

When time stands still in meditation, really still, the illusion of time is not there. And we begin to experience Reality. If you could meditate into the eternal now, your patient would have an instantaneous healing. Jesus lived in the eternal now, that's why his so-called patient's recovered instantly. He brought them form a concept of time, to the real eternal now, in an instant. While they were in his consciousness they felt that miracle of instant healing. Jesus taught them that, few there be who can follow the straight and narrow, and few there would be who might find it, because the straight and the narrow is the now. Now gives us a total new world. In now, we find the secret way. Only now, only now is God. If you want God, you have to go to now. Now is Spirit, now is the Kingdom, now is not yesterday, now is not tomorrow, now is not a second ago, or 1 second from now. How are you going to find now if you can't hold now right where it is? When you find that illusive now, you will find perfection in the Kingdom of God.

I challenge you to find now. I challenge you to accept that challenge, and we will find it together. In that split second, a panel opens in the atmosphere and you are out of time. Out of the universe, beyond you find the timeless, the now; me is gone, I am now. In the absence of me, Spirit functions. Thought is gone; no desires, no future, no past. In this eternal second, which is the same as the infinite now, your daily bread flows in abundance, regeneration comes, fulfillment is continuous. Look forward, anticipate the breaking of time and the open door which embraces you, in which the now engulfs you, when you experience it, you experience God.

We are going to break through the illusion of time very frequently. It will come slowly at first, but it will accelerate. We will be in the reality, which is all around us awaiting our perception, and we will practice the presence of God, without opposite. We will make God the center of our life. We will see God's perfection in all things. You will begin to experience these moments when the hypnosis parts like a veil. When these moments becomes more frequent, you're close.

I'd like to suggest that between now and the Chicago seminar, you work several hours a day, well, several hours a week, on getting out of time. It's a blank wall at first, but when the wall starts tumbling down, you'll know that you're more than halfway home.

This series so far, has revealed that spiritual progress has no closed end, the end is open. I believe we've come a long way.

In Revelation, our responsibility is indicated by the depth of the insight we can receive and as we receive it through Christ revelation, we must share it with the outer world. We must ask ourselves, "What am I here to do? What am I trying to do?" As for healing, if we have patience, we are not trying to bring them good health, they have it. We are trying to open up their being to a new way of life so that they see it. We are freeing man from the world mind, by freeing ourselves. This is a beautiful process! You are leading your patient's to understand that they are God.

You can't do it all at once, but you can start in your family. You certainly can train your children to know the truth quietly, silently, within themselves. You can train them not to broadcast, not to go out into the school and shout, "I am God." You can train them that other people do not know. A child's' mind is open; open for your teaching. And you become a healer to your family and you have a responsibility to them, which you didn't know you had. No you don't pile them in the car and drive them to the hospital or the doctor. Your responsibility is to teach them truth. Not to sit them down and insist that they learn, but to intrigue them with truth. Wet their appetite. Let them ask you questions. Show them how the questions are solved. Always a finger to their lips and to yours. Yes we have a responsibility as healers. We can train maybe two, three, five hundred healers, people who are not hypnotized. You see, that's our subtle purpose. When they are not hypnotized, when they can face universal beliefs, when they can stand in their own Christhood, knowingly. And so you must be an example. You must be trying to live the Christ way.

I wish to assure you that certain things will happen. Oh you will go so long and you will think, "when, when, when do I enter the Kingdom? How, how, do I enter the kingdom? Where, where, can that Kingdom be?" Obey My commandments, abide, dwell in the Secret Place. Faithfully, be assured you have a trustworthy teacher. Christ within is on the job throughout eternity; take advantage of It.

Let us meditate now with the firm knowledge, that I am Christ. I am Christ. I can never die. Wherever I go, Christ is within me, and whoever I see, Christ is within him, within her. Why have I lingered in judgement of a so-called enemy? Haven't I known I was violating God's divine law? I was looking at God, I was seeing a man.

THE END OF PART I

PART II

CHICAGO HEALING SEMINAR
CHICAGO 1990

BY HERB FITCH

FOREWORD II

By Bill Skiles

"And a certain man was there, which had an infirmity thirty and eight years. When Jesus saw him lie, and knew that he had been now a long time in that case, he saith unto him, 'Wilt thou be made whole?' The impotent man answered him, 'Sir, I have no man, when the water is troubled, to put me into the pool; but while I am coming, another steppeth down before me.' Jesus saith unto him, 'Rise, take up thy bed, and walk.' And immediately the man was made whole, and took up his bed, and walked: on the same day was the Sabbath."

– John 5:5-9

"No words, no thoughts, no might, no power. You are in the Consciousness of Sabbath. For six days you have labored to train yourself and study. Those six days, remember, are many, many years. But *there comes a rest to My people: there comes a Sabbath*. And that is when you stop all of your struggling, you stop and relax, and let Grace live your life. When you come to the sixth day of your practice, you just smile, "I do not have to pray for anything, I already have hidden manna the world knows not of."

– Joel Goldsmith

This series of talks called, the "Chicago Healing Seminar," took place in 1990 and the students attending these classes had already been prepared by listening to the Chicago preparation talks the year before. Consequently, it was not surprising that many of the people experienced some kind of healing while at this seminar. Indeed, we can hear Herb as he asks a lady to stand up out of her wheelchair and walk down the isle toward him and she does just that. Yet, a serious student will realize that the healing of a broken body is not the purpose of this seminar, it is only an "added thing" of living in this Consciousness.

I invite you to make this journey now from sense to Soul, stop all your struggles and rest back on that Sea of Spirit which is your Consciousness as you enter the Sabbath.

Bill Skiles
Robbinsville, NC
05/12/13
Link : http://www.mysticalprinciples.com

CLASS 1
Physician, Heal Thyself!

Herb: I'd like to thank the Chicago group for inviting me down here and thank Howard Samuels in particular and Ruth.

We would like today to investigate our understanding of the Bible and to be sure that we all know the things that we are expected to do. There are many loose points, many uncertain passages and I find that some of the people are not moving in the right direction, so we have to alter that. And I hope today to set the way for us to; in French they say;

"Reculer pour mieux sauter."

My French isn't very good but I know the meaning of that and it's to draw back in order to jump further ahead. And I think we must make the effort to jump further ahead.

I would like to dedicate this class to Joel Goldsmith for bringing the spirit of God alive on the earth, making us more aware and pointing the way to what each of us is hoping for and that is the achievement of life eternal. Jesus had said;

"Whoever hears my sayings will not see death."

During the next hundred years every person on the face of this earth will be dead. And every person has been exposed to Jesus remark which was the very opposite of what we are going to do. Some of us have discovered certain requirements on the path, Paul summed it all up in Corinthians, and I'll like to read his passage to you;

"For we know that if our earthly house in this tabernacle were removed, we have a house not made with hands eternal in the heavens."

And then to point the way more sharply he said;

"If we are present in the body we are absent from God."

And if you will note the subtle changes and phrases. Jesus is saying that if we listen to his sayings and hear them we will not die. Paul says that we have a body not made with hands and then he says that if we are present in the body, the human body we are absent from God. Now it all adds up to one simple thing. If we are present in the immortal body we survive and if we are present in the mortal then we are retreaded, come back, try again.

Now Jesus did not say that if you hear my sayings you will not die and therefore you will die if you don't hear my sayings. What he was saying was that we all start out the same, unchristed and as we go along we are either Christed or not. If we are Christed then we do not die. If we are unchristed then we come back again and try again until we are Christed and if we're not Christed again then we just keep retreading and swimming the same pool. And in our first lesson I thought it would be wise to get that out of the way. You cannot live in a human body and make a transition. You may as well face that because it's the truth that you've been facing all your life and for many lives. The only way you can make a transition is to be in your immortal body.

Now it's the same thing with healing. You're not going to heal a human being of anything until you're in your immortal body and if you're not aware of it, now is the time to face the fact that in your human body you're one of six billion people who will disappear from the face of the earth.

Then the question remains if we are to be immortal and must leave our mortal body to do it, do we set our priorities on that or do we just go drifting along hoping today to have a kinder experience, a little more harmony, a little more dollars in the bank or do we make our complete effort of our complete life on immortality. Now those of you who have not been faced with this decision will find that your difficulties always arise in the mortal body and in the mortal mind. There are three or four causes for every problem in the universe and the one is that;

1. We believe that we are a human life.
2. We believe that we are apart from God or at least God is another individual.
3. We have a human mind.

You can trace all of your problems on this earth to the human mind, the belief in life apart from God and that our life is human. They're all untrue and we have to correct them.

Now in doing so, if we look at the average person, he is living a life that is false, he is moving through it as best he can and he's going to terminate some day still living the false life. Then we come along and we think that we are making some progress, we find that we know a little bit about this and a little bit about that. We're spiritually minded to some extent and we have some indications that we are favored in some way. And as we show this little improvement it takes us only about 15 million years instead of 20 million years. We have to make radical changes.

Our destination should be this incarnation - immortality. This incarnation we transcend. This incarnation we see God face to face. And so that's going to be the kind of class we have. A looking at things squarely, facing issues and then taking the great leap, following the Masters instructions implicitly. What did Jesus mean when he said;

"Those who hear my sayings will never see death."

How many can you name who have not seen death? I don't believe that we can anyone of us can say that we can name about fifty or a hundred but we have six billion people on the earth. And so maybe in this room we are a group of people who consider ourselves ambassadors for God.

And maybe by turning our attention to helping others in need we'll be helping ourselves, because the requirements to be of help to someone else means being very adept at divine truth. As a matter of fact if you're human you are limited in the help you can give to another human. It's a case of, "practitioner heal thyself!"

Now there are several things that are to be required in order to be successful in healing and the first and foremost perhaps, the cornerstone, maybe something that even good practitioners do not do; we must see each individual as the Christ.

But that involves more than saying, "I know you are the Christ." It involves accepting certain things about that individual. Many of the healers pronounce the words, "Ye are the Christ," without any feeling of love at all. It's like reading a science book. There must be three things present.

1. You acknowledge the Christ and
2. You love the Christ and
3. You believe that Christ is perfect.

Class 1: Physician, Heal Thyself!

Perfection, acknowledgement and love. All must be directed at the Christ of the individual you are trying to help. The minute we establish these three viewpoints and practice them, we find a great change in the amount of healing work we do, because we start to find love going out from us and we're recognizing our own Christhood as we recognize the individual Christhood of the patient. And so we've got the two and all of a sudden you see two in my name or more. And words have a new meaning for you. In fact it's one of the big secrets of the healings of Jesus Christ. At every turn though not a word is said, Jesus knows 'this is the Christ', he's got a crippled arm, he's got a withered arm, he's got eyes that don't see, whatever's wrong with him, 'this is the Christ' and he knows that before he even sees the patient because he knows that only Christ is on the earth.

And so in order to start healing you've got to be aware that everyone you see is the Christ. So you don't resent him calling you. You don't think, "Oh well, they've got to have that problem." You don't think of him as different than yourself and as you begin to practice recognition of the Christ in every one, the first step in healing him is to be aware that he is you. He is the Christ, you are the Christ, under the skin you're the one Christ. Now without that recognition there's no healing. Now, this is beginning at the top part of the healing. But as we go along filling in learning more we'll become acquainted with the way one goes about the healing process.

Now when the phone rings in your house the last thing you're thinking of is, "This is the Christ on the other end of the phone," and you're not thinking at the same time that I am the Christ too. You're thinking of the everyday events, child going to school, you're making a hurried omelet in the kitchen or whatever you're doing and these are the things you're thinking and the phone rings and this person says, "Help me." And you've got to be in readiness to help right then and to know that this is the Christ who is perfect without even taking thought about it. Instantly you've got to zero in on who's calling and it can only be one person, it doesn't make any difference who it is. You've got one caller that day, if it's ten times or fifteen or five. That caller is always saying, "I am the Christ and I need your help," because the Christ is my identity but my outer self doesn't seem to know it, I can't realize it. I know my inner self is the Christ but I can't realize it in the outer self.

Now, how does it work? Let's try and find out. The best way is to close your eyes and to know that you are the Christ. You can't be anyone else. And it doesn't matter if you've got a toothache, or you've got rheumatism or you've got anyone of a hundred different ailments, they're not you and you've got to see through they're not you. You've got to go directly to who you are, the Christ and you have a call from a man. Wherever he is, is unimportant. He's saying to you that something hurts him or something is critical and you're listening and you're saying, "Your words are coming into me, but my Christ mind doesn't hear those words. I hear everything you say with the outer ear. My Christ mind has already started on you with the knowledge that God gave you everything that he gave to me. We all start out identically. But you pick up this and I pick up that and we all pick up certain concepts. They don't change us, they just change the exterior. So a few thousand years go by and there we are a lot of different exteriors. But our interior is still the same there's still only God on the earth and that makes each of us the invisible Christ and we are still perfect."

Now when we in meditation are not pushed into a frantic move or thought pattern in which we try to figure out certain things that won't make any difference anyway. Our human thoughts cannot help the patient. We can't be mortal and help someone spiritually. We have to first be what we are, that's the requirements for being a healer.

Be what you are.

Now as the Christ, and this is how you must be willing to address yourself, your function is to bring a patient closer to his immortality, closer to his eternal life. You have to be able to unleash the forces of God. And as a spiritual healer, you are not interested in healing this individual between the head and the feet. Other healing methods can do that, but that's not your purpose. Your purpose is to bring this man closer to his reality. If you do all the things you are supposed to do, he will be healed and he will be just as well off as if he were in a different kind of healing. But your main purpose is to bring this man as close to eternal life as you can. To make God effective in this man's consciousness. To bring his spiritual consciousness up, up. To eventually make him realize, and don't laugh, make him realize that he is the Christ. And you may get people who are far from that right now. But while you are doing that you will be learning

Class 1: Physician, Heal Thyself!

how to look at a man and to look through a man and to see who the man is without any process of thought.

So when you heal you are helping yourself because the hardest thing to do is to learn how to see the Christ of an individual. And when you must see the Christ everyday, every moment, in order to be a successful practitioner or in order to heal yourself, then you see that healing has a purpose which is far greater than just healing a limb or an arm or something of that nature. And so we start off in spiritual healing knowing that our destination is not to just restore the use of a limb and restore the use of an arm, I mean a leg or any other part of the body and to make it function. We want to do that, but it is not the prime purpose. If it were we'd be short changing the individual.

Now, in order to understand the basis of this you have to go back and see that there are several levels to our lives and that your life started out without a beginning. There's no place in time in which life began. There is a place in time where human life began, but life itself has no beginning and we were all there and are there right this moment, but there has been a generation acceptance of a level below divinity and a level below that level and so it breaks down into the seven days of Genesis. Those seven levels, and as you know we're in our fourth level, the human mortal level and we came from the top the Christ, number seven and number six which was the spirit, number five the soul, number four the mortal, number three the vegetable, I mean we still consider number four as the animal stage which developed into the mortal, and then number three the vegetable and so on.

Now, as you come down the ladder, as you come from the top down and then return you go down to zero, then we started again, up and it's this ascension that we're concerned about. And in our fourth level now we have three more levels to go. We're three levels away from perfection. But while we are moving up the ladder it's only an image of us, it isn't us. From the top, down, up again to the top. The levels are all images, concepts, but the one individual being is always remaining the Christ at the seventh level which encompasses all levels. So that the Christ which is your name has always been the Son of God, has always been perfect, has always been immortal and then there's a mortal image of you going down and then going up. And this mortal image of you hasn't the vaguest knowledge that it's a mortal image, it considers itself the person, the life, the everything else, but you see God life doesn't go down and up. God life doesn't make these descensions and ascensions, God life is always God life. And your life starts as God life and ends as God life and is God life in between. So while you're correcting these images you're not correcting anything but the image and your healer who is in physical healing is working with images and if he's successful people are smiling and they're healthy and then they go and die. But our function is to restore the awareness of who I am. The awareness that now I am, who I always was, now we are the Sons of God. And as you maintain this awareness while treating, that this individual is the Son of God, you'll find if you can't be swayed from who he is or who you are, that's the beginning of your healing process. So that's where you're going to stand and the person's going to come to you with any ailment whatsoever, you're going to know one thing and that he is the perfect invisible Christ and that momentarily the outer self appears to be a human with an outer problem but you're not fooled by it.

Now, that is a rough perimeter. We have to become a little more familiar with that, so that it's easier to feel it, to know it, to be it and let's practice a little because what we want to do after that is going to depend upon our ability to look at the human picture with the knowledge that we are looking at images, that the images as a rule don't know they are images. They're killing, they're loving, they're hating, they're running schools, they're running churches, they're doing all kinds of things with a total unawareness that they are divine life under the skin. We're not concerned with what they appear to be in their bodies of skin. We know the body of skin will disappear. And before it disappears we want to set in motion the awareness that I am the life of God who never dies. There is no question but as you set in motion that awareness that you're the life of God who never dies, that you're fulfilling the statement made by Jesus that those who hear his sayings will never die.

Now, I don't want to go out of this room before we've all established that in consciousness. I want you to forgive yourself, I want you to meditate upon a person you know very well, I want you to meditate upon yourself and start casting out the things that are not true. Don't worry that you can't demonstrate it as you cast it out. The demonstration will follow, just declare the things that you are not.

[silence]

Class 1: Physician, Heal Thyself!

If I were to do this here's what I'd be saying to myself.

"I hear Jesus Christ and on simple faith I will accept that I cannot ever die. If I can never die what will I be when my body departs from the earth? I'll be alive. What will I be? Well, if I've accepted and attained the knowledge that my body is immortal, then I'm accepting the fact that I am the Christ, but if I haven't attained the knowledge that my body is immortal then I am rejecting the Christ."

And that's what I said at the outset. You can say, "I am the Christ," but are you the Christ body? Suppose you went a step further and said, "I must be the Christ body right now, then what will I do with this body?" Well, I don't have to do anything. I am the Christ body and I happen to have a mortal image. This mortal image in time will fade away. Now I must learn how to feel the presence of my Christ body. I've got to feel the presence of my Christ mind. Always bearing in mind that I have a mind and body that will try to keep convincing me that, that is me. But I cannot be a Christ mind and body and a human mind and body at the same time. So as long as I'm in one, I'm not in the other. Paul tells me that when I'm at home in the body, a mortal body, I'm absent from God. Now how can I continue to be at home in the body and absent from God? That's the very opposite of what the teaching is all about. Conversely, if I'm in the Christ body I'm present with God. Here I've been declaring, "God is present, God is present," but I haven't been declaring I am the Christ body. If I get a sore arm what do I do? I wrap it up, I do this, I put something on, am I saying this is my arm? I certainly am. But then if this is my arm, then Christ isn't my body and I am absent from God. Do you see the dilemma? Everything we accept of a human, which we call ourselves, perpetuates our absence from God. Paul says he'd rather be present with God and absent from the body, so would I and so would you. We have to be absent from this body to be present with God and that's just a simple fact.

Now, how does one go about facing the fact that you cannot live in a human body and be connected with God? You cannot be in a human body and be under the law of God, if you're absent from God you're absent from his law, you're absent from life eternal, you're absent from all of the wonderful divine things that are true if you're absent from God. And if you're in the immortal body, the Christ body present with God then you're under the law of God.

Now maybe you've never been faced with a necessity for being present with God, being the Christ body, being the immortal body, but if you're going to do healing that's a different story, then you're going to learn how to be or else you might not as well start. And furthermore, if you're going to do divine healing, spiritual healing, Christ healing, mystical healing the only help you can be to a person is if you are in the Christ body and if you do recognize the Christ body of the individual and you come right down to those two, "Which were ever two who were gathered in my name." Two Christs, he's Christ, I'm Christ, two Christs,

"There am I in the midst of them."

And you're in possession now of a crucial fact. When Christ of you recognizes Christ of him or her you're on the way to the real healing.

Some people say, "Well can we repair eyes instantaneously? Can we do this instantaneously.? Can we do that instantaneously," and so forth, you'll never know until Christ recognizes Christ. Because I tell you that Jesus who's Christ recognizing Christ in his patients and that's why he had instantaneous healings. And you can't just out of a hat do that. It takes practice, practice and more practice.

So that's the value or at least one of the major values of going into spiritual healing. In order to do it, you're going to have to develop your Christhood and behold the Christhood of the individuals requesting help and that's enough payment right there. Anything that makes you do that, will eventually bring you into the awareness of eternal life. If I'm Christ and attain the awareness that I'm Christ, that's eternal life. And although I can't make him a Christ, he is one, but I can't make him aware of it, he'll have to do that himself. And at the last moment when a person has advanced that high, you'll find that you can be of help in another way.

So then our job as you see is really an undercover one because we're learning how to Christ the world. We're learning how to recognize that the world is Christ. And I think that there's no nobler profession in the universe than this kind of necessity to reach an awareness that everywhere we look, everyone is the Christ veiled. And we can pierce the masquerade and see beneath the veil with the inner self. Now we're going to change the world.

And the first change you'll notice is yourself, because when it comes upon you there's no way to describe the way you feel. You realize that all things are possible and that you've just been a slow learner. But now as you face the fact as you're directed to the true facts, as you bring into play the truth, you find a new harmony in your life immediately. And it's there as long as you have the ability to not waiver in your convictions. And as long as you have the ability to find that inner opening that takes you past all of the opacities of human life, I think you'll find your search has been worthwhile. And not only will you be helping yourself to reach the ultimate goal, accelerating your transition, but you will be helping people you never thought you'd help, all kinds of people and they'll come from remote corners of the world, but you've got to be faithful and you will be as long as you see these changes in yourself happening to lift you above your present ability. There's not a person on the earth who can heal anything but the moment he gets into this transcendental type of consciousness he doesn't become a human being anymore with human limitations...

∞∞∞∞∞∞∞∞∞∞∞ End of Side One ∞∞∞∞∞∞∞∞∞∞∞

You've got to be in constant awareness of the presence of Christ within you and outside of you, throughout the length of the village, the town, the city, the universe. This is your invisible ally and invisible identity. We'll have to now come to some understanding that the Christ is a reality. It's not something we talk about. We need our conviction that Christ knows, that Christ does, that Christ is. And we need our conviction that wherever there is an individual who doesn't know the Christ that's a dark spot and over there another dark spot and over here and there, but there are some light spots. And we're going to multiply those light spots. And we're going to recognize that where the dark spots are the light is.

And we want to establish the one important thing to a healer, that you're not doing the work, no individual does it, this network of the invisible infinite Christ is the healer and it is here, it is now, it is real and the infinite Christ when you are connected to it by simply accepting he is and I am and dwelling in that, the infinite Christ will ignite. It will do incredible things. We're going to try to see if we can't find part of that feeling in ourselves and practice it. We have certain rules but we'll get to those later.

Let's dwell on the fact that Christ is your invisibility, but it's also my invisibility and it's Johnny's invisibility, and it's Mary's and everybody's invisibility, and they know it to a degree or they don't know it. The degree to which they don't know it is the darkness and the degree to which they do know it is the lightness. We all live with the same Christhood and therefore the same potential to achieve the knowledge of our Christhood. It doesn't matter if you're a Saint or a sinner, if you've got a million dollars or ten dollars. Everyone has the same Christ. And your idea is to get so conversant with it, and you are the one who can do it, no one can do it for you because his life for me doesn't go on until I see it, until I'm aware of it, until even if I don't see it I accept it. My faith must put in operation what I cannot see is in operation.

Now if we build our lights into the one light, by recognition only, you will have the network. And what you do for that individual, this one individual, you will have a universal network saying, "This is the Christ." All the power comes from this universal network, it's not local, it's universal and it's mammoth you can't describe it.

Let's dwell on it, under the assumption that I will in time learn to have faith in the universal Christ and I will learn by being the Christ, to automatically hook into the universal network which can produce a healing in any place in the globe at any time. And only through my awareness of it can I make this happen, oh, it might happen for someone else but not for me. It can only happen through my awareness. It will happen through someone else's awareness for them. But if I'm aware of it then I've got a universe at my command, and believe me that's what Jesus had at his command. And it is no different for Jesus than it is for John and any person in the universe. I have this potentiality but so have you. And I'm sure this is what Jesus was saying. You see to never die means you've overcome all the things that there are to put you down. So when he's saying that he's saying you will overcome the world.

"I have overcome the world."

And I'm your teacher why can't you follow me? Why can't you say to Pilate what I say to Pilate? Why can't you say to anything what I say to anything? I am your teacher and I have overcome the world and I promise you that if you believe in my sayings, if you hear my sayings you will not

Class 1: Physician, Heal Thyself!

see death. I accept it. It's so simple, it's so clear. And then they pursue the thoughts and they say, "Get rid of this body idea you don't have one."

"Well, alright, I don't know how to do it but I'm going to. How do I get rid of this body? Well it's an image, I don't have to get rid of it I just have to know it isn't truth. I can only go with truth. So I've already overcome the image because I know it's an image. Oh yeah, it gets pains and things, everybody gets pains. So you get a pain and you say to the pain, 'I don't believe you.' And either the pain backs down or you back down. I mean it you say to everything that isn't so, "Sorry you're just an image."

What did he coin a phrase a 'white poodles'. Look at all those white poodles. Images trying to have power and of course they have power because I believe them,' so you start unbelieving and you find some of the images do back down. Couple of days you get rid of something that usually takes you a month.

Now what about things we have wrong with us right here in this room. Nobody knows it but yourself. Let's look at these images and see what they are. Something is hurting you, what do you mean 'you', it's not hurting 'you' at all see, is it? Is it hurting Christ? Well you said, "I have this and I have that." We all fall into the trap don't we, oh, we don't mean "I" am hurting, we mean me is hurting, this image but I can't hurt I is God, I is the Christ and if you know that is who I am, then I don't hurt, it's true isn't it? So you learn to say,

"Yeah, there's a pain but I, spirit of God, the immortal body, I don't hurt."

And that's one way to get started with your immortal body. To catch the difference. What is hurting is, there's an idea in the world mind and it transfers itself down to your mind, your mind buys the idea and incorporates it into your being and you get a cold or something else. You have no defense over it because you think that's the way it ought to be and this is me so they go together. But this isn't you. Start realizing it's not you and if you're wise you'd take that to heart right now. You say alright;

"You can't sit through this two hour class."

You mean your body can't, see what I mean? But you're not your body. You are the Christ body and because you're the Christ body this body can't sit through but why do you let this body pose itself as you? What do you have to do about it? Well, if I accept this body as drinking water, as doing this, doing that and doing the other thing, naturally I'm going to get fifty or sixty years of believing in a body, I can't drop the idea that it's not me quickly, but I can start. Because if you let this body be you it's going to die and that's the very thing. We have a building not made with hands. A body temple. Holy in the heavens, eternal in the heavens. That body isn't the one you're talking about when you say, "This body can't sit here." But that is a concept and so you must eliminate it. It's just regiments, after about the sixth hundredth time you'll realize wait I'm through with that. I'm just not going to save my body that way and it will not be very long before I catch on. And there's a place where a truth that you can't accept becomes acceptable. A place where something that was impossible at one time for you to feel, "Well I'll get over that," no, there comes that place where all of a sudden you glimpse possibilities. I can't trace how it happens, I could possibly... something spiritual happens to you and it gives you the start and you come to another event spiritually. And finally, you can see the horizon where you could overcome this belief that this body is mine and ultimately something happens in the real body. (Gives examples)

You're walking down the street and a man comes at you with a knife and he swings and you don't know how it happens but you're still walking down the street, and he missed. You don't know why he missed or how he missed but you're still walking down the street. You think "Wait what happened could it be that my real body got me out of the way?"

I know of a heart patient. And one day his inner self said, "You don't have a heart problem, you don't even have a heart, your heart is fine." And that patient reflecting at least a second said, he's free and he was.

This is how it comes about if you're trying, really trying, Spirit has some way of knowing it and being all power, all intelligence, it has a way of getting across to you that you're making progress. So I'd say that the purpose behind your activity should be, "I'm going to realize that the immortal body that I speak about is everywhere. I just become aware of it over here, but there's no limitation to your immortal body, I mean it extends into infinity and down here this little, little, bitty, bitty sense of body is substituting for the real all body. Now when you get a glimpse of that I'm telling you it's fourth of July lit up. And you will get a sense of it because it's meant to be. We're meant to be that. And that's why we're going through the transition in consciousness. We all come into this awareness in the dark, in relative degrees each of us, depending on our past image life. And so our function is to outgrow this image and to become an immortal body. That is all our function is on this earth is to come into our immortal awareness of Christhood of our being. And when we do that we come into the Soul awareness you just can't hop that fast but you do come into the Soul. And I'm talking as dead serious as I can, because I expect to see everyone again, and I expect to live in the Soul realm with the various people that we talk to.

Lord knows that we're not playing games and we're not meant to play games and we're to take this teaching as seriously as it was delivered. And when Joel brought it to us it came direct from one of Gods ambassadors. I got flowers from Joel at today's meeting. They arrived at my room upstairs, it said, "From Joel" and don't think I don't know who they're from because I know. It said, "From Joel," that's all. This friend knows Joel well and wanted me to know that in her awareness Joel was approving our talk today. I thank you for those flowers.

I think we're on a wonderful road. We have a million opportunities, we have certain responsibilities too. But we have an opportunity to open new lives in people to let in a little light. It's just like growing a garden, you know there's nothing there and then you come along and so we have a human garden and before I came to the seminar I had a couple of AIDS cases. One was very quick and he's in Europe, he went there on a vacation to celebrate that he lost AIDS, he took his mother to Europe.

The other one was interesting. I think you'd enjoy knowing some of the little details. This individual from Baltimore, I tell the case because you've got to learn to be discreet in your teaching to others, for instance, he didn't even know about Infinite Way. Now we can't turn him down for that and he was recommended by someone who was an Infinite Way student. And this came by way of our meeting in San Rafael and then out of this, this one individual had another one call me. And I could see he was an intelligent man but he didn't know anything about Infinite Way and I said, "What do you expect of me," and "Well," he said, "What are you going to do?" And I said, "Well I'm just going to try to realize that you're the light." It's difficult to talk to a person who doesn't know the language, so we have to sort of maneuver around it. We can't say to him, "I'm going to find the Christ of you," because he might not want to be a party to such a thing. You know this might be something he doesn't want and everybody has different ideas of who the Christ might be. So I just said, "Well I'm going to find the light in you", "Okay."

So we went along fine and I didn't say anything and I rarely spoke to him when he called me up and he said, "I feel pretty good." And then I didn't hear from him for a month or two. And the man who recommended him called me up and I said, "Where is so and so and he said, "Oh we have a problem there," he said "he read Joel's book, he just started his book and he says there's a conflict. He can't see that teaching at all." He didn't even know he was being trained by an Infinite Way teacher, he said. "He read certain things that just were in total conflict to his... he's interested in astral something." And I said, "Well, okay anyway would you tell him to give me a buzz and explain what the conflict is I'd like to know."

And he called me later and it turns out that he had a conflict in the reading of Joel's book, that on page such and such Joel made this statement and on page such and such he made the opposite statement, and he says, "I don't understand that man." "Well," I said, "When I started out I had the same problem. I found the same thing but when I found the third thing it answered the first and when I found the third thing it answered the second and then I saw Joel's plan was he had two opposing ideas but when it brought me to the third thing the two ideas didn't oppose anymore." "Oh," he said, "Well I'm glad you asked me to call you because my liver is bothering me." Well I don't know if liver bothers AIDS cases but I went to work on his liver and he called within a couple of days, he said, "I don't know how you do it but there's no liver problem."

Well I imagine through the experience of that, that he'd be open to a few more thoughts I might have. You see how you can't push too far with an individual. You've just got to go at a certain speed and you can't decide for yourself what you're going to do with him. You've got to wait till spirit makes it possible. So you've got to be patient. And I sight that as a beginning case where I didn't even mention Infinite Way, didn't tell him what I was going to do. He strictly left it up to me and I haven't heard from him since then, but the liver ailment went away.

And then there was another girl, she called about an internal problem and I asked her what she did. She ran a dry goods store and so forth. She didn't know what I was going to do and she never heard of Infinite Way at

Class 1: Physician, Heal Thyself!

all. But through one way or another she got a hold of me and she wanted to know what I was going to do and I said, "Well I can't explain it to you. At this point A plus B equals C and you'll have to settle for that and if you feel better, you'll be better." So when the problem disappeared, she now learns that she was healed, she don't know how she was healed but I told her I study Infinite Way and that Infinite Way healed her.

So you've got to start slow, you can't bash the person on the head with something. Now they're open a little to more and that's the way you're going to have to go about it. Now if we want some rules, you can't heal everybody. If this person hadn't called me I couldn't heal her. And if someone else called me for her I couldn't heal her. If someone hadn't called me for the boy who had AIDS I couldn't help him. The person with it has to call you. Just as if you're going to operate on... someone calls you and says, "Will you operate on him," if you're a doctor, well you can't do that you've got to get his permission. So, the same you don't operate on a body that hasn't given you permission and you don't work for an individual who hasn't given you permission. In this work you just don't touch those things.

Well, if that person is here who had a brother who got sick along time ago, when he was healed she wanted me to heal her boss and I refused. She got mad and all that but she learned later that we can't heal if they don't ask us. And she says, "How can they ask you if they don't know you?" And I can only say, "It's not my problem." It's not your problem until the person says to you, "I want you to help me." It'll just be a torment to you if you have to do it because there are many complications when you start helping people that didn't ask for it. Legal problems. A relative will call you up and say, "You told him this and this caused him that. I'm going to sue you," and all that stuff. So there's enough people who are going to ask you to work on it. If you want to do something privately and not take credit for it that's fine, go ahead and do it but don't make any issue out of helping anyone who didn't ask.

They're going to ask you how much is it going to cost, well I only know what I've been told. We don't charge fees. So if you want to charge fees, if you want to make some money out of this thing I'd advise you not to go into it. You just do your work and your payment is whatever that person decides, if they don't decide anything that's your payment. You just heal and you're happy that you can do it and if this person doesn't pay you maybe that one will and it's not as important as it sounds when you're on the line healing people. You're interested in the healing and somehow the income takes care of itself. You'll find that you're never poor and patients who are aided will be grateful and if they're not grateful they usually aren't aided that's why. So that's how finances work in this.

Now, we would have some rules I guess. When child comes and the child was sick, the parent asks you to heal the child well obviously a child can't ask you for help, so that's considered perfect authorization. So you accept that case. But if that child is twenty three and he doesn't want your help and he'd rather have AIDS than have your help that's his business. I'm trying to say we don't intrude on peoples lives without an invitation and then it's not an intrusion anyway because your work is silent and your work is usually for the betterment of the individual.

I can't depart yet because we've got to come to the realization that there are certain factors which make success impossible. If you try to heal an individual and you don't love that individual, you don't believe he's the Christ, **if you don't believe he's the Christ, you won't heal him.** And you say, "Well, if he's the Christ why does he need healing?" I mean that would be a question that you've got to have answered. If he's the Christ why does he need a healing? Well, he doesn't realize that he's the Christ. Most people don't. You can think of a time when you didn't and I venture to say there are some who still don't. So you're going to need healing while you're the Christ but the Christ is your invisible self. The Christ is never visible except in a rare case and then the Christ was invisible. Everywhere you're walking you're not seeing who's there, everywhere you're walking perfection is and it's not visible. So although he's the Christ invisibly, he needs help in the outer. All you're going to do in the outer is change the image, but you're restoring him to that opportunity that you have. The opportunity of being the Christ knowingly so that you can come into those things which are your birthright.

Now then, the individual who has a problem doesn't know he is God life. He doesn't know that he is not ever separated from God because how can you separate God life from the individual who is God life. But he is living in a sense of separation and why did God do this? Why would God put me through these problems? Why would God do this? Why would God do that? He is completely apart from God he thinks of God as another self. And the whole human race is living under the impression that God is another self. But you are living in the impression, out of your inner experience that God is who I am. God is who he is. The invisible life of every individual is God. There's only one life and if all of the individuals on earth pass away that's still God life and it's still present. And the next crop of individuals gets the same opportunity, there's still God life and that's all there is.

Now, when you are taking a person into human life and trying to make it better what are you doing for them? So you're thinking I'm not God life, thinking my life is a human being and I'm just one of another. This one is thinking he's apart from God, why what else would I be? Don't I pray up to God and don't I go to church? Or that God will be good to me. You're not making that mistake. You're taking the separate life and a separate person bringing him into the realization that this is God life and there is no separate person. There is one life, God. But the physician must heal himself.

You must realize this truth about you first. That God life is your life, there is no other life. God life is infinite, there is no other life. A person can never be alive, there isn't any such thing. There's only God life. Now these are all things that must be worked with until you know instinctively that you are the one permanent, eternal, God life and if you don't believe it, you're just a mortal being that's going to die. Look back at Jesus's teaching, look back at Paul's teaching, see that all of us are the life that never dies. And you start it at least, on knowing that I am permanent life and as such I have the power to establish in the other individuals the same truth that I am learning, that they are permanent life. That they are the Christ. And in so doing you will establish the cornerstone of a productive life under divine law, that goes on and on and on to the fifth level, to the soul level. Where then of course, you're in a position to wait for the bridegroom and then you're in a position having achieved that unity of Spirit and Soul to still go higher into what is Spirit and Soul but the Christ. And to finally know that I am that life of Christ which Jesus came to teach was the life of all men. And finally through your deeds and actions, you will be doing precisely what he was doing, bringing attention to all men that the Kingdom of God life is the only Kingdom there is, and it's right here and then we see how fast we can move up. Now those are the basics of what we are about to do.

If anyone has an objection or feels that there's any reason why he can't work on the fact that he is God life, I think he would do well to see me or to correspond with me and I will try to set him straight. I'd like to feel that everyone is working on the knowledge that God life is on this earth. It's the only life. I am it and I'm going to expand my awareness of it and I'm going to expand other people's awareness of it using caution, discretion, only when they ask but I'm going to not talk about it, I'm going to prove it. And that's why healing is important.

I could say a million things to a lot of people, wouldn't mean much but if they get healed of anything at all, "What did that?" "Well that's called spiritual healing," and they're interested. That sounds pretty good to me and how does it work? Well, we go into the Christ and oh, it lights them up. What is illumination? They're all running around talking about illumination. Illumination is Christ realized. In any religion it's Christ realized. Maybe they don't call it Christ but what's the difference. It's the realization of divine identity but, that's only a part of it, it's the realization that divine identity is the only identity on the globe. And as it's everywhere you can cut it with a knife everywhere you go, there's divine identity everywhere. You can't hurt it, it's perfect. It won't die. It doesn't decay. It doesn't get sick. That's our identity. It will always be our identity whether we die a hundred times or not. But there must be the day when you come into the realization of your identity and maybe that's now.

Let's in our meditation make a silent promise to ourselves. "I'm not the best person in the world but I can pledge that I will try to except everyone I see as the invisible light of God and that if I'm called upon by anyone to help I won't rush into it. Try to prove that I'm a great healer, but I will take certain steps, and among those will be, "Yes, I will heal you." Now, if you're phoning me I'll hang up, call me back in a week or ten days or two hours, but if you're writing to me I'll do the same.

Very few cases are handled right, person to person right now, but it's possible. Most of the stuff will be done all over the world just as perfectly as if you could do it in a person's living room. So we'll talk about it from that standpoint because the person in a foreign country certainly isn't going to write you that they're dying. They're going to get right on the phone and you're going to get a call in five minutes, you've got a problem someone's dying, you didn't have it five minutes ago, and if they're dying you're going to panic.

Well, let's get straight on those things then. There's nobody dying see, that's what they think. No patient is ever dying. If you're God life how can you die? So, there's no death. Nobody in this world will ever die, not a single person. They'll always come back, always try to find the light that they haven't found. And then they'll come again and again and again. There's no world going to end. There's none of the atrocities and the horrors. There's not even a whooping cough. There's the light and the darkness and that's all there is to it. The light in most cases is inner so that there's plenty of darkness. Now, when you are taking this little pledge to yourself - I don't want to call it a pledge because it's only something you know within yourself you're doing - you're agreeing that you're going to bring light where there's darkness. And you're not going to hop to it every time somebody tells you there's something wrong, you've got to go about this slowly and carefully.

Now, when you've got a particular case you've got to be sure that you're obeying some of the necessities of success for that patient's sake and for your sake. You know that you've got to know that this person is the unrealized light of God. The light is there but the person doesn't realize it. The outer appearance of sickness is just the outer appearance, the light never changes. That's your steady, your forever, the light never changes. So while he's saying, "I ouch, and I ouch here, and I ouch there and I got this pain and that pain," he's talking about all the things that are in the outer and he's the light which doesn't know he's the light. That makes him a prodigal. It makes him unaware of the Christ, which is the light of his being. See what you've got to do to heal him, you can't talk to him. There's nothing you can say to him that's going to heal him. So we don't bother to say anything. The patient can go read a book. The patient can lie down. The patient can do anything the patient is comfortable with. You don't even have to have a long conversation with the patient. In fact, when he establishes with you that he wants a healing you can drop the patient altogether there's nothing you can do with him. And it would vary, some practitioners will say give him some advice and I say a minimum. The advice isn't going to heal him either. He's still going to be faced with the fact that you have to recognize his light. So, I think just forget the patient. If you want to do something to set him at ease do it, but the healing is going to depend on what you do about him that he can't do for himself. So there's no point in talking to him.

You're now establishing who he is, well you should have established that before you started, that he is the Christ, he is the light of God, he is perfect, but there's a misperception that makes him think he isn't. He believes he's the image of something, but it isn't of God see. He may call it that he's the image of God but he isn't he's any old image you want to call him, but he's the image of a mortal mind. Anyway your job is to quickly get inside yourself, and by that you get outside of yourself. You're not this either, anymore that he's that.

Now we all know what it's like to meditate and find our within, in which we get outside of our body so do that. You meditate you get out of your body and you get the click, the feeling, the awareness and you might get it rather quickly sometimes, if you happen to be in the right frame of consciousness, you get the feeling of the presence of Christ in you and you're lifted to that level and you get the quick peace. He's got to feel it. He's got to feel better. And you'll hear a call real quick, "I feel a lot better." But you, I'm thinking about you what you must do to yourself, not to the patient, you don't do anything to the patient. He calls and asks for help and you say, "Yes," but you don't do anything to him because there's nothing you can do. He might be in Tokyo, there's nothing you can do. But you can touch your Spirit to his...

(tape ends abruptly)

CLASS 2
HEAL THE SICK

Herb: A very good morning.

And we will dwell in the silence for a moment while we seek that individual realization. That what I see is not, what I hear is not, what I touch is not, whatever I sense is not for what is, is always invisible. There is nothing visible in this world that will not decay. It is our function to lift ourselves above this world into the changeless perfect forever universe of God.

What we should carry into today is the knowledge that the invisible universe is real. But we should have an understanding of why the visible universe is here. To call it unreal is true but it's a reflection right back to the Christ and from it Christ knows where the human race stands, where each individual stands. It is our function to transform the world. Each individual has that function. It is our function to clear the cobwebs of imperfection that appear to us that the light may come through and in taking on a healing ministry, even though you're individuals without a pulpit is to take on God's work because the Father says;

"Be ye perfect,"

And this is echoed in your heart, and each individual has the job of clarifying that perfection and maintaining it. Every individual we face will not know about our mission. He will believe that he is sick. He's nothing of the sort. But he believes he is. He's unaware of the invisible Christ of his own being. We're either partly aware or fully aware, are aware that what ails him is an illusion. Only Christ stands there. And that becomes the way we think, the way we feel, the way we look at things. While you're looking at me and I'm looking at you we should be thinking Christ stands there. Until we can some day get past that thought even and know Christ stands there. And get past that thought and see ourselves as the one Christ standing everywhere. Let's hold onto that because we must build a relationship with everyone we are called upon to heal which is built before we meet them. We're not going to wait until he calls us and then go through the steps. The steps will all be amalgamated into our individuality we'll know every time who's calling us and why. This individual is the invisible Christ thinking he's a visible person. If he would just know he is the invisible Christ he wouldn't have to call me. But he doesn't know it. He is asleep to Christ. And you have a world that is asleep to Christ even while mouthing the phrase.

When you, knowing the truth, you look right past the human being who's telling his sorrows, his conflicts, his pains and it's difficult to say to yourself, "There's nothing there but the Christ," but it won't be that way for you tomorrow because you're going to practice until you know it's true. And you've got all the Biblical back up you need for it. You can't go on a page of the Bible without finding out that there is something going on there that is not meeting the eye. Why even this prophet was brought here for a purpose. Always to reveal that this is a perfect universe and that we are seeing it wrongly. Paul called it a glass darkly, it doesn't matter what you call it just as long as you can see with your inner eye the perfection behind the visible veil. Now when we have a knowledge that mortality is part of the visible veil we can understand then why we're to shuffle off mortality by the immortal self is the reality of everyone in the world. Everywhere you're looking at immortality and seeing mortality. You're looking at perfection and you're seeing some good and some bad. You're looking at the Spirit of God and you're saying, "This one is a thief, and this one is a robber, and this one is a politician," but you're not seeing what you're labeling it not even once, because you're not equipped with the five senses to see it, and therefore your function in this plane of existence is to develop your spiritual consciousness because the next phase of existence for us is the soul level we've got to start seeing with our Soul. People have seen in this world with their Souls and they have seen Gods handiwork and therefore we know that if all belongs to us that is Gods there's going to come a place and a time when we can see too. When the inner eye is opened. When we can think passed the brain. When we can think Gods thought. When we are taught by God. Now why would God say;

"That ye shall all be taught by God?"

Class 2: Heal The Sick

Because there is in us the capacity to be taught by God and it's your Soul. It comes into the influence of the Christ who is always present everywhere and as the government of God through Christ takes over your being, this is the washing that you must go through to reveal your true Self to you. And so when we become aware of the general plan that we're here now, that the Christ must take over and govern us, but that we are the Christ we see that there is an invisible universe of God and an invisible Christ, and there are - pardon the expression - robots living in this universe of Christ who are passing through and each must be wiped clean of all illusion. It's a plan you wouldn't expect the world to know and that's why it's so difficult to explain it to the world. You can't take away a persons mortality unless you've got something to give him. And you can't explain mortality in any other terms than itself because the flesh is thought of as Gods endowment to man. You cannot explain immortality to the flesh. And so the flesh never gets outside of itself, it's always sleeping, it's always unaware of the Christ, except as an external Christ and that's the way the world has been going since you and I can remember. The good people of religion see an external God and an external Christ and an external everything, not aware that the perfection of God is on earth where they are seeing the imperfection. In their unawareness, in their sleeping, they can be untrue to Christ, unfaithful to Christ.

Now there won't be many who can join you but there'll be a little X over their door. I think that Revelation says that about a hundred and forty four thousand in a symbol of course. We are the one hundred and forty four thousand all on the earth who are aware of a Christ presence in themselves. Now let's be sure we know what the Christ presence in ourselves is about and that it's function is to shatter that glass darkly. It's function is to take us out of the dream. It's function is to open our inner self to our Christ self. And if you find you're beginning to know this well there's an instant recognition of someone who also knows it well. So that the union within makes possible your union without. Christ within becomes Christ without. When I say Christ without the manifestation of it becomes part of your being. You feel an automatic friendliness with someone who's in Christ. You feel somehow that you can trust this individual. And then you begin to feel your own Christhood and you feel the miracle of it. You feel a divine plan working. And one day it's clarified for you, everyone on the earth has the same opportunity I have to be Christed, to thin out the veil of mortality, to thin out the veil of flesh and somewhere in the background you say, "Oh yes I was told that wasn't I?"

"Henceforth know ye no man after the flesh."

And now you're doing it. You're doing it because the man next to you appears as flesh but he is not. If you take away the flesh there will be an invisible something there that you cannot see, beaming it's love upon you. Everywhere you go that invisible someone will be there because you carry it with you. Wherever you go you carry this invisible someone. More accurately the someone is carrying you. Now start to transfer the feeling of yourself. This is actually what you're going to do in order to ascend the illusion of mortality. Become aware that your sleeping days are over. You're beginning to open your eyes to the withinness and the life and the reality of it.

Now everyone you're called upon to heal when seen this way, will come to you as a person who only thinks there is something wrong and will be coming to the Christ of you which knows nothing is wrong. They buried my Father yesterday, my son was taken to a hospital, my other son was killed in the war and on and on and on. Not in Gods universe it didn't happen. And Gods universe is the only universe there is. You've been looking through a glass darkly. You have been breathing through a glass darkly. You have been fearing through a glass darkly. When you awake you find just as Job did everything is perfect, cattle, family, everything just right, better than ever. His spiritual awakening changed his inner vision to see the truth where as he had been accepting the lie.

Can you accept that you have no parents? That everything you have, everything, without exception, is going to fade and die? Because you don't have it, you only think you have it. You're not going to lose anything that you really have. You're only going to lose what we borrow from the illusion world.

And I think we had better learn how that illusion world works because it's an illusion on an illusion on an illusion and if you don't trace it through and understand it or a semblance of understanding you go right out grasping for it. You want more of that illusion. You have a world mind and there it shines and then have an individual mind. The world mind casts an illusion, the individual mind picks it up and does something with it and

Class 2: Heal The Sick

then you have a human race and that's another illusion. The whole thing is an illusion a masquerade. And one illusion looks at another illusion and illusions think reality is everything they're looking at. So this illusion says, "I'm well but my sister is sick, or I'm well but my father has just died." You were told specifically you have no father but one, and that was no game, that was no pretense, that wasn't symbolic. It's the Gods honest truth.

Now when you go to a patient - and let's hope you have a lot of patients - it doesn't matter what they have, from the most critical, to the cold or the little simple problems of a cut or whatever, to the most critical. A illusion is always an illusion and one can be appear to be severe, one can be appear to be not severe but it's still an illusion. Of course an illusion of a world war will seem like the end of the world and you'll fall for it but an end of the world wouldn't be too bad if it would be the beginning of reality. So we learn not to grieve, not to fear and it may take you twenty five years before you'll actually believe that there is nothing to grieve for, because what you're grieving for isn't there. You can't grieve for an illusion unless you think it's reality. So when you accept the illusion of death you think someone has died. But God doesn't kill. God doesn't have a world in which killing is possible, it's part of the fourth world appearance. And you are not in the fourth world, you're image is. You can't be anywhere but in heaven. You can't be the child of God not in Heaven. So you're looking at an image in the fourth world thinking you're it, while you're in the seventh world which is the only world there is. The reality that you live in is called the Kingdom or heaven. When you're told it's at hand, it is at hand. It's that simple.

Let's transfer out of this image world for a moment. You're going to come back into it just by walking and talking. But let's know for one moment that the reality of us is here in heaven, now! We who are going to be ambassadors for God must know the reality. And you'll find that every time that you're aware, that you're in the Kingdom, in heaven, that you are, because of the fact that only Christ lives in the heaven, that is your name, you'll find that you are thinking along these lines, you'll find that whatever happens to you is quickly transformed into a heavenly activity. There is no such thing as an activity on earth unless it's the earth that is Gods, the invisible earth, the spiritual earth. Your little switch button should be handy to switch off from one to the other as quickly as you realize you've strayed back onto a make believe universe. When you get planted in your real universe and you're aware of it you'll feel the miracle of everything transforming what you had thought of as the earth is the place where you have been living. It looks the same but coming through it is the transforming Christ. No matter what station you have in life you're translated into the Son of God. And you'll continue on the earth until you perfect this understanding of the Kingdom of God on earth.

You continue to work at the same job, see the same people but there'll be something about you that's different. And that difference will be you are awake. You are awake to Christ and Christ awakens to the universe of God without a flaw. Which has never changed since before the beginning of time. No matter what happens in this world the Christ of you is changeless and ultimately there's no anyone but the Christ of you. We have a glorious [quotes] "future." The Father has told us to be perfect and he's not waiting for us to be, we are. You simply have to know who we are.

Now let's try to live in our Kingdom and let's not be tempted by the so-called evils of the world or the perils of the world. Let's resist not evil because why should we resist that which doesn't exist. The resistance gives it a sense of existence. The minute we grieve or fear, we're only grieving or fearing because we think this dire tragedy occurred. But there's no dire tragedy in Gods universe. So we must be living in a world which is not my Fathers Kingdom. But we don't want to live in the world. Now we start not identifying these problems and we practice not identifying these problems, and we come to people who are knee deep in problems who are asking us to heal them. Well how do we heal them? We don't go and change their problems because they have no problems, they only think they have. They're using that mind which is an automatic translator of everything into the non-Christ world. We've made no concessions to it. We simply recognize it for what it is and what it has created for what it is not, because it has no power to create anything. It's blowing soap bubbles all around us and these soap bubbles have got a name. Armageddon, war, annihilation, cremation funny words, they all take on a hollow ring. When two people can meet each other and see without even taking thought that each is living out of the Christ light then you have the power that can finally say;

"I have overcome this world."

Class 2: Heal The Sick

And I know that some of us have the confidence that we can do it and others are lagging, they haven't enough experience with it to feel that it's attainable, but that's today. One moment a light opens up and you see that the greatest dreams you ever had were nothing compared to the truth,. The truth of God, divine truth. What can have power against it? It can only pretend to have power because there's nothing there. Divine truth isn't sharing any position with any other kind of watered down adulterated sense of truth. Right where anything appears that is false the truth is. The truth is that we are perfect but it will take time to realize it. We will appear to be sick and it will take time to realize that. But it won't take time to realize it unless you start realizing it. Then it'll take less time and finally time will be shown as part of the illusion.

Now I'd like you to meditate please because we want to meditate for the people we're going to meet in our work, the people who are going to declare to us that, "We are sick." Let's make sure that when they declare, "We are sick," we are prepared for them. And that when they declare, "We are sick," there is an answering voice in us saying, "No there's no one there to be sick, a phantom." The one who declares he is sick can he be there if everyone is perfect. That is how we can meet those who tell us we have to help them attain a higher degree of freedom, perfection, mobility.

"Pick up thy bed and walk,"

Was the sign; you only think there is something wrong with you and you're so completely hypnotized that the world reaches through that hypnosis. But he could have said, "You only think you're human but you're not." And we can think to ourselves, "I only think I am a human but I'm not". Certainly I can't be what God says I'm not. God says I'm not a human but I've been saying "I am so. God doesn't seem to know anything about who I am if he thinks I'm not a human, I'm very human. I do all the things that humans do and that's whats wrong with me." God says I am not a human. God says you are not a human. Where does God say that?" When God told you;

"You are my Son,"

He was telling you, "You're not human." Can immortality have a mortal son? Is there a mortal who would say he's perfect or can be perfect and then go and die? God was telling us you are my Son, you're not mortal, you're not what you think. And the world has kept on insisting we certainly are mortal and the world has suffered for it. It's gone through the millionth illusion. It lives a false life in a dream world that God says has no existence. But we will right all that, we'll start living in our Kingdom. And then when we hear from the patients who say, "I have cancer. I have this, I have that," we'll know it's something archaic something from a bygone era. When there were human beings on the earth. And I'm not jesting we've got to reach that state of awareness, of awakeness, because the fifth world, the soul world is a complete departure from everything we have done. Just as it was a complete departure for the world of manhood, mortality from a previous world. Even in the fourth world where there were animals and then men appeared. Where you could walk out of being a chimpanzee and in a future generation you were a man. It was a total difference between one world and the next but it's just the same difference now. This is mortal and the next is immortality.

When we live in the Soul world it won't seem strange to you because you won't be looking at mortal beings. You'd be looking at other individuals like yourself but you'll be that much closer in your awareness, that I am God. I'm just aware of the Soul at the moment but I'll be aware of the Spirit, I'll be aware of the Christ and they will all amalgamate in me and I will be a true Son of God. These are not parts of my being but they are parts that I become aware of as parts until I see the wholeness of myself while first think of myself as a Soul not as a Spirit, but I am Soul-Spirit, then I'll see myself as the Christ but I am Soul-Spirit-Christ now.

So we act from the highest level which is a true level and as Soul-Spirit-Christ I can't look out of human eyes because Soul can see better. I can't be flesh because I am Spirit. I can't think with a human brain. I am the Christ mind and when we put them altogether the capacities of Soul-Spirit and Christ, we see that they are the capacities of God which is what the Son of God should be and this is what we are. And when the Bible teaches us to not commit adultery it's not referring to our relationships in the human level, it's telling us not to adulterate, not to live in the Spirit, in actuality and then to live in mortality and the flesh in our daily life because that's the adulteration, the higher form of adultery. The accepting a mortal physical world. Each of the commandments as you know has a higher sense than the physical sense. We are told not to steal, not to rob. We're told that we are really the person we are robbing from, Christ under the

Class 2: Heal The Sick

skin and the human flesh is hiding it. We are told not to have a grievance against our brother. Our brother is our self. We used to think of that as I can understand it but maybe some day I'll have a realization of it. There's only one being and everyone is the same being. All the things that you don't like in your neighbor, he doesn't have those things at all. That's what you see and that's what I see and in fact he sees too. That's mortal hypnosis. The truck driver and the professional man are Christ invisible.

Now everybody has an immortal body and you've got to be aware of it. An immortal body is the only body they have. They don't know it. Come fix my rib, come fix my shoulder blade, come fix my heart. I'm not going to stop and tell him he has an immortal body. But supposed you're faced with it what are you going to do? The truth shall make you free provided you know the truth. And so you start to know the truth. The man doesn't have a physical body. It doesn't sound so foolish when you're aware of the fact that it's the truth. The illusion is so great that we still believe in death and we still believe in birth. But Christ isn't born, Christ doesn't die and you're merely saying this baby isn't Christ, this old man isn't Christ, that is total illusion. There is no birth and no death. There are no limitations on the Christ. He exists before birth, he exists after death and you have a Jesus coming to show his existence after death. How can he exist after death. He doesn't, he didn't die, death was the illusion. Death will be the illusion for you too. And if you can release birth as a fact and see that it never happened, all that happened was the birth of an image. And you've never had the necessity to feel or to face the fact that the image that was born was not the image and likeness of God.

∞∞∞∞∞∞∞∞∞∞∞∞ End of Side One ∞∞∞∞∞∞∞∞∞∞∞∞

(starts abruptly)...Have to continue our meditation and I'd like to do that now with the understanding that the person who is meditating is going through changes because the meditator is always the unreality. And while you meditate you're seeking the light which is transforming you. And for a moment you're apt to think humanly and draw the wrong conclusions, and it's best to just rest in the Word until it identifies itself, because when the Word does speak to you, you know that no one in the world can correct it. You've got to go to the source. The fountain has to be proceeding from

God and that's where you go right inside yourself until you are out of the way, and all that is left, all that is standing or sitting or being where you are is the absence of a mortal being. That's how you know you're in meditation until then you're merely trying to.

Now when you're in meditation you are the power, you are the Word made flesh and it's different flesh. The Word made flesh is divine flesh which is nothing like we know about. The Word made flesh receives the complete information necessary to that moment. Whatever must be done in your life, said in your life, thought in your life, realized in your life, that moment of understanding when the Word comes to you, that moment will be a moment of God.

That's the top, you reach source.

And that's the sign that you have been chosen. You need a lot of these signs. You need them for confidence that what you're doing is what you should be doing. We all need that confidence many times because the world and it's hypnosis can wear us down. Can make us in a moment think that something is happening to us. It can suddenly threaten you. But the times when you have this experience within will come to your rescue, this threat, this external threat, it cannot make an impression on the Christ of being. The Christ of being knows only that which is real and which is happening. It automatically filters every unreality out of your life. So I say you need many of these experiences because then you don't have to look at the threat with human eyes, you don't have to resist it, you don't have to quiver, you don't have to respond, the Christ of your being will not even notice it.

I'd like to look at Jesus for a moment. You didn't see much of his meditation. He had reached the point where with his eyes open he was in an inner state of realization all the time. But we still have to close our eyes most frequently anyway. And while we're in this state of preparation to receive the voice of God we have to be totally silent, not only in movement but in thought. We have to fast from thought. This is a very important fast because when you're fasting from thought you're clearing the channel which is going to hear the Fathers voice.

When you sit before a patient or you're on the telephone with a patient and you hang up you must fast from thought because you've got to sit there until Gods healing grace is upon you. Sometimes it takes longer than you want it to take, sometimes it's instantaneous, and when it's instantaneous you know about it. You'll have those moments and you'll be grateful for them because they'll be phoning right away to tell you that something has happened. And all that's happened is you had a direct line direct to the source of being. And when it happens, why whoever happens to call at that time is automatically reestablished into a new frame of consciousness which they themselves are not frightened by the activity of their body or their mind.

I've had a heart attack stop the moment it started. When somebody called and told me that their husband was having a heart attack. The moment she called he was better. By the same token when the same lady called a month later it didn't happen that way. She couldn't recover as quickly he did. Now whether the channel for the voice of God was not clear or the lady's receptivity was not clear, I don't know. But I know it didn't come through me as clearly as it came through for him.

There are moments of human fallibility to consider. You're not always at your peak. You're not always able to dismiss the world. And that's why you practice. You'd like to be at your peak. You'd like to be able to not have to fight down ten thoughts before you can get quiet enough. And so it's important when you look out at the external world not to be living in a state of constant reaction. If you're a sensitive person you'll be in a constant state of reaction. You'll be saying, "Oh those Lithuanians and Russians stealing all the headlines with their problems. And they're doing something down in this Peruvian country and my friend had this happen to her here." If that's the nature that you're in you're just living in the unreality. And then when the call comes to you, how do you get rid of it? How do you just stomp it out? And so you automatically adulterate because no matter how long you're staying there in silence if you have built up this attitude of reaction to the world you're cleansing period has to be long and thorough before you can simply do as another person might do, and sit there in ten seconds, somebody else may hear the voice whereas you may never hear it. You're so busy with the world. So how you live is important.

Now we have to get back to fundamentals because how you live depends upon how you feel about life and yourself. If you haven't come to grips with who you are then there's a whole pyramid of negations that follow you around and every time you try to be still for the Word you have this whole complex - it's like a Chinese laundry ticket practically - its so long. And you don't know where to start to get free. As a matter of fact you find that getting free is very difficult. Even to meditate is difficult. So I think we're going to review now the process of meditation from the standpoint of a healer. It's relatively the same as with a non-healer but your work demands that you be free and it's not only for yourself that you're being free it's for the person who will be calling you, and so we've got to be sure that we know what we're doing.

Send out your vibrations to the rest of the world everyday. I am free and here's why I'm free, I'm a free soul in Gods paradise. And start seeing truth within yourself. Today there's going to be so many people say they're dying. So many in the hospitals they can't be counted. So much is happening in the world but what's happening in my Fathers Kingdom, that's all that's really happening. So you are quickly taking a shuttle from this world to your Kingdom. You must get into your Kingdom as quickly as possible. And if you are a businessman you'd be wise to do it. If you're a reverend you'd be wise to do it. If you were a housewife you'd be wise to do it because that's where you're going to meet the Christ today. That's where whatever someone says to you will be the Word of God. That's where you won't have to divide your life between good and evil because it doesn't exist in the Kingdom. Get to it and how do you get to the Kingdom?

Simply accept that you are the Christ. Christ lives in the Kingdom. And if Christ is your name you are in the Kingdom instantly. But even Christ knows when you're saying Christ and when you're feeling Christ so you'll fool nobody. But if you want to be in the Kingdom the instant Christ is who you are. And you must live out from that because otherwise you'd be a figment of imagination.

What is Christ like? Are you willing to go through it to find out how much of a Christ you are? Well you've got to do it someday, now is a good a time as any. You don't think you're the best person in the world, well you're wrong you are, you are the best person if you're the Christ. You've got to start purifying who you are. Let's go through what we will be thinking if we were the Christ.

I can help anybody in the world. Well can Christ do that? Anyone who came to him he helped, it's still the same. So then maybe you can't do it now but you're the Christ and you're trying to realize it and the process of realization takes you up the ladder of thinking and then out of thinking. Do you feel that you can't do it? When you feel you can't do it you're about to do it because Christ will. There is a point in which you realize what am I talking about, there's no me, who is me? Christ isn't me, Christ is I. And then the words become self explanatory. You're not playing with words, you're playing with being and non-being. If I am Christ I can do things that no person can do. But if I can't do those things then how can I be Christ? And you run into all these problems that you mull over, you can't figure out. You seem to be pretending. You'll have to get passed that stage the best you can and come finally to the place where God's Word decides who you are. What God says is all there is, you're non-being if you're not. Well finally you might accept the fact that as a Christ I have the potential in my human understanding to go all the way with no limitations. I don't have to build a bank account, I've got all that God has. I don't have to store in barns. I don't have to put away for a rainy day. In Gods Kingdom there's no rainy day. Can I talk with others who also are the Christ? Try it and find out. Do you know anyone who is like the Christ or is the Christ or wants to be, talk to him, you might be very much surprised. Your neighbor might be a lot higher than you thought he was. Try to expand your Christ household and try to be worthy of it.

Now anything can happen in Christ, human limitations don't enter into it at all, and they happen rather quickly too. In those who are Christed the changes are quite abrupt. But always they're not better humans, they're not trying to be, they're something that a human is not. They become aware that they are not humans and you begin to find that there is another breed of man on the earth. There's immortals and there's mortals on the earth. But you can't see the immortals. because they are not flesh. They have outgrown the need for improvement. They're too busy doing Gods work, living Gods life, living the God life.

The Christ can be disguised to you as a simple housewife who makes good pies. They never do things badly I tell you that. No matter what they do it's always as perfect as it can be. You recognize one by the perfection not that they talk about, the perfection that grows around them. You'll recognize the Christ in the making for sure. It's very hard to get a Christ to be critical. You'll recognize that the people you seem to like who are uncritical have a certain other qualities that come to your attention, honesty. They never overestimate what they need, they just know what they need and that's all they want to do a job. Whenever you can find one you're going to be blessed by that individual. They're not given to taking worldly positions in very high places but they blend in the atmosphere so that you don't recognize them as Christ or as an individual living by the Christ but they do their job well, they're coordinated.

Try to surround yourself with such people if you can and try to be one because as you are accepting yourself to be the Christ there's a change taking place in you. You realize that God is running the universe and it's a real universe. And God has reached you in some way to gather you in. And as you look around you at the world and realize that you are here to be helpful to it, to transform every individual you meet even if it's just a shade. Transform every individual you meet without he's even knowing it and without you even trying to change him. Just by being the Christ you will act as a state of transformation to other people. You will lift them silently without trying. Your being will be the lifting and they in turn will begin lifting others. This is an age when the world begins to transform. As we become aware one by one that the Christ has been in us from the beginning and then as we become aware of the Christ in us from the beginning and live closer to it we are able to receive the directions from it which govern our day. You'll see people who like to get off by themselves a little bit, there might be a reason, not just for the quiet atmosphere or they might say so, they want to receive the Christ Word. They want to live by guidance. They want Christ to emerge from the sleep that they're in and take over their lives. They know that Christ will live it correctly.

Each of us will become more loving, not in the sense that we love a person but in the sense that we can respect who one is. When I know that my neighbor is the Christ and he knows that I am the Christ I won't be fighting him, I won't be stealing from him and he won't do that from me. Now when one is the Christ and the other one isn't you have the Christ protection. So even while you're still loving him and he's not loving you back, you have the Christ protection. You need never be concerned about your neighbor. As long as you know who he is and who you are. You find little animals they jump up to greet you, it's so clear that they're seeing something nobody else sees. The Christ individual is always at home with the animals because the animals recognized the absence of human impurities. They don't stop and figure it out. Their purity responds to your purity.

So then we have thought of certain characteristics of the Christ and I'm willing to bet that you say, "Well I measure up pretty good. I have that quality and oh I'm beginning to see now that I'm talking about human qualities." Well Christ is going to lift you into superhuman qualities, into divine qualities that are not even on your books. You begin to think, to act, to a higher level of yourself that you never knew possible. Maybe you felt that already.

The one difficult thing as a mortal being is to expect something in return for your favors. The day you have done a favor and look for nothing in return you'll begin to realize, "Now that's not like me. I like to get paid for my work. I like a pound for a pound." And you realize that somethings come over you. Giving is more fun. Giving is more rewarding because when you start giving you find you want to give more and it becomes different. Now what you're giving is your attitude, your statement to the other individual, "I recognize you. You're somebody. And I treat you like somebody because you are somebody and because I treat you like somebody, what you've got to give comes back to me. Somebody can give something to me. He can give me qualities that he couldn't have given if he didn't have the nature of God in him." And so as you recognize the Christ the Christ recognizes you. There is no selfishness in Christ. There's nothing to be selfish about. If there's something left to be selfish about then you haven't climbed the ladder. What can you be selfish about when God has given you everything. When;

"All that I have is thine."

Maybe some of these things you're finding out about yourself are signposts along the way to tell you the level of Christhood that you've attained. You really don't have to want anything usually that's when you get it. We become certain that there's my name somewhere and that what belongs to me must come to me. There's nothing in this world that can stop it. You don't go out and fight for possessions. You know very well that whatever is allotted to you by the Christ will come to you. There's nothing can stop it and you are able to relax in the knowledge that everything I need is now mine until the day when I make a translation in the higher universe, the real universe, because the universe I'm living in is in the conscious outdoor visible world. It is not God universe.

Out of this should come a peace. The peace does pass understanding because you yourself look at the peace and say, "I don't have a thing in the world to worry about. This must be done, I'd like to do it," but somehow it's being done in the invisible, "And I'd like to go over there," but somehow I'm going to be there if I'm to be there and I may not even have to travel to be there, I might just be there. Space becomes different. Time becomes different. As the world around you changes it's complexion as I in the midst of you lives you, you start feeling the growth of Christ in you, the growth of the Christ understanding, you find that your emotions, your thoughts, your intelligence, everything seems to correspond so that they're all on the same level of performance. You will see openings you never saw for you. No one to compete with you. There's no competition in the Christ world. But yet you're still here, you're still here in this appearance world but you're living in Christ in the Kingdom of God while appearing here.

"And behold I make all things new."

It was a word in the Bible, it's an activity in your consciousness now. The I is your Christhood. The newness is the expansion of your powers. You always had these powers. But as you come into Christhood through your consciousness you'll find that the Christ powers will do the healing for you. You'll try at first to do your own healings but you'll discover that Christ heals. and as you empty out a way you are transformed to the Christ which heals. And things that were impossible to your mortal self are not to your Christ Self. But you can't control your Christ self, it controls you.

At this state now we could be sitting and a call could come and you find you are a better healer than you were a half hour ago, because what would happen at this state would be that the individual calling you would be the Christ that you are. You've already achieved the oneness and so this is when you have the instantaneous healing. The person calls up but the truth of that person is Christ. They call you who are in a state of listening for the Word and the healing is an automatic thing. It's automatic. No matter who is afflicted they are affected by the Christ.

Now when we come to the world of people living almost a world under you - that depends on whether you've attained a feeling of the Christ or not - you must realize that everything that happens to them seems real to them and their world isn't real at all. You've just come out of it. You come out by knowing that you are the Christ, being lifted by the Christ and they tell you this is wrong and that's wrong, yes it would seem that way to them. In fact it would seem that hardly much could be considered right. Everyday brings a new worry. It's amazing how many people are free from worry on this earth, there's so few. No matter who they are their worries are constant, but only because of the absence of Christ in their consciousness. The minute they become aware of Christ as reality of their being then there's no point to worry anymore. The Christ is the all knowing, the all perfect, the all power. You get to see that what you've been searching for is simply the Kingdom of God. Where it's all perfect, all moving along with Gods rhythm.

If you ever want to see it in action, - very quickly, I've mentioned this before but - if ever you want to see Gods perfect world in action, when you're driving on the highway, just realize that;

"Everybody is God driving a car."

The fellow in front of you. The fellow behind you. Get that realization. You'd be amazed what happens after you get it. You look out and everyones driving at the same speed. Their distances apart never change. Never more, never less, never speed up, never slow down, they proceed like automation. You look at it and you're fascinated but everyone is proceeding in automation, at the right tempo not to encroach upon anyone else's space, and that only happens when you get into the realization of the Christ. You sit there dumbfounded, no accidents will occur, nobody will get run over, nothing like that, because when you establish Christ in one that Christ governs all the rest.

But it's the same with other factors like weather. The Christ in you controls the weather because weather is perfect in Christhood. Test them out and you'll be surprised at what can happen. Now when this happens once, twice, three times, that a person gets well through your efforts you'll fall into a rut and you'll think you'd do everything the same way. "I'll just do the same thing I did the last time. It'll be the same thing", but no matter how many times you have to handle a case or cases nothing is done the same way. You go through the forms of doing it the same way, but what Christ does you'll never figure out. Christ does nothing the same ever, but Christ gets the results.

Now then if you have accepted that the responsibility is not yours to heal, it's the responsibility of Christ, and then you have that difficult step where, "I'm not me I am the Christ," and then after you let Christ heal, you will see that people will announce that they're well while you have done nothing. And you'll know Christ has done it, but you have cleared the way. It appears that you clear the way through human procedures and all that, but Christ is running the perfect universe of God right now. And Christ will take anyone into that universe who wants to be, sincerely wants to be. Who is willing to give up all else that isn't Christ. That's whats slowing us down in our human realizations. He is willing to give up everything that isn't Christ to live on that plateau.

Now what I'm telling you is that these feelings that we have are possible for each of us. That we have this invisible Soul to run our ship. You don't need a compass, you don't need the wheel, you don't need the ship, just this Christ. And wherever you are there will be an activity of God present. You have the savior with you. The only savior there is, is the Spirit of God in you.

CLASS 3

THE MIRAGE OF ME

Herb: (tape starts abruptly) ...we meet again.

We are about to commence looking at the Christ in a different way. We might preface that with the thought that in our own individual lives we have made a discovery. The only thing wrong is always in our visible life. All over the universe the only thing wrong in anyone's life is visible. The invisible remains calm, peaceful, contented and divine. Now when you segregate your problems also see that your invisible as perfect and your visible is not. And now when you become aware of that you make an inner decision, not so much to make the visible more perfect but to live in the invisible which is perfect. And so I had an experiment with myself and it turned out rather successful. I suggest it to you.

For the moment divide your life into your invisible life and your visible. Put them about two feet apart in your mind for a moment. Let's say you put your invisible life on the right side, the visible on the left side. And you begin to sort out certain things in your life. If you have a problem, you don't have it in your invisible life. You have it in your visible life so you push the problem into that. And every problem that comes your way goes in the left side, in the visible life but your right side your invisible life remains without a problem. And soon you begin to realize that you're putting all your problems on the left side. Why isn't the right side? Why is that problem less? And you begin to work for that. And without any realization on your part you're beginning to think in terms of my invisible life which is perfect, and which you know is real until you feel the reality of it. Now that's our preface. I want you to be thinking of that later. On your left side about two feet away your visible life, on your right side your invisible life. See if you can sort out all your problems into the one because there are none in this life. You're eventually going to drop the illusion and there will be left the perfect life, but not at the moment.

Now let's look at Christ who had already done all this, and he hears about a boy. The boy was born blind. And his disciples come to him, want to know, did the father or mother sin or was it a karmic experience from a previous life. Christ thinks about it a moment and tells them, "The boy didn't suffer a karmic experience. The parents didn't sin. They haven't been punished by God. This situation is entirely different than you know about." He says, "But I'll tell you one thing you want to know. God gave this boy vision and there's no power on earth can take it away. So it's still there." When you think of the things given to you by God that are perfect and that seem to be impaired you are wrong in that assumption. The qualities of God are in you but they never change and they're never impaired and they always remain. If you live five hundred more lifetimes in five hundred different bodies, you will still have the same perfect qualities given to you before the beginning. So when you're told that something is incurable you're laughing inside, because you know that the perfect qualities of God given to every individual are identical to what they were five trillion years ago or a minute ago. Nobody has lost anything. But they've lost it on the left side in this world of visibility, the world that is the illusion. "But that isn't possible," say the disciples. "This boy doesn't see. He never saw anything." And all the people who were there are of the opinion that because the vision of the boy is gone, because science today would say, "We can't do anything about it," just as science said then, they were to assume that Christ was going to meet an unsolvable problem. And the man himself who was now blind we never hear much about his thought processes, what he was thinking. But in those days to be blind was to be lower than a rodent. You couldn't see; you couldn't scrounge around for food. You had no status in the community. People weren't happy to see you. You were helpless and to your opinion worthless. And this man himself had little hope of ever seeing. It never dawned upon him that it was possible.

Christ said, "There will be a moment of light within you." Christ was the invisible self. Christ was saying things that nobody knew about. They only heard the words of Jesus outside. But Christ is the inner man, the reality. And so when they heard Christ they only heard Jesus speaking, but Christ inside was active ever. Jesus was not doing the healing. Jesus was standing outside. And it's important for you to know that Jesus was made visible to you so that all the activity going on in the Christ of the boy would be heard by you. For instance whatever Jesus said if he hadn't said anything you wouldn't know anything about the Christ activity, but whatever he said was the Christ activity invisible outwardly making that statement. So you get the idea that Christ is always acting inwardly but there's no channel for Christ to come through to make statements, to do anything. That's why Jesus makes the statements and that's why Jesus is made visible. Jesus is the visible self. Christ is the invisible Self, the invisible Self which is always perfect.

Now he says, "Go and bathe in the pool of Siloam," after he has made a few outer expressions, like spittle, clay, throwing it on the floor. And the man goes and bathes in the pool of Siloam and he comes back seeing. He hadn't lost his vision; it was still intact. And this was a dramatic statement. No one loses anything. You have the opportunity to recoup whatever has seemed lost to you. And because the miracle is not done by a human being the possibility of that miracle ever remains. To all things you must describe the possibility of being achieved because to God nothing is impossible.

Now the miracle is done; the man sees. What has Christ established for the world? When you know why and how then your hope is renewed, that everything that my life has lost, everything in the degree of perfection that is no longer visible, everything will be restored to you as you rise higher in consciousness. You may say, "Oh I've aged so much. I've lost my right ear; I can't hear through it. I don't walk as well." That demonstration was to show you that it doesn't matter who you are or what you have lost, it will be retrieved, restored, renewed, yours to use as in the beginning. The demonstration of the boy's eyes being restored is a demonstration of renewal for all. If you think something is lost irretrievably, you can stop thinking that. For as the Christ is realized inside you, whatever Jesus performed in the outer was performed by the Christ. All Bible miracles are Christ miracles performed by the invisible Christ. And as you are enlightened, as your enlightenment increases you will receive the assurance that you have lost nothing, absolutely nothing. Your eyes will be restored, your ears, your power of hearing, your power of sight, but you'll be looking for it as human vision and it won't come that way. It will come in a way you know not of, and the human vision will not be needed. You will need divine vision if you're living in the Kingdom. Everything that you are will be divined to live correctly in the Kingdom of God. All of that from this one demonstration of a Christ miracle. So none of us can be approached by any patient when we are under the belief that something needed for a patient is impossible, we have not learned our lesson.

Everything is possible to God.

And the patient will always come to you with things that to you may seem impossible. I can think of a number of them. An amputation; you can't restore the leg. Christ will establish the reality of that individual and that individual will be capable not only of walking but of appearing anywhere in the world that he wants to, when he wants to. Prepare for your miracles. At least that's what Christ is a miracle worker.

We must now develop the awareness that as we increase in the ability to know the truth, we will be approached by people who instinctively reach out for your consciousness because there's a law. If your consciousness is higher than another's, it will attract it to it. If I be lifted up, I will lift all men unto me. You will find that your consciousness is a magnet and you will be approached at first very slightly, but they will find a reason and an avenue to your person and they will make a demand upon you. And that will be a Christ activity, something that you can put down and say, "In some way the Christ spoke to me and he has asked through this individual that I utilize my new capacity to bring a little light." And this will grow daily. There may be times when you seem inactive but as you show more enthusiasm, more confidence, more integrity it will grow. And in short time you'll find you have a little group, a household and this will make you grow. And soon you'll discover that you really think of yourself as an individual who can heal. But you must know that if you're still healing with your brain, you're limited because we have been given a demonstration of Jesus doing healings over the world, but we must remember that the Christ of Jesus did the healings. And the Christ who did the healings is the same Christ who will do the healings when you are called. You must be meek unto the Father. You must be willing. There is no personal thing in healing; it's a stepping out of the way knowingly that the Christ can step forward.

I would like you now to pick up the thread of healing from a place where you left off. You were forgiving yourself at one point in our discussion. I want to resume that forgiveness. You must learn to forgive all the inabilities

Class 3: The Mirage Of Me

that you have ever had. You must learn to forgive all the so-called false thoughts that you have entertained, all the false ambition, all the vanity. All must be approached now as:

"I am the living Spirit. I dwell here on this earth but I am learning to walk invisibly. I'm not going to do it all at once but I'm going to learn that I am an invisible being."

No one has ever seen the Christ, even when they saw Jesus. They were looking at the Christ but all they could see was Jesus. And they're looking at the Christ when they look at you and all they're seeing is you. You're walking invisibly now; you're learning that your being is Christ invisible. And because you can't live in the invisible twenty-four hours a day yet, you must practice that because I am invisible I must live that way for some time during the day. And I know you're going to find it difficult to do. But it's important that for one hour a day you give attention to the fact that you are living where no one can see you. While you're right out front talking to them, doing things with them, participating in Government or education or whatever you're participating in, you are involved in an invisible activity. You are knowing as much as possible what Christ knows about the Kingdom of God while you participate in the visible world. If you do not do this, it'll be difficult for you to learn what Christ does; it'll be difficult for you to be silent and let Christ step forth and perform the miracles.

Now let's say you're living in the invisible world. At first you say to yourself, "I'm sort of living as two people. I've got to remember that I'm the Christ and I've got to live in the invisible world." That's how it seems at first. But after a while you will realize that you're living as Christ in the invisible world, not as you but as Christ, and then you won't be separating these bodies, into one on the left which has all the problems, one on the right which is invisible and has no problems, because the moment you practice living in the Christ body you will realize that this is my real body and my only body, and now the outer man, the image, the self I have lived in all these years must decrease, while the inner man the Christ that I am learning to live in must increase.

Let's try it. Let's see how we would react to living in the invisible Christhood rather than the visible mortal. And let's see how unimportant you find the mortal is, how hollow, how incompetent, how completely irrelevant to your Christ life.

What is the mortal going to do today? He has three meals. He'll go to the office, sign some papers, make some phone calls, get some people to do something that he wants them to do. Then in the afternoon he'll repeat the process and on the weekends he'll go out and he'll entertain himself. What will the Christ be doing? The Christ will be bringing light to your soul, oil from the lamp. The Christ will be building your Spirit, your consciousness of reality. The mortal will be doing things that mortals have always done. Maybe it'll be an inventive mortal. But while the Christ is building your complete eternal life into a reality, the mortal is living a temporary life.

Let's turn off the mortal for a minute. Let's go back to our Christ life and see that as we live and practice Christhood we are living and practicing eternality; we are practicing infinity. We're building a whole new living vocabulary. We are practicing harmony and we are practicing something that'll come up later - which will have a special meaning for you - we are practicing wholeness. We are using facets of our life that we have not used intentionally or knowingly. The roots are going deeper and more and more we'll find that we don't borrow as much from the mortal aspect of life because that's not where the source is. Deepen now if you can; feel the stability of your invisible life.

Think for a moment that you don't have to worry about your invisible life. You don't have to take vitamins for it. You don't have to go to any medical profession for it. It doesn't have to be entertained. It doesn't even live in a day and then another day until there are no more days. Now you're going to make a transference to that invisible life until you feel it and know it. Until you find something in you that is able to voice that invisible life, act from that invisible life, and cohabit with the invisible life of others. And when an individual phones you for help or writes you, you'll come to him from a different level of yourself. It won't be person meeting person. You'll begin to feel the invisible yourself of you while the visible self of you is saying to the patient words of comfort or words of good cheer or words of hope or whatever you do say even if it's briefly, "That I will be with you." When you turn it over, you turn it over to that invisible self. That's where your healings emanate from. The human of you does not do the healing. That's why the invisible of you must come alive.

Class 3: The Mirage Of Me

Now let's see if you can turn your case over to your invisible self. Start in the attempt: "I must be healed; I want you to heal me of my problem." We'll say it's a leg infection. You don't know anything about leg infections. You don't even look at the leg or at least it's a cursory investigation just to ascertain that that's what you're working on. Then you forget my leg; you even forget my name. All you can think of and all you must think of is the Christ must be brought to handle this problem. The Christ must be lifted up in me. Then you go to the Christ, to the perfect one, to the one who will not accept an individual as hurting or pained or in a problem area, who sees him as perfect and now the case is beginning to go out of your hands. And yet you're the visible healer just as Jesus was. And the Christ is saying to you, "I am on the scene," or maybe you haven't advanced to the stage when the Christ talks to you but you feel the presence of something which you have turned it over to. And you're relying on that presence to take it from you and bring about the desired healing. The Christ then will go through various activities and you in observing them, in witnessing them, in beholding them, in keeping your attention riveted on them, you'll perceive that Christ will function in such a way that the patient will not know someone is handling his case, called Christ. He'll look at you and wait for expectantly, but there's not a thing you'll be doing except staying out of the way. Christ does all the work. And the patient doesn't enter into it and you don't enter into it. That's where the hope is. Christ does all the work and that makes you a very good healer because you have learned how to live in the invisible and to turn cases over to Christ, which is what a healer should do. But Christ is that part of your being which has lain dormant so long because you were not awake to Christ. You're not turning it over to a stranger. You're turning it over to your true self which is Christ. And now the mortal, the physical, the human, the mental brain, the human brain, all of these qualities, the judgment which you always entertain of the other fellow, judging him good or bad or sick or well, not necessarily a judgment of his character but he's sick or he's well, well he's neither, he is the Christ too just as you are too. And you are learning that you are the Christ while you bring the Christ to him, in the awareness that he is the Christ.

The miracle then is not accomplished on the human scene. You're not working on his mortality. It's only the result that shows forth in his mortality. His immortality becomes the thing that he becomes aware of and then his mortality shows forth the fruits of his immortal recognition, his acknowledgement. Perhaps he doesn't know that he's acknowledging the Christ while you're healing but it all turns out when he is better; he feels better. He feels grateful to you; you feel grateful to him for having brought you that case. But the world is aware of an increase in Christ realization. And every increase in Christ realization raises the level of human consciousness. He'll play a greater part in any other way of a human. You're dealing in the spiritual universe of reality. You're opening the door to people who can learn that the Christ in them - because they will learn it ultimately - the Christ in them is a reality and you're learning that the Christ in you is the real healer and the miracle worker and therefore you know that now anything, ANYTHING is possible to me, because everything is possible to Christ.

Now when you look at any healing in the Bible then, see it from the standpoint now of what Christ must have done. All Jesus did was say, "Lazarus come forth." But the Christ of Jesus who was very powerful, the Christ of Lazarus was very receptive and when the Christ stepped forth the world saw Lazarus, but the Christ did the miracle. The Christ knew Lazarus was the Christ. And again Jesus was teaching as he was always teaching that we may think we're in the grave but as soon as Christ is born in us we stand forth like Lazarus even though we ourselves may be bewildered by it. You have no area of your life which cannot participate in healing work. You have no lack of ability in any area of your life that cannot participate in the most incredible healings, because you're not limiting your healings to yourself. The human of you becomes a channel, steps aside; the Christ steps forth, the Christ does the work.

I suppose then it might be important to learn how to step aside. How there should be an ability to be something to someone and yet something to the Christ. You've got the patient's confidence to win, you've got to be your human best, you've got to go through certain routine things, you've got to talk to the patient, you've got to say things that will win the patient's confidence in your ability. It all comes down to being a good human being and while you're being a good human being, you've got to be the Christ. And when it's possible to be the Christ and be a good immortal being that will be our next step.

Class 3: The Mirage Of Me

And now let's stay with our patients. Anyone from any part of the universe is your patient. Any age there's no one excluded. And this is so serious a matter while you're in the process of awakening that once you decide to bring it out in the open with anyone you're going to have difficulty. The chances are that the individual won't know what you're doing, won't have the initiative that you have to do it, will be a curious onlooker. Spiritual work is done in private, and seriously it's nothing to share with a mortal being. Don't make that mistake. There are rare times when you can share and you will learn about which times to share and with whom. But you will know of your failures and you will know of your successes; no one else need know anything. And eventually there'll be successes more so than failures and when you have tasted what you can do you will know that you have penetrated the invisible world and from that moment on you will be led where you must go.

I want to recapitulate in ourselves what it feels like to be the invisible Christ because it's a new phase of your life that must be undertaken and will be undertaken by some of us right during this seminar, by some of us at a later date even though we may try during this seminar but we all should know what our future is. Our future is our present brought to light. We are going to have an opportunity to be our Self.

∞∞∞∞∞∞∞∞∞∞∞∞ End of Side One ∞∞∞∞∞∞∞∞∞∞∞∞

Now let's see how you start a healing career. Start with a child. He only looks like a child. There are no children. The Christ has no age, neither five hundred, two thousand or a day. Go past the illusion of child. Take a child that has an appearance of sickness. He's had this infection a couple of weeks; nothing has helped him. He goes to school; he has to stay home. Your consciousness now flatly accepts the child as the Christ of God. Through omnipresence you're not concerned about the fact that he isn't next door or he's not in the same city, he's anywhere in the world, but that child and you occupy the same space. To you, you must know through omnipresence you and that child occupy the identical space.

How is it possible to occupy the identical space? He's not a child; you're not a man or a woman. You are both traveling under false colors, when you accept the Christ where you are or where he is as the one universal Christ.

That makes his sickness impossible in reality, and because you believe it makes his sickness impossible in reality, you know that there's no sickness. You could think this all day with your mind in the world and it would not out-picture. And so you go more into yourself until you can feel the depth of your own being.

Let's say you're not able to hear the voice but you have a feeling that in some way you're in the presence of the presence. There is something in this boy here that is different than ten minutes ago. And while you're resting in this feeling it's automatically deepening. And soon human thought for you is almost impossible; you just can't think, not that you want to, but it won't work, it just won't come out. You find that you're deadlocked into a different situation than human thought and human appearances. In fact the human is diminished to a point of a particle. Even the boy is now playing a role. And on to some strange inner feeling that comes to you, there is the knowledge that there is no boy here, his fever will go away. He was never there; he was an image in world thought. And although he walks the earth everyone had accepted him as a reality, but in your meditation as you come to the depth of your being and Christ in you awakens, you realize that Christ in him has awakened; there is no boy. Only the Christ is present in him, in you; the work is done. Sometimes it goes just that fast. Healing is effortless. Healing leaves no feeling that you've got to strive, you've got to push him over into another place, that you've got to do something to take the sickness away. No healing is just the Christ recognition, the acknowledgment and the realization that follows and it's just a matter of being patient. This has been available for centuries. It always is an unusual experience for even the practitioner who's been through it many times.

Now if he had said that he was a boy who had died and that he had been buried or about to be buried in a coffin and his mother was a widow and the procession had proceeded out of Nain, out of the city toward the burial ground and they had called you to do some impossible thing, the Christ of you has already done that. The Christ of you has performed every healing in the world that has been done spiritually. So you're not turning this over to you; it's not a new case to Christ, and you must remember that. And that's why your capacities are infinite. Christ has handled every case before. Christ is always on the scene. Christ is omnipotent. Christ is

Class 3: The Mirage Of Me

perfect. You have this infinite ally who is your identity. And I'm sure if you receive this into your consciousness and developed a capacity to face the world with Christ in you that the world will be very sure to bring all kinds of treasures to your door for your ability to bring this light out where this person seems to be.

I want you to keep trying tonight. I want to repeat this as often as possible. I want the process to be simple, to be understood.

Now you get a call and it's three-thirty in the morning. The person is dying. You're flustered. Everyone gets flustered when someone is dying and you start doing all sorts of things. Your mind whirls and you wonder what was the principle that I was supposed to remember and all of that. Just stop a moment. It's the same always; this is the Christ of God, this so-called dying person. You're seeing something completely opposite than what the world would see. And you can feel the parents' anguish, of the husband or wife or the child, this person who's dying and instantly cool off that opinion with the knowledge that this person is not a person, he never will be a person, he never was a person, the Christ is not dying, that's number one. But he may still die. But even then he's not dying. You'll have to get clear on what dying is. Dying as the world conceives it is the loss of life. But the world does not know about the Christ life, which is the life of everyone and does not die. So he is not dying to you. And if you can, find the capacity to make no judgment about what's happening. To know that Christ is life, you will do what the Bible suggests. It tells you to "Judge no man," and instantly to acknowledge his Christhood. Now that's the point of miracles which are being called upon to accomplish even as a beginner because you never know what will come to your attention. You only know that you must learn the principles that he is the Christ, that you are the Christ, and that all power resides in Christ and to look at anything else with not even closing one eyelid.

You're standing in the secret place. How many times have you stood in the secret place? Nothing less will do. It's as if you were that boy's consciousness, that dying person's consciousness. You're standing where he would be standing, but you're standing in the secret place for him. The secret place is Christ life. If you're standing there with him in your consciousness, it's the equivalent to him standing there. Through the Christ omnipresence, Christ omnipotence, through your steadfastness and ability to hold your acknowledgement of Christ as the only presence, there can be an alleviation of the problem. There may not be. You may find you have not the ability to get the full light or there may be an appearance of death but actually a transition, and there may be a real death, the way people think of death because somehow you haven't been able to release the problem to the Christ.

But at least you are learning in this moment of concentration on what the facts are; you're learning what can and cannot be done. And someday you'll find that saving life isn't as difficult as it would sound. You'll see through the fact that the life is not going; it is not dying. You won't feel this inner pang of futility which translates into losing the case. It will be a simple matter of realizing impersonally that this is just another problem, like a mathematical problem. And if I react not, if I know the truth and if I'm patient, I can be a factor in the release of this man from the belief that he is dying. It'll feel good for all concerned. Now I know it has to be done before it can be appreciated, but all sorts of strange things are done.

I've often told the case of - it was like Joel's case and that's why I tell it - of this child. This child, her mother is pregnant and at the moment of pregnancy the child is a breach baby and the child won't emerge. Everybody is frantic and the attending physician just does everything he knows. Nothing will happen; the child won't turn around. And there's only one way to handle that and so you get the call, and even though you're not very advanced in the work. But in a short time the baby turns around, the infant turns around - I suppose infant is the wrong word - the embryo turns around and then the birth is a normal birth. And all that happens was that you stood for that moment or two or ten in the baby's Christhood and your Christhood and the infant turned around and was born.

Now when you see these things happen that you had no knowledge of, you have no ability to make it happen, but they do happen, you realize that life can be different if we bring the Christ into the picture. We're working without the light. We're absent from God and when we bring the Christ into the picture the whole world changes; impossibility has become normal. And I suppose you know of incidences of that character. That was only one that I know of, I mean that was one that I do know of and I know of others but when you participate in them and you find that you have this immense power just by virtue of knowing you're the Christ and that the

Class 3: The Mirage Of Me

other fellow is the Christ, and you don't forget it and that you treat them as the Christ although you think he's the lowest level of humanity, you mustn't have any point in your consciousness which says, "He's this but he's that." You draw no distinctions of any kind there are none in Christ. And that's the hardest part to have a purified consciousness which you can face these problems with no judgments, quickly transfer over to Christ and rest in it and as time goes on you find a way to transfer over deeper and faster. We're going to heal people. And I hope everything is clear so far because this is the whole foundation.

Now you can heal then physically, you can heal emotionally, you can heal financially; anything that is wrong is not wrong. You must learn to stand in the fact that there is nothing wrong in God's universe and just stand there and as the Christ plays on it you will see your miracles.

Now let's stand still in our own miracle. If you are the Christ, we'll all be satisfied with the word. The Christ is the Kingdom of God and the Kingdom is infinite, so you're not an individual person. And if you are the Christ, your mother never gave birth to you; she gave birth to the image of you that you thought you were. Let's trace our ancestry to God.

"Call no man your father on the earth for one is your Father in heaven."

You may not even be willing to do that but it's the requisite of the Christ healing. You must trace your ancestry to God, for God is your Father. And if God is your Father, then you must be the Christ. And if you are the Son of God, you take on new responsibility as a man or woman.

Now the Son of God does not think with a human mind. You're not being asked to. If you're let's say an accountant, you're not being asked to not do accountancy because you must use the human mind but you've got to be aware of the fact that you have the Christ mind and you've got to know when to use it. I don't think you have to bother the Christ mind about doing accountancy for you. The Christ is interested in activities not of this world. All you've been doing, if you're an average person, is activities of this world. But now with the Christ mind you can do activities in the Kingdom of God. One doesn't necessitate your dropping the other. But don't make the mistake of thinking you can do things with the Christ mind or do things with the human mind at the same time. Now Christ life is not human life and so you do have the Christ life and you walk in the belief that you have a human life too. I'm not telling you to drop one.

But remember that your Christ life is perfect, that your Christ life has no beginning or end. And that you are moving toward your realization that your Christ life is your reality and your human life is at least ten shadows away. Slowly but surely you learn to accept the Christ of your being as a wholeness and to lessen the human self of you because it isn't there at all.

I suppose there'll be many questions and you'll figure too that I have certain information now and I've got to live with my family and my family doesn't understand these things and my sister is of a different type of thought than I am now. Well then there's no need to upset the apple cart. You can still be friendly, you can still love, you can still do the things you do. This is your secret life, secret until you are so confident at it that you care to have other people see it. So for a while we'll keep our secret life to ourselves. And if at the age of two our son is - he should have died as people do but he's not - they're not able to kill him, we don't say, "This is the Christ." If at the age of six he performs a miracle we don't say, "This is the Christ." If at the age of twelve he's doing things that no boy who is twelve years old does we don't say, "This is the Christ." Our secret is our secret and his life remains secret with us. But we do the work. We have the Christ as the fulcrum of our existence and we look at everybody with the same attitude, the same realization, because we're living in the invisible. And in the invisible all is Christ.

Out in the visible world a person may look this way and act that way but in the invisible this is the perfect Christ. And so all we see in our invisible world as Christ. And when we're not seeing Christ, not accepting Christ then we're not living in the invisible world. See if you can learn how to accept Christ in the invisible world and every person on the face of the earth in the invisible world as the Christ. You'll be in such a degree of truth that your transformation will be startling.

I think possibly we can rest in this which I have given you as nothing more than information but what we want to do is rest in it until it settles down within our consciousness, so that it is a practical way of life that we know we have this way of life in the invisible. It is a side of us that is going to enlarge and enlarge and enlarge, but it must be used. You can't let it grow stagnant in your life or you'll find that in the Christ you have refused to acknowledge and to let work, won't take it lying down. If you

Class 3: The Mirage Of Me

desert Christ, Christ will desert you. And though your Christhood will be your reality, it will go right back and you will sleep to Christ.

Now take your hardest problem tomorrow or tonight and look at it another way, the hardest problem you know you have to face. I imagine there won't be one or two problems there'll be a hundred and fifty different problems. And when you face it quietly within yourself, ask yourself, "Who has the problem?" The answer will startle you because you know very well you don't have the problem because you are Christ. "Who then has the problem?" You have a problem that has been manufactured in the world mind and you have said this is my problem. You don't recognize it as an illusion, and it's very real to you. Now turn to Christ. And this should not be thought of as turning to a Christ that is a stranger to you or external to you. You're turning to the Christ of your being which is all you are, and ask Christ, "Do you have this problem?" And there's the source of my duality. Christ doesn't have a problem but I am Christ. Someone else has a problem that I have been accepting as myself. If I am Christ, where is the problem? My continuance in the problem is saying that I'm not Christ. By saying, "I have this problem," I say, "I am not Christ," because Christ is perfect without problems. If I say I have this problem, I will continue to have this problem because I'm making an illusion a reality in my consciousness.

Now reverse it. "If Christ doesn't have it and Christ doesn't, how can I have it when I am Christ?" The problem is the inability or unwillingness to accept that I am Christ. Now face that tomorrow, face it just that way. And after you've decided that you are Christ or not Christ perhaps the problem will look quite different. That's an assignment, to face a problem, a major problem and I'm hoping some of you say, "Well I don't have a major problem I'm Christ." We'll see.

So I'll see you in the morning and now that we have more or less done a good deal of the groundwork maybe we can get ambitious and try a few things that we wouldn't have dared when we first started. Until then I'll say good night and thank you very much for what I consider to be a perfect opportunity for all of us to make some progress.

Thanks a lot.

CLASS 4
RAISE THE DEAD

Herb: Good morning again.

You may never think of yourself as raising the dead. That is what you will be doing the moment you go out and agree to sit, stand spiritually with another individual, to help lift his consciousness. That is all raising the dead ever meant. In the healing ministry we are raising the dead, those who are asleep to Christ. And that is what you will be doing when you open your healing heart to other individuals who need a boost along the way who have to be reminded that somebody cares, and that somebody is the Holy Spirit.

Christ left the earth when he stopped being visible, when he stopped throwing forth that image called Jesus and then he reappeared. The reason it was three days was because he appeared to us as a mortal and then the three days during which he disappeared were the Soul day, the Spirit day and the Christ day. Those three worlds were transcended and then he appeared as a man again to the disciples, to remind them to teach us, that as he had not died we could do the same. He gave us a glimpse of life behind the scenes to show us that no one in the world ever dies. Even if a fellow went to a place that they called purgatory, if he were dead he would not suffer, he's alive in purgatory. So the point is that whether you go to a higher level or to a lower level you're still alive.

Now on the lower level which strangely enough is called the world it's really the underworld, and that's what we're in, we're in the underworld. We have the option of God or mammon. The option is always present. And then comes the Christ to show us that it's possible to raise yourself to a level out of the flesh.

"Henceforth know we no man after the flesh," we have known Christ after the flesh, "Henceforth know we him that way no more."

Class 4: Raise The Dead

For above the flesh is the Spirit world where we will have our fifth experience. And so, we are now a group with one intention, to raise the dead and that means our human selfhood and because we cannot leave our fellow man behind, we must raise the dead universally. And every man must feel the Christ. And then as Christ in Jesus showed us that life is eternal, Christ in man will follow that course and will attain the eternal life.

If that picture is clear, it becomes so simple to rearrange your life, to cover those important bases. Our function is to remain awake to achieve total awakeness. To lift ourselves from the fourth realm of mortality which believes that it dies. And yet it doesn't die because when it's so- called... it's meaning of death is different in the spiritual world than it is in this world. In the spiritual world death is known as an experience, in the physical world it is known as the end of life. When matter dies we think a person is dead, but the matter was never alive to die. The supreme illusion is that we die and we're dead. If we're lucky we get selected on the basis of our so-called merits and we go to a place called heaven which we all bought at one time. So we're not very far off from yesterday's illusion. Strangely enough there is a quantity, a physical quantity which has made it impossible for most of the world to see the spiritual nature of man. And if we look at matter and break it down we have been relegated to a place where we are that matter. And then when the matter goes we go with it, it decomposes, it joins the rest of the universe and there's no us anymore.

The scientist breaks it down a little further, he goes down to the atom and for a long time we thought we knew something. So we were atomic and I was an atom a compilation of atoms and you were a compilation of atoms and then finally we became micro-atoms. Finally we were the smallest particles known to man. People thought that this was what life was made of and people, largely, the majority of people in the universe still think that is what life is made of. That you are made of these tiny micro-atoms. And until you can see through that illusion you're going to fear death. You're going to fear that his body of yours is going to be taken away and it's composed of micro-atoms.

Now when you go out to heal you're going to bring that fear of death to your treatment of a patient and that's going to deter results. You must get rid of the illusion that is called fear which is based upon ignorance.

And all our fears are based upon the ignorance that this is me and that when the life of this goes, me goes.

Then it was seen that there is no life in matter. We understood why Jesus wanted to raise the dead. The belief that there is life in matter leaves you as a prey to every illness in the world. Every possible sickness that can occur, every conditioning is based upon the fact that I live in a body of matter. And the thing I'm really living in is in my belief that I'm living in a body of matter, because I see myself as a body of matter, because when I go to the store my body goes to the store. You may as well say, "I am the body and the body contains a brain, there I am." And man has lived this way, he's cut himself off from the true universe. When he says;

"God or mammon."

He's saying mammon is the universe you live in without God, absent from God and absent from life because God is life. We are all guilty. We have all wandered around the universe as a prodigal, absent from life, absent from God and there's that deep hunger in each of us. We all feel it. We're all searching for something, something to stabilize us, something to hang on to. And finally we hung on to an atom and a micro atom, "Oh that's us." It wasn't, but we thought it was. The atom was another illusion. Oh, it's just as real as your body, to you, but it isn't here, it isn't there. The body that seems there slowly decomposes and what we thought was there, isn't here anymore and we think we have gone and we were never in that body, NEVER! It wasn't possible to be in that body. We have built up a concept of ourself and then we see it, we feel it, we hear it, it moves it breathes it does this, this is a perfect counterfeit, a perfect counterfeit! So that you cannot tell the difference and you are not in that body and you are not that body. And as astounding as it was to us to learn that, astounding as it still is why in the world would the Christ tell you; withers."

"Know no man after the flesh." Why would he tell you that, "Flesh is grass. Flesh Because there's no life in flesh. There was an illusion of life, because the flesh seemed to move, we thought that man is alive. And now you're desperately reaching out for something else because you've got to live. You can't forever remain in illusion. And the answer is that this was the fourth phase of our return to the heavenly Christ. We have to go through it. I assure you once you're home again you'll never wander out,

Class 4: Raise The Dead

there will never be another illusion in your life. We have to learn what truth is and we have to use truth, let it use us to lift us. We all think Jesus said;

"I am the life. I am the resurrection."

Infinite Way has taught us that Jesus didn't say that at all and nowhere is the distinction more important. When you read that in the Bible you're reading the words that were spoken by Christ. The universal Christ. The Christ in every man. And then the translation becomes so utterly clear.

"I-Christ am the life. I-Christ am the resurrection."

And suddenly you've discovered that I-Christ am the life. Not I-Herb, I-Mary, I-Joel, I- anybody, I am the illusion, but I-Christ am the life. And fortunately for us I-Christ is our name. And when the life tells you who it is, but you don't know that you are the Christ, then where are you? And so Christ says now;

"Know no man after the flesh, know Christ." Plato says, "Know thyself."

But who is thyself? It's not this bundle of bones. It must impress upon you the undeniable fact that the living Christ is the only identity to which you can answer and say, "Yes I am that." And then it must be impressed upon you that you must spend your time developing a relationship with the Christ, which in turn will supersede any relationship and you will be that Christ. That is the only way for survival. That is the only way to get out of the wheel of death and reincarnation and death and reincarnation. You must be that Christ, and you are.

And so it would be well if we would move things out of the way, that stand in the way that prevent us from realizing where our work must go. It wouldn't matter if you were an Infinite Way student or not. Christ is universal. The Catholic, The Protestant, the Jew, anyone is the Christ, so we throw away the labels and we claim identity as the living child of God, but not for ourselves only, every individual we see. And because Christ is the name of each individual, you can't claim it here and disavow it over there, because I am over there and I am over there. I am omnipresent and therefore you cannot claim that I am localized because when you claim that I am localized you are stepping out of the realization of identity. Identity isn't one person or another,r identity is the immortal human race. The human race has to awaken to the fact that it is not the dead dying matter, it is the living eternal Christ. And every recognition that you give another is raising the dead. When you become infatuated with the idea that you have this power to raise the dead to life, you have something to give every person in the universe. You are the bringer of good news and the funny thing is that you can't even take this to everyone. You can't say, "Let me tell you something, you are the living Christ." There's no preparation for that in the human consciousness. And so at an early age you start to be still about who you are and about who he is although you know who he is. And soon you lose the he, the him, the her, the me into this larger concept;

"I am the Christ of all men."

And when you do, you open up a whole new universe for yourself, because that is when God proves that everything is possible to God. Let's assume that you agree and that you try to follow and that you realize that you are the universal Christ. What change would that make in your human life?

You are everyone you see - I don't mean it as a symbolism. I don't mean it as an idea that we're to think about - I mean it's the fact of life, you are everyone you see. That man over there is no less you than what you had called yourself, because yourself isn't this body. You are the infinite invisible and it's silly when you have all, to be settled down into a microcosm that has a tiny bit, a tiny bit of nothing. All substance is you. There's not another substance in the world.

And when we get back to the atom and follow it down lower to the micro-atom and then it disappears and that man is considered dead we have forgotten about the essence of that man, which is not dead, which is the substance of life which we are. And once you become imbued with this idea – oh, it'll take some time - but when you become imbued with it and it slowly pulses through up to your soul and the realization strikes you, "I, the universal Christ?" It may take you a year before you even can get yourself to believe it, but someday you must because it's the only salvation we have. And then when you're the universal Christ we see how stupid we have lived. We've lived by the sweat of our brow, by our intelligence, by our will, all the things we thought we had to do to survive, to forge ahead, to protect ourselves. We all live with one eye on tomorrow and one eye on yesterday, we don't know who is coming up behind us. But our being includes all that is called time. It is all myself.

In your meditation now, we want to slowly realize that the universal Christ is here. All of the universal Christ is right here. All of the universal Christ is right there, and all of the universal

Class 4: Raise The Dead

Christ is in every country of the world. The infinite Christ is everywhere and everywhere it is, it is infinite and it is I. That's the miracle of infinity. I am perfect in Alaska right now.

[short silence]

But you're speaking about the individual you once thought was God in the heaven to be worshipped externally, but God is right here and strangely enough the ground you are is Holy, because the you and the God are one and the same.

[short silence]

We have been out with the swine, eating with them, but suddenly there are no swine we are home with the Father.

Now, if you believe a wit of this, it will take you and it will slowly drain all of the iniquities out of your so-called brain. It will drain out of you all of the things that you are not and you will stop riding two horses. You rode those two horses because the world made you, the world you created. You thought you had to ride on the horse of good and the horse of evil. And you thought you had to live in such a way that you kept the evil out and the good in. In human duality we all live on those two. It's the same as the tree of good and evil, but where is it? It's in our imagination. There is no evil and there is no good, there is only perfection. And we must make an earnest effort to uphold what is.

[short silence]

You're taking all this and more to your patient, so you have a double responsibility to be what you tell your patient, to lift your patient as you have been lifted yourself by yourself.

[short silence]

The difference between a poor man and a rich man is not the amount of money they have, because neither the poor man nor the rich man have reality. But the Spirit of man which is the only man is the rich man, for the riches he has are the divine, which will never be taken from him, the riches of the human will be taken.

[short silence]

Hold to the new idea that your Christhood extends all over the universe. That's why you're Master of the tides, that's why you live above time. All things that are temporary have no power to one who is the Master of himself. And the only Mastery there is, is to know the truth. To be the truth you know. And eventually, as all of the truth becomes part of your being, you will find that every emotion, every activity, every thought is divine.

[short silence]

Now, I am not painting a picture of a future event, nor am I trying to instill in you the belief that you are someone you are not, or the belief that you are trying to impersonate, or trying to in some way convince yourself that you can do these things or feel this way. I am, not I will be. All that you will be is what you are. As you climb, climb, climb higher you're only climbing up to what you already are, completed. It is finished.

[short silence]

Man is the Son of God and when you know yourself to be that, a lot of the foolish things that we do we won't do. That's the beginning point of life, that's when we start to live, when we start to explore. We start to have things come to us out of the blue, wonderful things, things that we need but can't find. The peace of mind we earnestly seek but can't find, lingering doubt, the things we can't control.

The worries we have about children. We have stopped realizing that the only way we can teach children is by example. They will follow a good example. If we can show children the value of Spirit, they have little choice but to want it and to seek it and to strive to attain it. If we can't show them the value of Spirit, why are we surprised that they turn to drugs? There is energy that they have to burn up, they're going to burn it up as they see fit when they have a goal that is superior to another, they will choose the one that's best for them. If they can surf ride they'd rather do it than not surf. If they can surf ride in Spirit they are going to want to do that. We have to provide them with alternatives they do not now have, and in so doing we'll provide ourselves with the same alternatives. The children are our inspiration to do as well as we can to invite them to our Kingdom. Let's not invite them to our world.

[short silence]

So when we look at "raise the dead" we begin with, "I am the life."

"There's not one among you," says the Christ, "if he's not living the Christ life who is alive." And who will someday be brought to a rude awakening. And so we have a manger which somehow we're led to and in that manger we are born of the Spirit of God. And do you notice how nobody can hurt that child. That child born in you is the same way. And it is born in a manger. In a manger of your consciousness where noone is present. And many many things in this world attack and still that child grows up because there is something sustaining that child, that is the Christ child and that's the same thing that sustains you as you grow up internally. There's always the Spirit of God protecting. There's always three prophets arriving to give you the myrrh, the frankincense and the gold. Along the way there's always the Essenes to raise you as you grow a little older. The Spirit of God is always with the child of Christ. And as that Spirit grows in you, when that child grows in you, it's growing into the fifth world of understanding. There's no impediment, nothing standing in its way. As this Christ grows you find that you and heaven are one. The Spirit of God is upon you.

I didn't read of any sickness in the Christ, any infectious diseases, any heart attacks, it must be that it didn't have any, and why? This is the nature of the Christ. And as this Christ continues to grow in you, it begins to draw people to it. At first they're offended, but as the word of

God comes through, as the blind man sees, as the crippled arm is no longer crippled, as all of the defects that mankind has known are not in this child, there must be a reason. And this child is a symbol of the child that grows in you, ever, ever widening out until your identity has over reached the shores of this world that we know.

"My Kingdom is not of this world."

I'm not stopping at a boundary. I'm not going to be a micro-atom or a combination of micro-atoms or a configuration of atoms. I am the essence of God, my essence is the light of the world, but I am only the child that grew in you, which automatically fulfills every divine law.

[short silence]

You thought you had wealth but now you have wealth that no one can take from you. If the stock market goes up or down it won't affect you, inflation or deflation. You are provided for by an invisible force and if we felt a little of that in our lives up to now, just imagine what you'll feel as it develops, as this Christ in you grows. None of this is fanciful or fiction, it is to be lived and when you have an element of it in you stabilized, so that you know it, you're a different person. And you know what I mean by that, that no one can ever take it away and you know it. And you go forth, and you now have the ability when you go forth to bring that light in you and to light the light in others. You're doing God's work. You can be as rich as you want to be, but you're doing God's work now, or as poor as you want to be, but you'll be provided for in health, in income, in companionship, in happiness, in harmony, in peace, in fulfillment because you're living a whole life. Nothing is missing. You don't have to go seeking for something else, the world comes to you. Everything you need comes from inside yourself. Your human mind would not have known what it needed, it would've thought it needed certain things. Your Christ mind provides for its needs and it reaches out for those needs in the inner world and then they manifest in the outer world. Whatever is needed must appear. That's the way life should be.

∞∞∞∞∞∞∞∞∞∞∞∞ End of Side One ∞∞∞∞∞∞∞∞∞∞∞∞

I've been getting a lot of questions about the next classes that we're going to have, but we're going to have one in San Rafael in California, that's up in Marin county, that'll be next Easter. And Easter 1992 will be in… I think we'll have a class in Poipu, Kauai and you can start putting away your sarong if you feel like coming and we'll see you up there, outside of that I don't know, then others have asked me any books? Yes, there's one book that will be out, I can't say when but it's written and we're having a conference on it Monday. And another book that's called <u>Forty Days in the Wilderness</u>. And the other book will be the <u>Revelation of St. John</u> and that will be the theme also of the seminar, the second seminar in Kauai, 1992. So between those two books we'll have our hands full, but things happen fast in this we're always developing something and we're always pushed in a direction we don't expect, so I'd say look for anything.

For the consciousness that we spoke of dawns in you, you'll know about it. You won't feel alone in the world anymore. Something happens inside you and there's no way to describe it, but you're suddenly about to burst and yet it's a controlled feeling of exultation. Everyone who has felt it knows what I am speaking of. That exultation is that at last I have found the Spirit in myself and it is now alive.

You see what we're doing right now is preparing you to go forth with the living Spirit, there's nothing else can heal. If everyone here would go

Class 4: Raise The Dead

forth with the living Spirit, inside of one year the world would know about it. Your influence will be felt all over the world.

An interesting thing about Spirit is that many people are frightened about old age. First of al,l industry doesn't what them anymore, they don't have anything to do except clippings. But you see Spirit has wisely left the best for the last. Old age is when you have the time and as you grow older and this grows in you, you are eternal youth and you're not old age anymore. There's something beautiful about ripening years and ripening consciousness they go together. Then lo, you find out you're not older at all. No, you're going to change bodies but it's no hardship, and many people wish you could do it for them, and wish they could do it for themselves. Because there is a Kingdom of God here waiting patiently, that Christ born in you is going to take you into that Kingdom.

Christ is always a present event, a here event, a now event and you maybe surprised to discover that Christ is working in you, in a way you hadn't believed. Your grief may suddenly disappear, love may suddenly appear. It is my function for you to always be in the will of God. Now can you imagine the will of God doing something that is not divine? If the will of God has been given access to your consciousness and your consciousness has opened, then you have heard the voice. You have heard the Spirit of God knocking and you have opened the door.

When Jesus sent forth his disciples without purse or scrip, they were surprised, they didn't know what power was in them.

"Why we can even tread on serpents."

And just a while ago they had just been human beings. There'll be a burst of new enterprise, new achievements, because there will be no boundaries to what can be achieved.

Now let's go into a patient, let's take a city with an epidemic, that's a patient. What can be done when an epidemic breaks out? One person in a group calls you probably for himself, but he tells you there's an epidemic going on. Well you work for that person, but when you learn that is an epidemic, you work for the epidemic too. Now, let's say it's diphtheria, you have the power to unsee that epidemic. You have the power to do it in your living room. Let's say it's malaria, whatever it is and wherever, when it is brought to you by an individual who has been infected by it, you have the right to treat it. And you treat that epidemic just as you would treat the single patient.

Where is the epidemic? It's not in a place, that's for the unenlightened. It's not in a place, because there is no place. There is no matter in your consciousness. Oh, they'll call it a city, a village, a town but in your consciousness that cannot happen in the Kingdom of God. And if you're living in the Kingdom of God you'll see to it that it will not happen in your Kingdom. But you can't be somewhere else, back in the world again. You can't be in humanity, you've got to be Spirit living in the Kingdom of God and appearing on earth. Who's going to do the healing of this epidemic? Why Christ has done millions of them. You are called upon to bear witness to the perfection of Christ, while the world is bearing witness to the epidemic. How will you go about it? Will you be overcome by the immensity of the task or will you just see it as just another running nose? What's the difference if it's an illusion on a small scale or a large scale? You don't believe it. You stand fast. Christ does the work. But you have to stand fast first, and while you're standing fast taking no thought, realizing that this cannot happen in my Kingdom,

"I come forth."

And how does I come forth? What brings I into the picture? Your consciousness has prepared the way. I don't believe this epidemic. Christ is the life, there is no epidemic in Christ.

"I am the life," said Christ.

That is the one eternal infinite life of the universe. Where's the epidemic? It's in the world of illusion but oh, it's so real to those people. Now maybe people are going to "die." Well they're living without Christ aren't they? In the presence of God there is liberty. You have to be the one, the enlightened one aware of the presence of Christ, because Christ comes through your awareness into the world. You notice how subtle it works?

Remember that stationary of mine of two worlds, two circles and the voice coming through the two circles? Two worlds next to each other and the voice comes through. That was given to me in 1964, that design, it was handed to me, it always symbolizes the living between two worlds, the middle path between good and evil. When Joel gave it to me I didn't even know what it meant, just a vague idea that some symbol says, "W,ell yeah I read about the middle path, and stuff like that." He had no reason to give

Class 4: Raise The Dead

it to somebody who wouldn't treasure it. So I put it on my letterhead. And it still means then, what it means now, because there's one time and that's NOW. It always meant the invisible Christ comes forth and you are the door of awareness which permits him to walk through your consciousness into the world.

It's a marvelous feeling to know that you don't have to stand by helplessly and watch a world suffer. That if you have access to the Christ, you have access to the healing influence. But the healing influence doesn't only apply to the person who calls you. The healing influence is in your life because I would assume that you don't have access to the Christ only to heal a phone call. The life that comes through you to heal the individual who phoned does as much for you.

"Awake thou that sleepest and Christ will give thee light."

Were you excluded? Was she excluded? Was he excluded? Who was excluded? It's a universal call to all men, all races. And here and there one person hears it and another person and now there are more hearing it. Christ is becoming a living treasure. Not someone reserved in heaven for those who are fortunate. A walking living Christ among men as Jesus appeared among men.

I can't wait for the next challenge, we don't know what it will be or where it will be but we all have that challenge ahead of us. And it will come to you sooner than you think and if you're not ready, it will come again, because you've already been touched by the Spirit, it has prepared you. But it has prepared you for something bigger than you can realize in a moment. It's prepared you not only to heal the sick, it's prepared you to raise the dead, and you will raise them every time you recognize that Christ is the nature of life, not will be, not tomorrow, Christ is the nature of every life now. How can there be a fire where Christ is realized? How could there be a robbery where Christ is realized? Do you see what you're coming to? Every iniquity in this world happens where Christ is not realized. Can you sense the scope of our power, of our responsibility and how in failing we put ourselves in the grave? Does God dispense with someone who's doing God's work? I mean doing God's work.

"Father thy will be done."

I'm building houses. They house people, they house God's child that's a noble work. I'm building good houses for good people. I'm flying an air route for an airline, I'm flying good people to their destinations, to do good things. And each of us finds that we are doing something and when we open the door to the Christ influence it becomes something better. It doesn't lose the original aspect we gave it, it adds to it. And as we ascend in consciousness, the things that we do in the world ascend in consciousness. We find that we are lifting the world, raising the dead. Awakening, those who have slumbered in their ignorance of the invisible Christ. I don't blame them, we can't blame them. It's difficult to know that there's an influence in this world that's being unused, but there is a major influence being unused. We have lived a false life and have not known it. Some label it successful, some label it not, but they all pale to insignificance compared to what we are doing with the Christ of our being.

I think we all have the general principle of healing and of living, that we know we must open the door to Christ in our consciousness. Perhaps you would like to know what will happen when you open the door.

"The Father who seeth in secret will reward thee openly."

There is an all intelligent eye, an omniscience and the instant one has come into Christ, that instant registers on the creator of the universe. That registration on the creator of the universe becomes the instant that you are under divine law. That means your plane doesn't fall out of the sky. It does if you're not aware of who you are. It means that you walk in an invisible cloud of love. It means that you bring this cloud of love wherever you go. It means that your heart does not stop beating until the Father has taken you into the highest level of the Kingdom where you are self sustaining forever. Are you aware that you can be self sustaining forever? That's the nature of God in man. The things you must do will not stretch out in time. They will occur in the now because that's where they have already occurred. If you think the things you have done are wonderful, you will be surprised to find that the things you have done in the invisible are more so. You will add an infinite dimension, which is no dimension at all, to everything that you have thought yourself possible to do. You will find that there is no sickness on earth that can reach you. Why is that so? Because the healing influence is always with you. Christ is there. And you say, "How will I know?"

I Christ speak, "I speak to my Son. Literally speak."

Class 4: Raise The Dead

And when you hear that word and you obey there's nothing in this world that can stand in the way of the Living Word of God, absolutely nothing. You find that without any form of ostentation or boasting or desire for personal glory, the power of God to bring you through the crowd, through the war, through the non-existent metal, will do whatever is necessary at the moment. It will shuffle all the papers to make new figures, it will make the computers say whatever it wants to say and if you don't believe it you'll be pleasantly surprised to find that the power, the invisible power makes an atom bomb look like a child. The invisible power can instantly reduce the atom bomb to exactly what it is, a great deal to human beings, but nothing in Spirit.

If you live in the earthquake area you'll find that even though the earthquake is there it cannot come nigh thy dwelling. In short, you are protected by an invisible light and you're aware of that protection. You won't have to move out of the twentieth storey floor of a skyscraper because you feel it will tumble with the earthquake or Spirit will move you out, but whatever you'll do in that area you'll be guided by Spirit and after the earthquake is gone you'll be there. If you're aware you can take all of the fear out of the earthquake before it ever happens. You can move that earthquake out of its unreal position into nothingness. You can reverse the tides, you can quell the fire, and you say, "Who me how?" I didn't say, "Who, you, how," you won't do it, you aren't there. You are the invisible Christ and if you're still the visible person you haven't caught the message.

The human sleep will lessen as we go forth raising the dead. I can pick out five or ten who will do this and I am sure there are those I don't know who can do his. It isn't going to be a limited effort, it's going to be a way of life to raise the dead wherever you go. Oh, you'll sense it the minute you walk into a family, someone there is alive and the others are not, they're sleeping. Now the some one alive needs you just as much as the others who are sleeping to bolster the confidence of that one. You always can be a better influence to wherever you go just by being there, in truth, knowing your identity and living it out. You must live in your identity.

Now, if you want to do a strange thing and join me. Our meditation will be for the unborn. For those who have lived many times but are now unborn, about to be born. The children of what we call tomorrow. They need our help too. Before they form and crystallize into a shape, into an identity, let's reach them with our love. The Spirit of God is their name too. When they are born with the Christ influence they bring to the world something that it has needed for a long time, and something it has not had, something we can help give it. The light of the unborn Christ is as powerful as the light of the Christ living in this world. The world will call them matter, fetuses, we will them the Christ. Wherever they are, in a communist country, in a dictatorship, in a democracy, in a republic, these unborn children are not political. They're coming in with a fresh consciousness to complete what they have not done before. We stand in the invisible Christ of our being, which is infinite, which means we are in their presence.

[silence]

Let's take a quick review of what we will begin doing as a result of these lessons. Try to get together with yourself, first. If you will in the afternoon, sit in your room for a little while, be still. There's a technique to taking no thought and you don't turn your mind off, but you develop a capacity to leave it open without thought. It's a very important technique. Later you will use it often, daily in fact. Your mind is open but awake, very alert and is tuned to something in yourself. And into that consciousness there will come a thought, but it will not be a human thought and you won't control it, it'll be an impulse perhaps, and it may take three minutes before it happens or five or twenty seconds. That impulse will be saying something that is shaping itself inside your consciousness. But I'll tell you what it will not be, it will not be a desire to go out and get something, it will not be a desire to hurt someone, it will not be saying any thought of this world. It will be something that you can't describe, that is just right for you. And you will sit there and you will say, "What is this thing I feel in me?" And you'll make a note of it and then you'll stay there a little longer and finally out of it, you will open your eyes and you will go about the world business. But now this something in you will direct you. It will keep you on a certain path, a certain level, a certain course until you have been drawn into a relationship, an activity, a job, whatever is needed at the moment. It will take you a step beyond with a spiritual impulse to guide you and you'll say to yourself, "Well, I didn't know I could do this so simply. I didn't know this could be done. I called the airline and I didn't plan to do it today, I was going to do it next week but they told me I was

Class 4: Raise The Dead

lucky and I got the last ticket," or something of that nature. "I called the hotel, yes they could get me a room with an outside view or a room by the water," or what not. Perhaps I called the hotel and they told me there's no room and I called another one but there was. They will do something within you, that is necessary in your living and you will develop the habit of everyday going to your within, for this impulse. It will vary, it will never quite duplicate itself, it may surprise you one day and speak to you. But you'll learn that your impulse comes from God. And as you follow it you are doing the Will of God. Again through your awareness Christ brings the Will of God.

Do you see how a world with Christ bringing into it the Will of God is a better world? Now, everybody won't do that in the world. So you'll say, "What if I get it and no one else gets it?" But you'll find out that as you get it, you'll be guided and your day will feel blessed, inspired a certain way, and your day will impress other worlds, other lives. And that way you'll get an impetus starting, and you'll find it is always in the Kingdom of God that it begins and when it ends in you, if you can continue it by enacting it, that is how you begin to do God's will. It may be a slight thing, unimportant to others but it'll be important in your life that God notices your ability to follow the commands. Don't take it so literally that you go out and follow a yellow taxi cab because it tells you to look for the color yellow.

Listen for the spiritual impulse. There are many people misled by the spiritual impulse. They got a psychic impulse they went out and did it, they ended up on the wrong side of the tracks. You learn to hear your Master's voice. And it's not easy at first but even if a dog can hear five hundred people and tell it's master's voice, you certainly can tell your Master's voice. It comes very subtly and that is the most important voice you will hear. Whatever you do then will be ordained and blessed.

CLASS 5
A MOMENT IN INFINITY

Herb: The best we can hope for is to be very good human beings, very successful human beings and someday very dead human beings. We have no choice if we want to be one with God. We must learn how to live outside of time. Most students are never faced with this issue. But then once we decide to face it, to see that what we are feeling represents the truth of being. To be one with the Father, one must be outside of time with the Father. Once we make our decision to face that issue we find unexpected health, but health which is so surprising that we find ourselves in another problem. And these represent the rocks, the reefs, the obstacles that we have to wiggle through to get to the position where we can formalize our oneness with the Father.

Now prepare for a few shocks because we have to go through these hidden mines that can explode any minute in our face. We have to see that there is no past. The past is absolutely nothing. Every yesterday is gone, and all your aches and pains in yesterday are gone with it. You may think they're yours that you have to live them but you're only living with the memory. Sometimes the memory will seem like a present memory, it will go with you wherever you go, but it's still a memory. Every ache and pain that you ever felt is in the past.

A woman wrote me that, "How can we go to God when this pain hurts me?", "You're living in the past and you're going to carry that into the future. And your memory is laying hold of an idea that repeats and repeats and repeats and you drag this repetition into every day. There is no past. It's quite clear that God has no past and you know God has no future either and neither have you, neither have I. There is no future at all. It's a myth. The past and the future are the parenthesis that hold man in bondage to his so-called errors and to his so-called ambitions. When you experiment with past and future you will see that they have no existence but in the human mind.

If you had an ailment as a child and think that the ailment has carried on and left a scar on your present life, give it more thought and dwell in consciousness on the fact that the errors of the past are no more. Just as the moment of light will break the shackles of memory, so will a moment of truth reveal to you that there is no past in my being. There would be if I were a physical form living in this world. Then this physical image would have a physical past, and the past will be as illusory as the present. But after you've come to the point where you realize the illusion of the form, don't you see that what was in your so-called past would have to be an illusion about the form that is not? Do you realize that you have shed the past when you have shed the illusion. You'll dwell upon it and you'll discover an unexpected freedom. You didn't live one minute before this minute.

The future is a future of what? The form, the life in form? But it's illusory, you're building a future illusion. If you're down to the rock bottom truth of being, all that exists is this split second now. And in the split second now is the only time that you will ever meet God face to face. Now this information can be used effectively. If you'll become a Master of the truth that God is in the now. God has never been out of the now. God can't go backwards and forwards because there's no backwards and forwards to go to. There's only infinite now, always now. It will be infinite now, a million tomorrows from now and a million tomorrows ago. God lives in the infinite now and when you realize it, after working on it, dwelling upon it, abiding and waiting for the Christ to clarify, you'll see that the infinite now is the only place you can find perfection.

You can face your entire past and you can't go back one minute of it. You can't go back into the past. You physical can't, all you can do is think about the past. You can't step into the future. You can think about the future, but you can't live in it. You may think I'll wait and I'll live in the future when it comes, but it won't be the future then it'll be the now. You can't go anywhere beyond this split second and all life comes down to this split second, until you learn the infinite nature of a split second. And when you learn it you're going to find a change in your life. You're going to find the power. You're going to find everything you ever thought was in heaven on earth. Try it and see what I mean. You might find yourself without a body in five seconds. It's the way you're going to learn to step out of the body.

I, three hundred and fifty pounds of such and such a person am standing here on the current belief in time. I'm in such a year, such a day, such an hour and I'm under the impression that if I wait twenty four hours I'll be in another day and another day and another day. But it's a strange thing about time. I can't step beyond this second, as try as I might I cannot step beyond this second and neither can anyone else. That's a prison. You're being held prisoner in this second. You want to escape? Try going backwards, you can't step a half inch into the past. You're a prisoner in one second or less and you thought that we had freedom. This image is tied down to where it is. It has a life of seconds tick, tick, tick, and that's all it has, and think what you'd think you're doing in those seconds. But Christ is not tied down to this second. Christ is not tied down to the belief in time. Christ lives in the eternal now. Man lives in the passing now. You see the difference? In the passing now you have the illusion of being free. In the eternal now you can roam Gods paradise.

Now let's see how we would step out of time. You can't do it humanly. You're absolutely bound to the parenthesis, parenthesis, parenthesis and your life in the second between. Now you remember those two circles and the voice coming through. Dwell in the Spirit and see how the Spirit liberates you automatically from time. Your body doesn't have to move in it. You can leave your body right where you are. Your mind won't help. It cannot move into timelessness. Your mind you'll have to leave behind in a few years, ten, twenty, thirty, forty. No, it can't move anywhere. It's bound to the earth. Your Spirit knows no boundaries. Your Spirit is you. Your Spirit can roam a million years ago or a thousand. It doesn't think of them as a million years or a thousand because it's all now. There's no space to your Spirit except infinite space. It's all here. When your spirit says, "Here," it means here in the infinite which is without boundary. It doesn't mean here in this one inch plot of ground. Here in the infinite which is without limit, I live. It doesn't mean in this hour or this day. It means in the eternal which is a normal thing, now in the eternal. Spirit lives in the eternal here, the eternal now and that's the scope of your being. Now! And you're going to rise to the level where you know that and experience that un-limitation.

Now your patient is stuck. He's riveted to the spot. He's riveted to the hour. It happened over here - he's got it over here - he'll have it over there - that's the sequence. In the now, in the unbounded space, in the unbounded time he's perfect. He's imperfect because he is accepted that he is the individual bound in time, bound in space with a physical body. He can't even move and get out of the body. He's stuck inside of it or in the illusion of it. He's got a physical body in time and a life in time. And in that time comes an ailment and he's got that in time. And then when he disappears from time he thinks, "I am not here, I'm gone. My relative went out of time." Why time doesn't even exist in God. We've got to learn to build our true life around the God who has the power. When Jesus stands before Pilate;

"Thou couldest have no power over me."

He didn't explain it. Thou could just have no power over me. Well now here's Pilate, a body in time and space with a beginning and an ending. He's trying to have power over infinity, over the hereness of everywhere, over the nowness of eternity. He can't even begin to see this infinity which he's trying to have power over. And in human pride he makes the boast that I have the power to do such and such. He has no power.

But what has that got to do with you if you can't emulate the Spirit who is demonstrating that Christ can't be contained in a minute or an hour or a day. In three days the Christ appears after the beheading; "Here I am." "We thought we killed you." "Yes I know.", "How do you think you would do that? Did you take a segment of time and cut it up, or a segment of space, did you think I was in a little space like that?" I can't explain to you what infinity is or what eternity is, but the Son of God lives in infinity and eternity. Even Pilate, "You are the Christ." Maybe by now I'll reach a student of a movement somewhere where he's learning a little bit of truth. Everyone was told by that experience that here means everywhere, in time hours that tick, are really not there and all of time added up wouldn't make a second in eternity, but that's our natural habitat. Seems late that we are learning it. But we have discovered that the process of learning is very exciting when one experiments.

Now Jesus had no concept of time and that is why his healings were instantaneous. Today we think it will take four days or five days to heal or maybe a week but we're still lingering in the concept of time. As that disappears you'll find healings are instantaneous too. And when you're out of the body you have no concept of time, that's why healings out of the body are quicker than when a person is lingering in the flesh.

The other day a girl was hypnotized by a group, they put what I call a curse on her, and she was so aware of this curse, and so fearful of the pain that it might bring to others that within herself she was petrified. Could hardly talk. And so she phoned her mother and wanted her mother to send down the money, certain amount - it was quite a large sum - because if she didn't send down the money it would be - the impression was that this girl would be - in danger. Her mother is one of the highest Infinite Way students and she laughed at it but it was still her daughter, so she couldn't laugh too hard she had to be concerned. She tried not to be but it occurred to her that maybe if she went down, she would talk to whoever her daughter or maybe even talk to these people. Anyway she didn't go down and we worked on it.

The way I worked on it was to stay out of time. You see that couldn't be happening except in time, but out of time Spirit lives. In time flesh lives. So we got out of the area of flesh which is the hypnotism into the area of no flesh the Spirit. And ultimately the daughter came home and then she could laugh at it, for after a while. The point is that the consciousness awareness of no time and no space broke what I think was the curse. I tell that to you as healers because you may be called upon to break the hypnosis of an individual, that someone is in danger and she has to be bribed to get the money down in a hurry and this and that. But it held that girls consciousness in such a way that she couldn't get out of it. And you know, funny thing, is that it's happened to some of us, we've all been in that fix. We all thought we were smart, nothing could fool us, and then along it comes.

When you find that you cannot break a case let your thoughts run to the Spirit. And let the Spirit infiltrate so deeply that you've built a barricade against any possible error. If the solution is time or timelessness, space or spacelessness. If it's any protection you need, the Spirit which is omniscient knows the direction to take, takes that direction and liberates you. It doesn't matter what your problem. Now that girls problem was that some other problem any other kind, Spirit would have had another solution for her. The important thing to you to know is that Spirit is never bound by any human power. No matter what the power is, it's not a power against the Spirit. And if you don't know the solution it doesn't matter at all. Spirit does know the solution. You've got to know these truths that Spirit meets the claim if you are in a position not to interfere.

We are now looking at the straight and narrow and it becomes straighter and more narrow than you can imagine. But the straightness and the narrowness is infinite and it widens. It widens to allow all of infinite Spirit to function within it's scope, so that whatever is needed by the person who is in it/problem or by the person helping the person you will find coming to your rescue in the invisible. And, that what is needed flows to this particular spot where there is a patient to do what must be done for that patient, no matter if the help is five million miles away it can instantly appear in the Spirit. You must build your faith in the flexibility of Spirit to perform whatever is necessary, anything even beyond the human mind can conceive. Spirit will literally appear out of nowhere.

We were given some glimpses of this in the Bible itself. We could not tell what Spirit was saying to us but when Jesus appeared and they picked up stones to throw at him, it says, "he disappeared in the midst." He just escaped in the midst. You can escape in the midst when people are going to take your head off with stones. It means he became invisible and so he escaped that way. Was he afraid of them? No. He said what he had to say and you know whatever he said was always pretty inflammatory. He wasn't afraid of them, and then he either walked away or disappeared. Where did he go when he disappeared? Just where you would go if you now became invisible. You'd be right where you are but no one could touch you. The whole Pacific Ocean could flow over you and not touch you. Because, there is no connection between matter and Spirit. You have no idea who is living invisibly right next to you, right around you, right where you walk there's no connection between the two. This make believe world will be here until it has served its purpose. For you it will be here until it has developed you into a first rate Spirit who can now function with infinity and eternity more directly than he can as an individual in a physical form.

Now let's get used to movement of Spirit throughout infinity and eternity. It is said that it is like the wind. We do not know the source or the destination and it comes when we know not. And the bridegroom comes for the bride when we know not, when ye think not. What are all these phrases doing in the Bible? They're saying something esoteric so that you will stop and look, and discern that all around you in the invisible are the everlasting arms of the Father. If you get from my discussion that when you go to heal another person you have the everlasting arms of the Father, infinity, eternity at your beck and call. Provided you are not in a state of thought because instantly when you think you draw the curtains. And, once more you are living in a world where man is tricked by illusion, tricked by false boundaries, limited to his breathing apparatus. You're back to being mortal. But the curtain can be pulled apart.

It is said that; "the pure in heart will inherit the Kingdom of God." The pure in heart are those who are willing to lay down their thought, ultimately to lay down their concept of life which is their thought and to let the Father guide them, slowly at first and their guidance will be in the direction of Spirit. Open their eyes, show them a little bit of heaven. And then you'll come upon an individual with a problem, and he'll come to you and you'll say to yourself, "I don't really know how to solve this problem." You'll say that for a while, but then you'll say too, "that Christ knows how, I think I'll turn to the Christ and I'll watch, I'll behold. How does Christ do it? Well Christ lives in infinity and eternity. Christ has the freedom." He also uses a human brain as a stepping stone to get into his Christ brain which you will have to learn how to do. You're trying with a human brain. Of course you're limited to human methods. And so maybe you would operate and this person would die, or maybe you would operate and this person will live, because human methods are fallible. Human methods are only temporary. Spirit is eternal. When your patient is healed by the Spirit your patient is also going to live forever because Spirit does not work on a human level.

If you decide to become an agent for the Spirit you'll be making a wise decision. Instead of boasting about I healed this one and I healed that one, because it won't last very long. Spirit doesn't want human healers. But you can be a great spiritual healer if you take the time to absorb certain lessons about the nature of Christ, the nature of divine power through Christ, and the absolute non-power of all human methods because they're only power in the world of illusion. This clarifies to an extent how you bring Christ power to work on a human being but you need practice. You have to do ten healings, twenty healings, thirty healings to get the feel of it, to see how

Class 5: A Moment In Infinity

you get out of the way and how you allow Christ to get in. The best way to practice is to try to do it in your own life - in your meditations to invite Christ in by signing off, by slowly learning the art of dying to the flesh.

I would like to experiment a little again. Dying to the flesh is not saying, "I won't do this. I won't do that." That's a negative way of doing things. Dying to the flesh is to make yourself available to the Christ and let the Christ sit on the seat of your consciousness. Let Christ be the voice that reaches your client or your patient although you may be talking you're repeating what the Christ is telling you to say, what the Christ is instructing you to do. You are taking no thought, using no will but you're the perfect instrument for the Christ. You're like a ditto machine. Christ says, "This is what you do," and you find your hands doing it. "This is what you say," you find your mouth speaking the words. It's so close that you don't even know if you're speaking the words, Christ may be. But something is controlling your work and you feel the control and you're grateful for the control, because you find yourself doing things you didn't know you could do. This is how you live to the Christ until Christ is your consciousness. Many inventor has thought he has stumbled on the discovery that ultimately made him famous, but it was in a moment when he thought not. That ability to self efface, to still the mind, to keep it alert while stilling it, to let it hover there until Christ comes through. We all know of cases like that in our own mind, lives even when we were lifted to heights that we could not believe you wanted to tell somebody about it.

Christ is teaching this class. Christ is saying these words. The Father is teaching his children the things he wants his children to know.

"Heal my Son. Heal the world. Take man out of bondage. And in the process liberate yourself from the belief that there is anything that can stand in your way. Anything that would stand in your way is a complete illusion."

We all want to be famous and rich. Well we are rich, we are rich in divine love and you can't be any richer. The Father so loves his Son that the Father has forgiven every error, every error that the image son will ever perform. The Father has forgiven completely because the Father sees through the illusions he sees the clear universe.

St. Augustine was rather a nasty fellow at one time, I don't suppose anybody was lower than St. Augustine was, or appeared lower. He became aware of the Christ, practiced the Christ, his sins [quote] were washed white as snow. There's nothing anyone has done that is considered a sin by the Spirit, "he's washed white as snow."

∞∞∞∞∞∞∞∞∞∞∞ End of Side One ∞∞∞∞∞∞∞∞∞∞∞

The subject of time and space, unless it's met now will keep us in a material universe, because time and space are the pavement on which the material universe runs. When you get rid of time and space you're automatically getting rid of matter. So the way to getting rid of the sense of body will come through your eliminating time and space. There is a necessity to dwell on this subject for a long time. But there is that necessity to do it because if you don't you're going to stay mired.

In the Bible we see many cases where individuals were captive in time and space, they received an ailment, they accepted it, and they went twenty five years with the ailment or they went five years or ten years, but they were subject to dismissal of the ailment at any moment that they realized that there was no time. The cripple who had been infirmed for many years thought he had it as long as he was a child, and he had it now, it never occurred to him that he had carried it with him as an image in his mind all these years.

Let's look at our own lives and the errors that we have experienced. Suppose we had had the ability to step out of time or to see that we never had been in time and that which we received in time wouldn't be true. I've known of people who have healed themselves that way. Let's take a young boy. In time he had a disease called - can't think of it at the moment - it was one of those paralyzing diseases, and he got out of paralysis but the effects of the disease still were with him. He didn't know anything about the fact that it only occurred in time and he had that problem all his life. But suppose he had known that what had first infected him only occurred after he had accepted time as the place where he was living. We all think time preceded us. We came into the universal belief of time. And if we were able to transcend time, not only would we transcend that which was a necessity for the illusion of a disease but we would have ascended beyond the belief that there was a body in time. We would have lost the opportunity to be infected by any disease on the face of the earth and we would have been free.

The concept of time is so completely illusory that man has never become aware of it. He thinks that everything that happens to him is happening, but the complete cycle of time life is the basis of the illusion. You were never in time. You were never born one hundred years ago. You were never born five hundred years ago. You carry the illusion of birth from one incarnation to the other because you carry the illusion of time from one incarnation to another. Why do we grow old? Because we think the years come one after another. When you break the illusion of time and see that it never existed you will understand why God has no age. God does not grow older in time and God never created anything in time either. God never created time. There isn't a thing in mans world that is the truth. Everything in mans world is an illusion that he must overcome and the sooner you get busy with the tougher illusions the easy ones will just follow.

What are we looking for? Our goals are all manmade goals and where do they get us? They get us in a corner. At the age of seventy mans manmade goals are kind of useless. He may have a few achievements between the ages of seventy and eighty and then where is he going to go, where is he going to borrow the energy. So we are digging our own graves literally unless we get out of it into the free universe of Spirit. If that universe is becoming real to you, if you're feeling the presence or some enchantment. It's something that never grows old. It's something that outlasts a man, not because it's a mountain or a body of water, but because it's something that spreads joy, and happiness, and harmony and never seems to stop. That's the world we want to get into. To lay down the garment of mortality which has bound the human race since it can name it's beginning and has chained everyone to a similar procession for a similar number of years. It really is now an old fashioned way of life. We're in a new age. We're in an age of Spirit where the young stay young - where the harmony of God becomes a living factor in peoples lives. Where life is not fourscore and ten. Where life is limited to nothing and where we do not have a parenthesis around infinity. Where we ourselves are infinite for that's the birthright we inherited.

I want to speak to those of you who know they are infinite. You are infinite in every perfect quality of God. You are infinite love. Not a little little love directed at one person. You're not that kind of love, a total love.

A love which seeks nothing. A love which gives all. A love which knows the thrill of sharing infinite deeds. A love that is as big as Gods love. When you give infinite love you have to step aside and let it flow through you. It's the kind of love that won't bring any harm to any individual. It's the kind of love that will see everyone living as the Christ whether they do in the visible or not. And unless you're expressing infinite love something in you is blocking your being, because it's your nature to express infinite love as the Christ. Infinite harmony is your nature. There's nothing else you can do. Infinite harmony follows the Christ wherever the Christ goes. Infinite intelligence always operating at the level of the need and so on down the line. The perfect qualities of God are your qualities, but they occur in a timeless world. The time world cuts them off - the space world cuts them off - and it limits your brain to concepts of things in time and in space.

Let's take a child who receives this kind of love. It's an unusual kind of love. It doesn't smother the child, doesn't instill in him human ambitions. It liberates him from all ambition. It frees him from all those things which would make him say, "Mine and I want," and in turn he receives the infinite love that God has to bestow. We don't see many children like that. But they're coming, already in the making and unless universal hypnotism comes into their home to hypnotize their parents these children will grow up with a kind of love that the world has never seen. We have that to give to them to show them that it is possible.

If we all think we're operating at our maximum, we'll be surprised to find that our maximum is not even one percent at the present time. We can all do one hundred percent better than we do, but we can't do it by repeating our human errors, by repeating our human ambitions. We must turn over the complete leaf and try to operate from a new level of Spirit.

Are there germs in your body? They're not in a spiritual body. Do you still feel the impulse to do what you know is wrong? Those impulses don't come to a spiritual body. Do you still look at your fellowman and decide you'd rather be in another neighborhood than he is in? You will find that your Spirit recognizes itself in your neighbor and lifts him up to the level of spirit when you do not act like a mortal. You will find there are hidden treasures in everything because the reality of everything is Spirit. Let's live in the new world and find out that it's the Kingdom. The only one who will determine that is ourselves. If we wait for our neighbor to do it, it will never happen. I want to live where God wants me to live. God wants me to live in his Kingdom. And I want to live in his Kingdom now so I can't go anywhere. I've got to recognize his Kingdom where I am. And then I've got to insist that my own behavior lives at the level which lives in the Kingdom, and I will find heaven here and now, and I will live in the Kingdom of God here and now, and I will manifest the things of God here and now provided that I say to the Christ of my being, "take over because I can't do it." I've never met a man or a woman who can do it without the Christ.

If we had the Christ we wouldn't be talking about no time and no space. We wouldn't have to talk about crime on the streets, or poverty, or any of the activities in the world that are un- Godly. So we're going to make our universe a Gods universe and we're going to live in it as Gods children. We're going to train our children to live in it. With the knowledge of truth and this takes twenty four hours a day. We're going to lift the errors of the world and reveal the Kingdom of heaven on earth. I think God is counting on you to be among the advanced guards, the true ambassadors of this divine Word. I don't know who would be the one that God would rely on if so many people are unaware of truth, but we have more than an inkling of it and all we need is the courage to follow through. You won't have to upset a home to do it, Spirit isn't that way. You live in truth that's all. You don't have to influence anyone to do it, but you live in truth. Inject that into your household, where you are living in the Spirit of God and observing everyone in that house in the Spirit of God. Getting into the habit of seeing the Spirit of God in everything, looking for it. And when your patient calls you that's the habit you bring into that meeting. Matter meets Spirit and Spirit says, "No you're matter." And then matter changes it's concept, finds it's improvement, and in time you may find a lot of people who once thought they were material human beings, doing things that a material human being doesn't do whether they call themselves Spirit or not.

We're going to look at ourselves again. I want you to see, like a purse, like a ladies purse. Just take out of your mind your beliefs and lay them invisibly in front of you. Do you understand that a person who has a physical problem is not really aware that he has no physical body? And therefore his physical body shows forth the problem. Do you understand that a person who fears death is really afraid of losing his body? A body he doesn't have. Do you see the core of all human fear is the flesh. Do you see that same individual, knowing that he has a spiritual body right where the physical body appears, but that the Spiritual body is not this size, this shape. It is infinite and his worry about a mole on his left arm is kind of ludicrous in the face of his infinite spiritual body will just not have any defect. Now you're not going to teach him that but you must have that knowledge. You must know that his spiritual body is perfect while he's trying to heal his physical body. And his physical body is just a concept about his spiritual body and the concept is in his mind it isn't there. You're not trying to heal his physical body. You're not even trying to heal the concept in his mind. You're simply trying to live out the truth of Christ. And slowly or fast, speedily through your awareness of truth and your spiritual development the idea comes into his mind that he feels better or well or right. And it happens quickly or very slowly but if you are persistent it will happen and when you see enough bodies reacting to your teaching and your faithful rendition of what Christ gives you to do you'll realize that Spirit is doing the work.

I want to go with you a little further knowing yourself to be infinite. In infinity you can't touch your toes or touch the top of your head and say, "That's me." You can't realize that your infinite with this little mind, and with a two and a half or three ounce brain. So what are you going to do to realize it? You'll never realize infinity with human thought. Why does the bible keep insisting that you take no thought? And why do you keep insisting that you must take thought. Your limitations are in having a human brain, no matter how brilliant it is. We are learning how to transcend the human brain and the human body and all of the things in between which have to do with human ambition and pride and so forth. And that when we have a Soul recognition of the infinity of being, in that one second we have travelled a thousand years. From that you rise to the Christ mind which is the creator of the true universe. And everything that Christ mind sees and hears and becomes aware of is reality. And there's not an ounce of discord in that reality. All the discord that we know is the counterfeit thought of the world brain and the human brain, so that several illusions away is reality. The world brain creates the illusion. The human brain then alters the illusion but it doesn't change the reality. You

Class 5: A Moment In Infinity

can count on what is. To always be what is. It is always ISing. And the moment you touch IS you touch now because reality is now.

Do you think in your recollections that you have ever experienced the living now? Travel through your experiences for a moment and try to recall what happened when you touched the living now. What triggered it? What made you suddenly see with such utter clarity that you know you weren't seeing with your brain or with your minds eye, or with your eyes. You saw right through all the clutter that the world could throw at you, and you saw something with such utter clarity - that was a divine experience - but what triggered it? There are such moments and in that moment you can see the equivalent of a thousand years in two seconds because time has been moved out of the way, and something not in this world appears to you. It's called a vision. But there's psychic visions and there's a Soul vision. In the Soul vision you get your first hint of reality. Is this worth laying aside the toys of humanhood? To live in the world where peace reigns. Where bombs don't drop. Where there are no labor struggles. Where crime doesn't enter the streets. That Kingdom is right here. You are walking in it and you may be experiencing some of it. Some of our students are quite advanced. They walk in the Kingdom at times and their reports are that they have seen the light. They have seen the sun behind the sun. They have seen the army of angels that are spoken of as the Hosts of God.

We want to transform the visible world of illusion into the reality that it is masking. Every little bit of progress we make makes possible of more progress. In "New Horizons", Joels chapter, we're given a hint of that of the new world behind the old world. In "The New Jerusalem" we're given more of a hint. And these were two chapters that Joel wrote based on his... in fact they weren't in the original "Infinite Way" were they. At that time he hadn't envisioned what came to him. But he did write the chapters into the "Infinite Way" when he was lifted out of the mental world. The delight of the individual who reaches that level is so great, so profound, that human pleasures are nothing in comparison. So I urge you to keep on with your study until matter has less of a pull upon you. Keep on with your material life transforming it daily to the best of your ability. And if you can, let the people call you for help because in giving them their help you have to achieve a degree of what I've been describing. And by giving them their help successfully you will have achieved that degree. And it's a very sensible way to accelerate your spiritual progress.

We're going to close with a meditation that the material world in time is not there. That means the Atlantic Ocean is not there. The Pacific Ocean is not there. We're looking at a world which is devoid of all material things. There are no planes in the sky. All these are precursors of the spiritual universe that we cannot see, but is seen by some. There is a world in which Moses and Elijah and the Christ Jesus can still meet, can still appear, can still talk with bodies that have been on the earth since the beginning of time.

[silence]

If moments of light come to you liberating you from a way of life that you have been living no matter how high or low, hold these dear experiences close to you. Share them only with those who can share them with you. We already had quite a number of those experiences reported during this class. Where people have spent a lifetime but during one or another of these classes they had an experience, not a little experience, but an experience which will change their lives. And it's all based on the knowledge that they are Spirit, they are Christ, their neighbor is Spirit, their neighbor is Christ and now it will be based on the knowledge that time does not exist in Gods world and there is no world beside Gods.

If you feel a slight movement toward a higher universe your movement is correct.

[short silence]

Blessings of love and we'll see you tomorrow morning.

CLASS 6

LIGHT BODIES

Herb: Happy Easter morning. We have the inspiration of Easter and our own consciousness to take us now to the point where the world left off.

They were given a message by Jesus Christ and it seemed to them that a man was standing before them. Those who followed him believed in him, but they did not know what they believed in. Hardly anyone on earth knew what Jesus was about. After his passing into a higher dimension the world wondered, what did he come for? Who was he? What are we to do now? And some were even glad that he was gone.

When he later spoke to John and gave him the revelation which John called the <u>Revelation of St. John</u>, no one received it. It wasn't shown to the world until the year 90, 92 or 3, the end of the first century. In other words over half a century passed before John even presented the Revelation to the early Roman church. They of course listened, looked, but they scoffed. They even thought that John was a bit touched, that he was a pretender, that what he had written was simply a trick, because there were many sects at that time and this was considered to be the work of another sect, a rival. Even the language was strange, symbolic, symbolistic, so forth. They looked at it all; they decided that John wasn't John. Why did he wait so long before presenting? They decided he was a fraud, a forger and besides what did he say in the Revelation? Absolutely nothing that they could understand. And so the early Roman church rejected John's revelation. They rejected him for three hundred years until the year 397. Then they reversed themselves and accepted the Revelation admitting it into the Bible as Holy canon. For one thousand years the Revelation rotted in the Bible. Finally about the sixteenth or seventeenth century scholars began to translate it. Until then most people didn't even own a Bible. It was about the seventeenth century nobody knew that Christ had communicated with John or what he had said; they saw only gibberish, meaningless visions. The world was not ready. It continued to live in darkness, the same darkness that veiled the truth long before Jesus came into the world.

But now a few Bibles began to appear. The printing press had been invented two centuries before. People started reading the Word. By the eighteenth century metaphysical interpretations began to appear, but the truth remained underground, because truth is too revolutionary, too upsetting and far too astounding, even now. Fortunately John left us another legacy which was not in the Revelation. In his gospel before Revelation he said:

"In Him was life and the life was the Light of all men."

I hope that phrase remains in your consciousness for a long time, until you begin to realize the truth that Christ life is the invisible, ever presenting its perfection in every man, because for two thousand years we have lost that Light. We have not understood it. We have not obeyed it. We have lived without it, but the Light is still you. It will always be you and everything that it is you are. That Light is infinite, perfect, eternal and when you can trace yourself back to who you are, you will discover that you are the Light of Christ, the Light we have lost, the Light that we must now find.

John the Baptist came to bear witness of that Light. He came to reveal that there was an inconquerable Light in man. We can compare it to a coffee bean. You run a cup of water over it and you adulterate the coffee, but you can get a cup of coffee. So with the light of Life if you put a veil of flesh over it you adulterate the Life. You walk around as a human being unaware of the Light within, the wholeness within, the perfection within. And because you live without the Light of your own true being and you live with others who are blind to it, you are said to see through a glass darkly.

I think the laser light is another example. It's a concentrated beam of light that works on your body and it does things that a normal light cannot do. Yet as powerful as the laser is compared to the Light of your own Christhood it's nothing. But it is an approach to the concentrated reality of the original Light. Nothing can remove or change that Light. But men live in a time where they're absorbed in their own work completely unaware that the Light which goes all through the universe and which is also at the center of their being is Christ; they are not aware of it.

Class 6: Light Bodies

Now you are becoming aware of this Christ. You are aware of the Great Light, the great secret of Life. That is a Light of all men. It is everywhere. So vast, so powerful and yet we cannot see it. It is thousands of decibels above our vision but it is here and it is us, and when we are able to make contact with that Light - like a central broadcasting station - it feeds the outer network, and one program sends out nine thousand across the country. One central, an infinite, omnipotent Light is what we are operating on and we are not aware of it. We are not making contact with it. We are stumbling in the dark.

I don't care who you are, when you are not aware of the Light you are walking in darkness. The sun may be shining but the darkness is your unawareness of the source of life. And while it perpetuates itself, constantly maintains itself, we see things through the glass darkly of human vision. We wonder, how did God create this and that and the other thing, those things that don't work? And we are looking through the eyes of imagination. All that God made is perfect. Nothing that is imperfect was made. God is not the creator of imperfection. So we are looking at the illusion of our own mind.

You made this journey through the illusion of your mind. You've come far. But now you have to get out of the illusion, out of the illusions of the mind and be born of the Word, which in the beginning was the Light of all men and which still is. We are going to look at the first chapter of John, just the first. We want to get a feeling of how John became aware of this Light. How John was able to communicate it in his Gospel, and still not be understood. So all this amounts to is a reminder of what we have failed to do, and every time we go through another day unaware that Christ is the Light of all men and that Christ is the Life of God, it's very clear that the individual who can accept that and can step out of the pack and live in the secret place being welded back into his own reality, that individual can change the world.

Now Jesus changed the world, but what he changed was something that he planted in the consciousness of men into invisible reality that emerged into visible actuality, which was the reason of course for the Revelation of St. John. It will further liberate mankind, but now it is abundantly clear as we look at these words in their simplicity, we have not seen them before.

"In the beginning was the Word."

And that Word we must call Christ. In the beginning was Christ, yes, "Before Abraham was, I am."

He, himself stated that.

"And the Word (Christ) was with God. And the Word was God."

So we are establishing now that Christ has been in the beginning, which means before the beginning. Mankind had to have a beginning. So it had one. And there was no beginning. God has not a beginning. Christ is always. If you remember, Isaiah had indicated that Christ the Light of God was seven times brighter than the sun. His meaning was to inform you that Christ will be attained by us in the seventh realm. We are now going through the seven realms. Four realms have almost passed, we're now in the fourth and we have three more realms to go. So when you know the mind realm is the fourth you start figuring that there are three higher realms: the Soul realm, the Spirit realm and the Christ realm, which is eternal life. This follows Isaiah's prediction because then you're a finished product. He also said that in your seventh level you will be transparent to Christ, and the twelve qualities of Christ or the fullness of the Light of God.

The twelve disciples then represent the twelve levels of pure truth that you will realize when you are in the Christ level. In that seventh level you have twelve precious stones or perfect knowledge and that corresponds with the twelve disciples. But they still didn't know what he was saying, so they had to have John the Baptist come down to say, "This is the one, follow him, because he is the Light." And that is what is meant by the straight and narrow. You can only follow the Light of God.

So at the beginning of the first century it was shown by John the Baptist that this is the Christ of God. It was also shown by John what the Christ was. Christ was the whole Light, and Jesus being a representative of Christ was a Light on earth. He was the one on earth who had attained the Christ. So although Jesus and Christ are the same, Jesus only appears on earth and Christ is infinite. Jesus exists up to crucifixion. His name then becomes Christ. To show that this is the Christ who had delivered to us the message of Christ as Jesus.

So we have John the Baptist coming to bear witness who points at what appears to be a man. Looks exactly as other men and says,

"Follow me."

Now where will you follow the Christ who will walk off the earth? And how will you follow the Christ walking off the earth? How do you follow the Light? There's only one way.

You must be the Light.

So you see a major transformation is in the making. Each one of us will be transformed. How? When? No one really knows. But prepare for it, know it is coming, each one of us at a different time. When we think not the bridegroom cometh. And this is something that we cannot see. We cannot avoid it either. Nor do we wish to avoid it. We can put it on hold and we're making a mistake. It must be worked at. It happens when it happens. But the transformation only happens when you are ready for it. You're not going to the next level while you are imperfect, I can assure you that. You've got to be perfect to go to the next level. And there's a reason for that. They do not adulterate things in heaven. Of course we have ideas about heaven, all fairy tales I might add. Heaven is going to be your level, your consciousness, which is perfect, that is all heaven will be. But that allness is everything. You're going to live, to go into a higher state of consciousness and when you are ready, when you have been pronounced fit, pure, perfect you will slide easily out of this consciousness into the higher consciousness and this is telling you how you are going to do it, how you are going to get ready for it.

Now we know why it is called the straight and narrow. Whoever does not receive the Light has no exit from the consciousness of earth. The only exit he's got is out, down and then up, in other words death and reincarnation. Whereas our true exit is vertical, a new higher consciousness, and although it's exciting and almost fantastic it is equally simple when we get used to the idea that we are states of consciousness being made ready for the transformation. The transition to Christ. The transition to Christ consciousness. And when you are aware of the Light of Christ that is Christ consciousness.

Now let's be careful about one point. John is trying to leave us a legacy that we can follow which is so self-explicit that we do not teeter off the edge and wander back into human consciousness but keep on the straight and narrow truth up, up and up in consciousness by assimilating the Light that we are and blotting out the light that we are not, the false light of humanhood. Having a sort of transfusion of light, and as we mount the ladder of consciousness, slowly becoming the Light that we already are, we are fed by the Light. Our bodies change, our thoughts change, the things we see and hear change. And this is the slow, graduated consciousness which takes us up to a level which can look out on a different world. This is how the vision changes, the hearing changes, everything about us changes and we become what we thought we were but we change to the divine image and likeness. When we are the image and likeness of God we see with God's eyes, we hear with God's ears and we find there are no eyes, no ears in this consciousness. We see without eyes and we hear without ears, because life is not reduced to just this and that. Everything you have is infinite, one infinite awareness.

Now let's be cautious. Let's proceed with the introduction of John.

"In the beginning was God, in Him was Life and the Life was the Light of all men."

You must be Christ now. You don't look it. You don't speak like it. Perhaps you don't feel like it. But you are Christ now. You're not a different Christ than He is, nor is He a different Christ than you are, because there's one Christ. Just as we breathe air, we all breathe the same air, one body of air but many breathe it. One spiritual body of Christ and all spiritual bodies are it.

Now when you get on this ship of Christ, you're on the right ship otherwise it sinks. Is that clear? There is one infinite ship of Light invisible and you get on that ship. How do you know you're on it? Well that's what the whole Bible is about; it gives you instructions on how to get on the ship of Christ. You do this, you do that, you do the other thing; it's all about your purity, your willingness to take orders, your willingness to lay down your life and pick it up again, which is the transformation to Christ. Everything that is in the Bible by way of instructions is for the sole purpose of preparing you to be acceptable, to be stepping on the ship of Christ. You see now that this pure total being, which is all being, cannot accept an illusion.

You cannot walk into the Christ as an illusion; you've got to overcome the illusion first. That's one of the required responsibilities we all share. The other is that as an illusion you've got a mind to think to function with, and you've got to see, you've got to judge and all of that makes you a state

Class 6: Light Bodies

of division. Well in a state of division you cannot come into the Light, because there is one steady beam of perfection. And so high or low, mighty or lowly you've got to come to a place where you can make the concession. You give up your opinion, your thoughts, all you can do to stand in the Light and accept or reject. As you accept it you become less mortal. As you reject it you become more mortal. We also have the capacity to know when we are in the Light. That's what the <u>Sermon on the Mount</u> is all about. Don't do this, do that. Go the extra mile. Don't pretend. Don't wear a false face to show that you've done some good tonight. Be forthright. When you steal from your neighbor whether it's legal or not, you steal from Christ. So who do you fool except yourself, because the Light knows itself. We become a transparency to the Light and all of our stupidities, our follies, our mistakes are totally forgotten. You cannot walk in the Light with any imperfection. And that's why it is taken what appears to be a long, long time. The imperfections have to come out. Only perfection is possible in the Light. It's automatic.

Even an airplane, now they don't make you walk on it if you have metal in your pockets. If they find metal they stop you at the gate. If we see all these precautions on the human scene think of the precautions on the divine scene. Perfection is required and protection to prevent adulteration of the Light. So entrance is impossible when you are not willing. Even your mind is an open book. They've got to know that you are not only in the Light that you are totally turned toward the Light, and you are not conditioned to be otherwise. You are not going to get a heart attack in heaven. You are not going to wake up and suddenly find something missing. All the imperfections of a person are weaned out of you. So when Paul says:

"Put on the garment of immortality."

He is informing you that your mortality must go, because mortality is a state of imperfection. Even the best mortal is imperfect. He doesn't have 20-20 vision when he grows older. He may have a hearing aid. He wears whatever one of those things are called that gives you an extra beat for your heart. Mortality never enters heaven. Mortality cannot be the Light. As it becomes clearer that there is a reason for these things then you are willing to accept them. As a mortal being you are not admitted to heaven. You are not admissible to the higher realms, because the higher realms require perfection. You can't survive in a higher realm without perfection. So ever so reluctantly you finally yield. You say, "Well I like what I have and I like to protect it but it's going to be taken from me anyway. I'm smart but I'm not omnipresent, not as a mortal. As a mortal I'm stuck in this chair, in this alley, in this street, I'm stuck wherever I am. I'm just a little sample of the bigger things to come." And they're not particularly proud of our human achievements because these human things become as nothing, as dust. We can be proud to an extent that we're happy to have made a contribution, but in the final analysis there is nothing of this world that remains when you have made your transformation. When each individual has completed the transformation to the Light, civilization will not be the same; it will not be there. What remains of it will be that which we see, either a shambles or another expression and then we'll be completely unaware of the universality of reality which we occupy as we leave the human scene.

One woman said - I can't quite remember it but I'll try - she said, "What happens if I die while I am still imperfect?" "Well you'll come back," I told her, "And someday you'll be perfect and you'll go into the higher consciousness, and that's all there is to it."

∞∞∞∞∞∞∞∞∞∞∞ End of Side One ∞∞∞∞∞∞∞∞∞∞∞

Without Paul, Christianity might have failed for a thousand years. With Paul even though the disciples did not quite accept him there were certain qualities in Paul, in his teaching that survived. Light shined through. At that time you couldn't say for sure that the others were necessarily in the Light but they were learning. What happened to his Light? What happened to the teaching? What happened to the true Light which lighteth every man that cometh into the world? How does one become aware of one's own light? Jesus said:

"I am the Light."

That's exactly his words and that's exactly what John discovered. That he too was the Light. He who followeth me will walk in darkness no more, but this is from self to self promised here right in this series of verses, for you and for me and for the world. A promise that we can count on to keep us moving toward the Light.

"But as many as received Him," - oh, there were few who understood him - "As many as received Him," - now that means a very special thing. Your acknowledgement that the Light of Christ is in you, that's how you receive it.

When Jesus says, "When as many as receive me," he is talking about the inner Light because he is the inner Light. The Christ within you is telling you,

"As many as receive me, to them gave he the power to be Sons of God."

So if you wish to translate this work into the Living Bible, the Living Truth that you can live by, you become the living Son of God by receiving the Christ Light within and you already are the Son of God because the Christ doesn't come into you, the Christ must be in you now! Do you understand that?

The man Jesus outwardly is speaking for the Christ within you. And when Jesus speaks outwardly, He is the Christ within you. The outer Jesus is the universal inner Christ and as many as receive Him to them gives He the power to be Sons of God. Do you see the secret message, the way it's tied up? Anyone who receives the inner Christ is the Son of God, anywhere. And you receive it simply by acknowledging it and listening for it and the world doesn't know it.

You have to open your consciousness to it. You are the Christ, but you are asleep to the Christ. And when you receive the Christ, you are awake to the Christ. And then you are awake to the fact that you are truly the living Son of the Living God with all the privileges there unto. It's all laid out for you. All we have to do is to prune out all those qualities that are unlike the Christ in order to become aware of what is Christ. To accept what we are through faith - though possibly it's more than faith at this point because we can see some of the miracles and that's not faith anymore - you have proven something. It's deeper than faith; it's faith proven, faith established as fact.

I think I want to meditate at this moment because there's something powerful, so powerful that we want to feel the essence of it. Yes there's something very powerful right here and now. As we go through these words we are being prepared for the true rebirth. I can hear Nicodemus saying, "Well what can a man do to be reborn?" We hear these questions. How can a man be reborn? We see the modern church, it glibly says, "I am reborn," by some external contact. They don't seem to understand.

But your rebirth will be when you accept Christ within and you become the Divine Light of God. That will be rebirth when the Light is actually received in your consciousness and then you are the light reborn to the Light.

[silence]

This is what is in store for you. I suppose it won't hurt to move ahead. When we pass from this plane as the Light, there is a preparation for a higher rebirth. This outer acceptance is the way you should show your faith, your willingness, your desire to be the Light. But you're not the Light when you pass from this plane, in the sense that you're a fully evolved Light. When you pass from this plane, there is what would be a long wait, a long period which you are prepared to receive the Light that you are willing to accept. That preparation will take two complete realms. In the Soul realm you'll learn all about the Light and when you're ready to expand you'll meet your own Spirit. This will engender a birth from the union of your Spirit and your Soul coming together, and this finally will be the seventh realm, S-E-V-E-N (spells), the seventh realm, and that's the final birth of the Light in you. Don't expect the Light to transform you totally at this time, but know that you must receive and live in the requirements of the Light and that is the straight and the narrow. You must begin to identify as the Light in order for your Soul realm to open.

There your Light is further unmasked. And that draws the Spirit to your Soul. These are Holy times. And by then you're far out of mortality; it's gone. And Christ is slowly being born in you. This Christ becomes the Christ that God made at the beginning, in the seventh heaven before the descent and the reascension. It's a glorious time. It's a challenging work and it's the identical challenge for all of us. All power is in the Son and it's not Jesus, it's the power of Christ. And Christ is Jesus and Christ is you and you and you. In fact when you're given all power, it's because you're not about to misuse it. You know the meaning of Christ power, of infinite Love; you're whole being is infinite Love. It's not a power to control anything in the world. It's a power to maintain the perfection of God's universe. You're going to repeat that phase because it is an important one; it concerns your motivation behind everything you do.

"As many as received Him to them gave he the power to become the Sons of God." At that time you're still not fully Christed, fully Christed.

Class 6: Light Bodies

"Given to them that believe on His Name which were born not of blood."

You see this is the second birth, not of blood, nor of the will of the flesh, nor of the will of man but of God. The birth of God in you preceded by the reception, the willingness, the belief, the understanding, the truth which God first puts out which draws you to the Light and you finally understand what the Light is. You feel your mortality when you're willing to let it melt out of existence as you receive the Light. You dwell in the Light and this is your birth foreshadowed because it's not happening yet, it's going on to the fifth realm. You're not in it yet but you're aware that it exists. That's in the fifth realm that you're now preparing for. It's called the mystical marriage of Spirit and Soul in the sixth realm and out of that marriage, out of that union, out of that oneness between your Soul and you Spirit you move into the second birth, the birth of Christ in you.

Your Soul has always been designated as female, your Spirit as male and as they become one they move into the seventh realm and then there's no more male or female. There's no more mortal to be male or female. And no doubt the marriage on earth of man and woman is a shadow of the marriage of your Soul and Spirit in heaven.

Many of the people we heal all owe the healing to Christ in us and Christ in them. But there's one thing you should know that they are healing us as we heal them because they are making us bring forth our Christhood. And if we don't bring forth our Christhood we don't heal. You see the double purpose? So you'd have the motive in many, many ways to find the inner Christ. The desire is born in you as a man. At this level you know where you're going, and how and why. You can endure many things no matter how difficult. Things you wouldn't endure without this great goal. You are trying to realize your Christhood and that is the purpose of life, to realize your immortal Christ Self. Once you accept that purpose, no other, then you have passed the point and realize that your life must change. This life will be a shadow. As you move up, Christ becomes the only life you have. You're changing your concept of life, the new life, the real life, born of Spirit and Soul, made possible as you receive the Light within, brings you into a realm where the Laws of God abide without opposite. In that realm no women die of pregnancy and other diseases. No men die. All are receiving the Light of perfection. Mortality goes.

Immortality takes its place. And that is precisely what Jesus meant when he said his disciples would lose their life in order to gain their Life. That is what you are learning to do now.

Let's be still. Hold the silence, find the inner Christ.

[silence]

Each of us is given the opportunity to proceed swiftly to the Light. We can keep this mortal form if we wish, by worrying about things of this world or we can focus our attention on those things that will enable us to prove our willingness to submit to the Light and not try to alter the Light, to live by the Word of God which is the Light. And being given this opportunity which is a turning point of every human life, what will we do with it now that we know where we can go, what we can be, who we are?

The Light in my consciousness is ready. It has been there eternally. I must listen to find it, to find out what the Light expects of me. What it wants me to do now! What is excess baggage in my life. What things must I drop. What things do I need to take with me. I'll get all the information I need from the inner Light and then I will proceed about living the Light. The Light has anticipated the questions I would ask. It has prepared a way for me in the wilderness. It prepared the Ten Commandments, then later the Sermon on the Mount...

CLASS 7

My Time Has Come

Herb: Is Carol here? Is Carol here?
Students: Yes
Herb: Where? Where are you Carol?
(Student gets up as the others applaud.)
Herb: Can you walk a little? Walk toward me if you can.
(Student walks.)
Herb: Great. Okay, don't overdo it, sit down.
(Students applaud again.)
Herb: We meditated with Carol for - about 8 of us - we each spent a half hour for three days, Friday. When did we have our first class . . . was it? Thursday night so we didn't do it. Friday we meditated with her in the afternoon and then Saturday and Easter Sunday. We put in an hour and a half. She flew in all the way from South Africa. She came in a wheelchair and she's walking. Jean called me from her room this afternoon and said she's walking. And I'm very happy about it. It sort of puts a good touch into the seminar, and we see in person that the teaching is correct that when you meditate for a person in the Spirit with the Christ that there's a response. We hope it continues and accelerates and that you recover your strength. It's going to be nice when you come home and say, "I'm walking."

The Word "now" is a very important word. Eternity as large as it is, is in "now." It's important to each of us because our so-called life in time is a misnomer. There is no life in time. We call it life, but if life is the Christ life and the Christ life is not in time, then life is not in time. As long as we remain in time, we remain an illusion. And I suppose it would be easy to be satisfied with being an illusion. But there is no God life that exists except in the eternal now. And although it seems like the eternal now must be miles and miles away and years and years away—several millennia at least—now in the eternal is now. And will it will astound you to know that you already live there and you're catching up with yourself? What is this now?

Try a meditation on now. It may astound you what happens. "Now I am the Light." That's the theme.

"Now I am the Light. Now I let my Light shine. Where is my Light? My Light is everywhere as the Christ. And when my Light shines in me there's nothing anyone can do to me, nothing any harm . . . no harm can come to me. I am lifted in consciousness. I am able to perceive things I couldn't perceive before. I have new capacities. I work beyond my sense level. All things are possible to me. I might start off with a minor thing but it will be something that was not possible to me before. Now I am the Light." To mouth those words may not do much for you, but they are truth. And I'm not going to say another word until you have lightly spoken to yourself and within yourself say it.

"Now I am the Light."

You have said an eternal truth . . . a truth that will always be true and will always be true of your being; and the key to that, the purpose of that is that you can always be saying truth to yourself, always be receiving truth from the Christ, and when you live in truth you can't go any higher.

"Let your Light shine."

We didn't know what that meant. It was a vague connotation about it. What was this Light? Oh we thought we'd sparkle a little bit maybe, or we'd be a little brighter or just brighter in our intelligence or we'd be cheerful or something like that. Let the Christ shine where you are. You were being told that you had a Light, in fact that you were that Light and to let it shine. You were told that you were infinite in that statement instead of this being who walks the earth. You were told that you were perfect in that statement instead of the person who reports occasional depression, pain, a little local arthritis. And when you're told to let your Light shine, you're being told that those things do not belong to you; they are not yours. You've put a name on them and you have said they are mine, but they aren't. You can't even make them yours. You are the Light. And as soon as you start realizing that every time you act in a way that is not the Light, you're not being yourself. You're not being what you can be, and you don't need anyone to tell you you can be better. The Father's Word is enough.

Class 7: My Time Has Come

And so you should be ready now to accept that this day, this day called Easter, I start off as the Light if I haven't already. And the Light is capable of everything. Now we'll slow down a minute; we won't use our will power to do things we'd like to do, but we'll give the Lord a chance to instruct us, and I want to listen to that voice because the Light hears the voice. I want the Father's voice to speak to me. I want to see that the child of God receives the voice. Listen for it after calling yourself the Light, and see if you don't have greater receptivity to the voice of God.

[Silence]

Who told you that you are the Light? Who told you, "Let your Light shine"? In the Bible it was Jesus, but Jesus is the Christ. Who told you to let your Light shine? The Christ told you. Who is the Christ? You are. The voice has been saying to you since you've been on the earth,

"Let your Light shine. Let me out. Let me be you. Why do you waste your time being a mortal being when you are the Light? Why do you waste your income on medical bills? Why do you waste your energy on convalescence? Why do you waste your ability to walk freely with occasional lapses when you do not work as well as you should?" All because you have not been practicing knowing and expressing "I am the Light."

Now the best you can do with the truth at first is to at least shake off the temptation to believe you're not the Light. "I have a headache. I have a cold." We all receive those inner impulses and we readily accept them, and now you face the impulse. "No, I don't have a headache. I don't have a cold. I am the Light." And even if the cold restricts your laryngitis and if the headache is burning, you still are the Light, and you still don't have the cold because I am free of all error. And there's a fellow with your name impersonating you who has a cold. And soon you get the idea that I have something to say about this. I'm not going to adulterate my identity ten times a day by stating that I have something when the Christ never has. There's something I can do about it. And lo and behold, as I do what I should do, the temptation goes away. You're startled perhaps, but the temptation doesn't linger.

And every time throughout the Bible where Jesus performed a miracle that was what was happening. The I of the patient made visible as Jesus was saying inside the patient, "No, I don't have a crippled arm. No, I don't have a withered arm. No, I don't have leprosy." And the world has not seen that these are actually self-healings, and that each one has the capacity because of the omnipotence of Christ to look at any ailment that faces one and to say, "No, I don't have it. And I don't have it because there's no such thing in the universe." It's coming up to me, it's wearing a mask, it's saying,

"I am this, I am that."

"It doesn't fool me anymore, I am the Christ, and I dare not think I'm not. If I deny the

Fatherhood of God, what's left for me?"

Do you see you've got to stand up and be what you are? And in the face of every form of error you must look at it and know, "I don't have it. Oh this body might have it, but I'm not in that body. How can I be infinite and be in a body? How can I be the Light and be immersed in a prison called body? Either I'm coming out of sleep or I'm just boasting."

Why not wake up, thou that sleepest, and let Christ give thee Light? Let Christ take you and show you the Father's way. When you get ready to admit to your identity, to be it, although you don't look it, you don't feel like it, you are it. When you are willing to say, "I am the Christ, and the Father speaks to me," the Father will.

And so I suggest now that you take into consciousness an hour a day that you are I, the Christ. And that when that meditation is over you're going to walk out as I the Christ, and that during that meditation you will be listening for the Christ voice, for the Christ impulse, the Christ direction, the Christ instruction, and you will do that for an hour one day until you receive a specific instruction. When you receive a specific instruction no one will have to tell you to go inside and listen for it anymore. You'll want to shout it from the housetops, you'll want to tell everybody you know. No one can stop you; they can just suggest that you keep it to yourself. Get a few of these words of the Father first and then only tell it to the nearest and dearest, but get them and be willing to listen.

There are better times to meditate than any old time. When you get to meditating very well it's any time. And when people call you, you've got to get to do it right then so you don't have a choice, but you can pick for your preliminary meditations those times of day which lend themselves to subjective thinking.

I find when day is breaking between, you know, the end of the day as the sunset goes down and it's just about an in-between shade of grey;

Class 7: My Time Has Come

night hasn't fallen yet but it's slowly falling, in the gloaming, you just rest there and, oh, it just slides off like watermelon out of . . . just . . . you can just feel the pulse, the weight, the presence of something grand and in no time at all it always seem to take off well for people when they get in there at that dusk hour.

And then when you meditate in the daytime even though it's light out it's better to get into the darkness so that there's no sun in your eye. And you'll find that in the inner shade with your eyes closed and particularly if you can get in a quiet spot it's just much easier. As I say you'll come to the point where, "Who cares where I meditate or when I meditate, I can always meditate, it's a natural thing." But when you're not doing well—the people know who I'm talking to, the people who have the problem and you're not doing well—make sure your chair is right, everything is comfortable, the room is quiet, the air is just right coming through the window, then you're lifted into it. Make sure you can stay in it if you want to so that you don't have noises around. You should be able to meditate now at a half hour stretch with just a joy. Not having to open your eyes, just listening, listening, listening.

There was a day when Joel said three minute meditations. Well he wanted to make sure that you did at least three minutes and he knew that you could do three minutes without getting tired or frustrated and so just three, and then later more, another three and then another finally he got to thirty meditations a day. We're more advanced now and those were wonderful as pick me ups. A minute, close your eyes and take off. But there should be a time during the day when you have a solid long meditation. I wouldn't sit down and do a talk, for instance, like this unless I had first been quiet and let the Spirit come. Let it give you the outline of what you're to say. Let it, perhaps, speak a word to you. Let it build up your awareness. Let it take away all extraneous thought, and then the talk has a smoother flow to it. Similarly I've been in business, and before I went out to see clients I used to meditate, and I imagine we . . . we felt the power of that.

Meditation is useful for every purpose. People were telling me about the neighbors next door making all that noise. Well it's true you could just call them up and tell them to be quiet please. Maybe you don't think it would work. You could call the police but we don't approve of doing that, but we do approve your being still, and you really don't have to think much you just be still. And I can recall a phone call I got from a woman. Her neighbors were always noisy. I might say this was in Las Vegas and they were up all night you know, playing machines and things and she was going crazy. And all she did, all I told her to do was to be still and know there's no neighbor next door. There really is no one there. You've just got a material apparition, and she didn't quite know what to think of this but she did it. And pretty soon the neighbor who was the obstreperous one, moved. She got a kindly neighbor, a sweet one and that was all there was to it. The point is that Christ is always working for the benefit of everyone, and if you are in your Christhood that which is obnoxious to you will be removed or you will move to another place, but you won't be there to listen to something that is noisy or whatever might be happening. Christ always listens. Christ always knows what's going on in your life because Christ is you.

Now we get into the habit then of having these meditations every day—not to let a day go by. It's only simple: When you're thirsty you drink water and you're thirsty for truth so you have to meditate. And it's amazing how it straightens things out right away. Sometimes in ten minutes your whole life is changing. I hope you're doing that.

But now we're interested in a relationship with the Christ. It takes time before Christ takes over your life, before there's nothing but the Christ where you are and not the duality of a human being. And be patient, it's got to happen. It might take you five years. I've known cases longer than that, but it's got to happen, and you will be a better person for it and then you will slowly find that you are not even a person. You look at people with a strange feeling of, "I like that person; he or she can't offend me. I just like them anyway," and you exude this atmosphere of contentment. You find that you're not tense anymore. You're not anxious. And all of this has a nice settling effect on various parts of your mirage so that it doesn't keep you up at night. It doesn't become a trip hammer in your chest. You don't have to complain to everyone. I know people who complain everyday of their lives, and often this could be eliminated by the belief that "I am the Light."

The speaking voice of Christ is going to be your companion. You won't talk about it because it will be too precious and you will lose it if you treat it any other way. Christ is not to be spoken of in the mystical way to anyone not going that way. But to those who are walking your path you can change all the notes you want. You can stay up nights and talk about

Christ, talk about the Spirit and you will find that in the middle of your conversation you're in the Spirit. I'll prove it. We'll talk for five minutes, and if we're not in the Spirit in five minutes I will be surprised.

We are without thought. We are listening for the Father's voice, some sign from the Father that the presence is here. And that the presence is here now. And that the presence is always here in the now. I must come to the now to hear the presence. I live in time; that's wrong. There's no time in the presence. No one can live in time. The part of you that lives in time is dead in time instantly. You die a million deaths in time. Every second you die in time. Every second you're born in time, dying and borning, dying ... every minute goes and every new minute comes and you squeeze your life into it like a toothpaste, and you think you're living. No past right now. We can't think backwards; hold it. We can't think forward; hold it. Draw in these two parts, the past, the present to the now, and don't leave the now. If you've got to spend two minutes in the now, do it. And then spend two more minutes in the now, in the now, in the now, now; now is God. Now is God. God only speaks in the now. You will never hear Christ except in that split second of now. And when you hear the voice in the now, the now continues; there is no time. That is feeding the Self of you. The Self of you lives in the now where Christ lives. And when you feel that now, you're entering the Kingdom of God. No, don't go into the future; stay in the now.

As you develop this capacity to remain in the now, wouldn't matter if you remained there for thirty years—the thirty years will go but you will still be in the now; you'll find a greater capacity to stay in the now. All the time that you are in the now that's the time that you are being the child of God. You have to practice it. You have to consciously sit down, step out of time and that puts you in the now but it is very elusive and you struggle to maintain it and eventually you really do, and that is how you communicate with God. All communication with God is in the now, where time is not. And as this grows with you, you can look at your life in time and realize it is not, and then you have the mystical truth that I do not live in time and that is why my life does not show because it cannot show in time.

The book of *Revelation* says: "Time is no more."

But "time is no more" is only for those who have become enlightened that their life substance is not in time. There's a ring to *now*, a sort of an extension into eternity that you feel; all things stand still and this now is where you hear the voice.

[Silence]

Speak Father; your Son heareth. You find something in you wanting to tell the Father that you're here. Oh, the Father knows that you want to communicate with the Father.

One student said, "Today . . . today you have dined with the Father." He heard it. And as the day went past we heard various things happen to people, images that appeared within themselves, joyously. There were many who could report and couldn't stop reporting because it bubbled out that things were happening, things that were of a nature that was a God experience. And I know from experience, too, that when you have the God experience it will never leave you, never leave you. It's telling you that, "I am come, and I will never leave you. I've told you that in words that you've read in the Bible, but when I speak to you I can never leave you and you know it. You know we will be back together again in conscious forever; even when I don't speak to you, I'm with you and you know it, and you really do."

That assurance from the Father comes every time you have the spoken word or even the slight inner influence and you can have them ten times a day and you're just grinning from ear to ear because you know something wonderful is happening, something beyond yourself, something from your inner self. And of course you then willing to take chances you wouldn't take because you feel the rightness of what you're doing; you loosen up. I have discovered what to me would be so exciting that when you receive a promise within, it happens, it always happens. It doesn't matter what the promise is. When the promise comes from within you can close your eyes and stand on a plank and jump. It will be there to catch you.

∞∞∞∞∞∞∞∞∞∞∞ End of Side One ∞∞∞∞∞∞∞∞∞∞∞

Incidentally one of the better books on spiritual healing beside *The Art of Spiritual Healing*, *The Master Speaks* is a compilation of techniques that is based all upon Joel's teaching. *The Master Speaks*. I don't know if Tanya has it, but if she I think you should get it because you'll use it all your life.

It's rather nice when a family has at least one person in it who can take care of emergencies, people getting sick, and bring a peace to them and a healing. Every time you attempt to heal someone even if they're not healed you've done some good, you know. Just the mere fact that you've worked at it. A person may not jump up. You'll find that something was accomplished in some way that you may not be aware of. You've got to give the patient the very best possible effort that you have, and often times there's not one meditation that will do it. As you just saw, we had three for Carol, and that's unusual too. Usually we work for patients week on, week off, week on, one week after another and they reported tiny bit of improvement. Some of the most successful cases have taken two months and if the patient is urged to call you back, to keep calling you back, you'll be grateful for it because every time they call you, you know that they really expect you to heal them, and having that expectation gives you the perseverance to follow through. Sometimes you may not even have the power and feel that you don't have the power, but the fact that this person calls back again and again finally makes you say, "Well I've got to get the power by gosh," and you stay up that night and by two or three o'clock you may have solved the problem, you may have out done yourself, reached higher than you have ever did before, but that reaching then becomes more normal for you and the altitude of your prayer becomes higher.

Sometimes when you don't succeed you wonder why. There's a tendency to say, "Well they're not receptive." I tossed that one out long ago. You can't blame it on the patient, you just can't. It's your consciousness and when you don't succeed you're just not where you're ought to be. It takes keeping the consciousness during the day. You can't just meditate for the person who is sick and then go out and play a round of golf, do something else, do something else and forget all about the Spirit and then expect the next call to be receiving your best. It's a dedication but you're the one who benefits because as you keep tuned up you find that you have kept ailments away from yourself and you've kept away from yourself all of the things to which flesh is heir. Some may not make it a profession; in fact if five do I will be surprised. But at least when you keep up the practice of listening to the Christ you will be free from the maladies that people generally succumb to. Christ should be your constant companion until you can proclaim that "I am the Christ." No one can say how long it will take, but I do know that each year you become better at what you do just like everything else.

I've seen many a domestic tangle untangle when one individual started being spiritual, and when two start to be spiritual they usually end up in a very companionable marriage. But we're not going to discuss the human benefits. There are many, but when the illusion is better or not better we cease to be concerned about it. We know that Spirit is on the path that I follow and to be spiritually well means to be totally well. Even the image acts alright after that.

It wouldn't be right to pass up Easter without some thoughts about Easter. Throughout the world there's a soft spot in man's heart for Easter because of the Christ and the seeming hardships he went through and the final dénouement when he showed that he personally could conquer death. When you think of Easter it should occur to you that your opinion, your awareness, your appreciation should be slightly different than an average person's. The New Testament teaches man a new way of life. It isn't common knowledge what it teaches but the new way of life is the inner life, the mystical life. And when Christ demonstrated that he could be on a cross one day crucified, and living while crucified, if we had known the truth we would have said, "Well he's not in the body. He didn't go through any pain." Once we get the idea that Christ could do that only because he was not in the body because the body was just another apparition, then we see there is a different meaning to death. He was trying to tell us about that meaning—that we can die because we are not in the body that dies.

Do you believe this? Do you hear it? That he didn't die and wasn't raised up by the Father but was not in the body that died, as you are not now. In ten minutes you can forget that you're not in the body, but that's the teaching that Jesus Christ gave to us—that the human race is not in the human body. Only Christ is in the invisible, and only Christ will be your rebirth, and only God is on the earth for the earth is the Lord's, but they're not talking about the visible earth. They're talking about the real earth, not the illusory earth, and you can touch it and you can grow flowers out of it, but it isn't there. Always there must be a sure remembrance of the fact that the material body is not the vehicle God gave you. All things were created by Him. And the answer to the material body not being created by him, when people ask you, you can't give them because you'd have to say,

"Well it isn't here. I don't have one. You're looking at the illusion of myself." And you'll feel funny speaking about it because it takes a long time before you get used to that, that there is no human race. There are no people. You're speaking every day to the Christ of God and if your tone is not the kind you'd use to the Christ of God then you haven't become aware that the Christ of God is standing straight in front of you. Now I know this is a mystical teaching. There's no other way to rise in consciousness than to abide by it and to live with it and to grow with it. So start looking at the world a different way. You can love someone even more if he's the Christ than if he's not. And the you that does the loving must be the Christ.

Another thing about Easter is that when Jesus taught us that he was not there but Christ was, when he invited crucifixion, he was telling us that there was no need to run from any evil that besets you. If there's no body there, what is evil? Someone picks up a gun to shoot you, someone picks up a knife to hit you, someone does something to misappropriate your funds but it's always a physical something and you're falling for the illusion. A drunk gets in your way in the street and you say, "They oughtn't have a city with people like that in it." Well they don't have one; you only think they do. Get so that you're aware of the truth at every time. Don't let the human illusion get to you. You may have tight shoes but you don't really have a foot to put in those shoes. And that's what Jesus was teaching the world, but he wasn't teaching it for that day. He was teaching it for those who would follow, those who would learn what he was teaching.

What does it mean to you when Peter kisses the foot of someone else? Or when Jesus washes the foot of someone else? He's paying homage to the Christ of that individual. He's saying just if he had said it in words, but he's saying for those who can hear him, who can understand him, "I'm not really washing your foot, but I am washing away your material body. This is a symbol of washing your material body away. I'm paying homage to the Christ of you." And we want to be alert to every bit of shade of teaching that comes because it will convince you finally that you know what he was saying, that he was teaching the world the invisible world must be reached. We must be living in it. We must be aware because we are going to raise ourselves up, to lift ourselves up. We're going to raise the Christ in us, and we're going to make the fifth level. We're going to find one day we are in our Soul. We're going to release it from the fourth world. And in our Soul we will have new power of speech and vision. You'll find your inner eye open, your inner ear. You're going to discover things you don't know that will amaze you.

What do you think about a body that would be twenty foot tall if you saw one? Why just a seven foot man is terribly high, but twenty foot. What would you do with him? How would we live with him? When we say that you are infinite, what do you think when you learn you have an infinite body? Can you imagine what it is and yet it's yours? Who possesses it? This five-foot-nine person or this six-foot person? Who possesses these infinite bodies? What are they made of? Let your Light shine. They are made of Light. You have an infinite body of Light that is not being used. It doesn't know a thing about the problems of the world. It doesn't know a thing about your human life. It's perfectly free, perfectly perfect, and it's real. Now you've got to learn to accept it in consciousness because until you accept it in consciousness you won't have the use of it.

Now you, an individual of infinite Light, called upon a person who has a sickness. Do you see how you have more opportunity to heal this individual than just another person? You must be aware that your patient has an infinite body of Light just as you have. And when you recognize it, when your spiritual consciousness can recognize it, that's when the healing takes place. How can an infinite body of Light live in time? The minute you live in time you exclude your infinite body of Light. An infinite body is in all parts of time so that time is no longer. An infinite body is where it was 2 o'clock, 3 o'clock, 5 o'clock—all now. An infinite body covers all that space is. There's no clocks in infinity. An infinite body will look at an infinite body and say, "Why we are one already, and just as I am you are."

All healings by Jesus Christ were in the now. There wasn't one healing performed by Jesus Christ that was performed in time. You'd never know it looking at the words of the Bible. If he had been in time there'd be no instantaneous healings; that's what was telling us he was not in time. It's a great secret. It's a wonderful truth, and it's worth spending five years just dwelling on it—that not only must you get out of time, you must lift your concepts out of time but the Christ that you are is not in time anyway. So if you attain Christhood you will be out of time. Everyone who was healed in the Bible was shocked by it. He didn't know for that moment he was lifted out of time. And I've seen it work on this local level just as

Class 7: My Time Has Come

beautifully as I could have hoped for, where you could try everything you want to try, nothing works and then you take yourself and your individual patient out of time and where's the problem? Just where is it? It dissolves; there's no problem. Now it's a hard thing to do and I want you to give it some thought. But remember when you take yourself out of time, you do more than heal a patient; that's when truth floods your being and you are immersed in truth.

Let's go over now to the secret place of the most high. Everything in the Bible has a way of coming back to the same thing. What is the secret place? Where is it? You've got to know. You can't go on not knowing it, you've got to know! Just one letter and one word: **I.**

And you've got to know the ramifications of I, because otherwise you still don't know the secret place. I, I Christ, Son of God. When you say, "I," and you mean I Christ, you're in the secret place, but if you don't know the fullness of the meaning of Christ, you've hardly opened the door. You've got to expand the meaning of Christ until when you say, "I," you mean all that Christ is. All that Christ does. All that Christ represents. Everything Christ is I am. Magnify the Christ. Magnify the Lord. And no matter how you magnify it, it all comes down to that secret place where I or Christ or Spirit is the secret place. The secret place is I but I is infinite, so that you're in infinity while you're saying, "I."

Now take the word infinity. Where on the globe are you not? So anyone from the globe, anyone in any part of the globe can call you and you are there immediately. The very place where they stand, you are. In that knowledge of oneness you're in a position to remove every error in their lives. But of course most people are not aware that they are infinite and they are not practicing healing either. But it is coming to the place where there will be more infinite I's practicing healing and this world will change because when people are living in the secret place they are invulnerable and they are everything that Christ is, which is omniscient, omnipresent, omni-active, omni-this and omni-that. We have a marvelous opportunity in the healing work to bring forth a measure of these Christ qualities in our patients. And if you're already in healing work, to bring the Christ into your healing is one of the great privileges, if not that greatest that you can offer to your community.

Our meditation tonight is once more a self-healing one. I've had people come up to me and tell me what was wrong. Well, let's try the self-healing process and see if we can't at least allay the belief that there is something wrong. We can pick out twenty different ailments and find them in the audience, but I can assure that there's less in this audience than there would be in just two hundred businessmen gathered together. Some of us can feel the living presence. What have you told the presence to do for you? I hope you've said, "Nothing," because the presence knows what you need before you need it. Then you say to yourself, "Well doesn't the presence know that I need a healing?" No it doesn't because what you call a healing is not a healing to the presence. The presence has pronounced you perfect and has said, "Be ye perfect."

It has no knowledge of your problems. It knows everything about you because you are the Christ and it knows everything about the Christ. It's going to take an effort to get you high enough where something in you shifts over and you realize that you don't need a healing; what you need is the truth. And the only thing that will prove that to you will be when your problem is gone, I'm aware of it. You can't deny that you have nothing because you feel you have, and that's why we're in the healing business just to remove what you feel you have, but never to convince you that we have healed you of a problem. We have healed you of an illusion. Probably don't care if it's an illusion or a real thing but you want to get rid of it and that again is your belief that you have something.

When you heal an individual and he says, "I am healed," or you see that he is, you have removed the five sense testimony which makes him feel that my eyes see, my body feels and so forth, this problem; you have removed the hypnotist. It's one of the most difficult things in the world to shake it off, but that's all it is. There is not a sickness on the face of the earth. All there is on the face of the earth is hypnotism—a simple word that means my mind experiences that which is not there. But of course the mind will experience that which is not there; it will see a body that is not there and it will experience a problem on the body which is not there. You might call that a double hypnotism. So we're not working with that body at all. We're not working with a physical body. We're working with the mind that is hypnotized into thinking there is a physical body.

Why does it think so?

The five senses say so. The "five liars," they are called in the Bible, even in the Old Testament. Joshua defeated the five Kings. Who were the five Kings? The five senses. He went out in every battle he had, he always beat the five Kings. He won a war once just by blowing a trumpet and the walls came tumbling down. He saw through the illusion and it fell apart. He never lost a battle because every battle was with a phantom. Every battle was with an army that wasn't there. He was always outnumbered, what difference did it make? They still weren't there. The Bible doesn't underscore these things, but when you become alert to it and learn about it, you become one of the many who have learned that the Bible doesn't say and underline the illusion for me because most of this real seems perfectly real to a human being. And it is only when I start to turn and look for the inner truth that the illusion becomes apparent, and even then it clings to you until one day you are aware that all on the earth is illusion. All on the earth is illusion.

We're waking up. And if you don't have a weak stomach and you can take learning about the illusions of the world, you can face them bravely. So far back they knew about them— *Don Quixote*, the buffoon chasing down every windmill. What was the author saying? Obviously he was making it clear that the windmills were an illusion and that's what life was to him. *Gulliver's Travels*—you can pick any of the classics that we're teaching, but still we didn't get it. We were still lingering in superstition; we were medieval in the present day. Thank heaven we have something called The Infinite Way. You may find other teachings that have the same understanding of the illusion, but this one certainly has and with it we are learning that we can be as free as Christ is because It is us.

I feel tempted to set a task for you to attain which I know is impossible but I'm going to do it anyway. Why don't you try for a whole day, a whole day. I'm not saying be the Christ for a whole day but recognize that everyone else is. Treat everyone as you would if you were positive that they are the Christ. Try it for a whole day. I mean make it something you're giving back to Jesus who was the Christ on this day and tomorrow give the day to Christ. Do it! And if you falter just like a kid on a piano, well you made a mistake, start over again. Play the mistake so you don't make the mistake. Treat everyone tomorrow as if they were the Christ. It will pay dividends. You will see people change in front of you and the change won't be only in their behavior it will be in your eyes too. Give it a whirl.

So tomorrow for us the last day of the seminar, the last morning of the seminar, let's make it a Christ day that carries over from the seminar, and let's take that awareness or that decision to make it an awareness back to our homes. This will be one of the best Mondays we've ever had.

I think I can continue tomorrow and perhaps we can find some of our inner self that we brought from home but didn't know we brought and that we can go home with it and feel different about ourselves. We're really wonderful people because we're immortals. And if we start feeling the wonder of our life we'll show it forth. Tomorrow we'll call it Christ day and make it as good a Christ day as we know how, and that's the day I'll see you.

Thanks again.

CLASS 8
LIVING THE GOD LIFE

Herb: Today is our Christ day and so I'm going to presume that we're all identifying ourselves as Christ. That means we have about one hundred sixty five individuals who are saying, "Today I am Christ."

And with that assumption we'll have to live in the Kingdom of Heaven. Our words, our attitudes, our activities as far as we can control them will be Christ actions, Christ words.

It might impose quite a strain on you because you can't act too quickly. You might feel that if I act too quickly I'll do something human, but that's not the case. You'll find that your activities will be guided and they will run more smoothly. It will be as if you had graduated from law to grace. Things slide effortlessly along, as long as you don't look back or look ahead but just do what you're given to do at the moment you're given to do it, you'll find you're living a charmed life. At this instant we're meeting, we're talking, we're listening and in this split second, is only second that God speaks to you. When that second is gone if you turn to the past or the future you're signing off from God. It's a habit you'll develop because you'll notice the difference is clear cut.

When I am living in the now, not in the past, not in the future, not an hour ago or not an hour from now, but in the split second God is my voice, my life, my everything. The split second is when God comes to you. You'll find that proven as you develop the capacity to live in the present split second, so that twenty four hours a day becomes as a many split seconds as there are in a day. Your split seconds one after the other, after the other keep you on the straight and narrow and you'll be surprised how grace will function your life.

The law makes you subject to the rules of matter and they go from one extreme to another. They contradict each other and they make of you a prisoner within the material body. The law of Grace is very different, you don't realize it when you're acting within the law of Grace that you're not in a material body. You don't think of it. You don't think of bodies, but in the law of Grace you're living in a spiritual body. And when it's called to your attention you discover something that has been true all along, the ground is hardly under your feet. You're walking about three feet above the ground it seems. There's no effort to anything, you're just doing things, but something else is doing them for you. And when you reach that stage where the wonder of it seeps through into your life where you know that, "I've got to have something over here right now" and then it appears there. As you begin to get these subtle feelings of "anything can happen" here but it will all be controlled. It will all be under divine control.

And as you feel this subtle guidance like you've turned on something automatic, then whatever you do under that influence is a God activity that will be bearing fruit, and it will bare fruit in such a way that you will be achieving things you hadn't planned that day. It'll just keep mounting up and mounting up until you're in a new plateau. You won't know what's coming next, just as you didn't know what was coming an hour ago, but something took care of it and it was dispatched rather easily and well and now somethings already happening for you in every second, it's happening in a divine harmony. And you're aware of it. You're just watching things go on around you, your hands are moving, your legs are moving, sometimes it's still then your body moves. But you don't move it, you're aware that you're not moving it, something is moving you. And then you say, "Can it be that Christ is living my life?" It can be and it is and the reason Christ is living your life is because you are Christ. You've attained that level which is not personal, which is not ego, the impersonal life. But you're still what you were. People still look at you and call you by the same name, but you've changed motors. Your motor now has more power, more direction, more finality, it has authority and it isn't imposing it's authority on anyone. **Not by might, not by power but by my Spirit.**

What is this wonderful thing called Spirit that operates below the eye level, but it operates with total love, total harmony in any situation and you have nothing to do with it? You're like riding on a crest of a wave. And then you'll know you're in Spirit and Spirit doesn't come about by your effort, by your physical effort or by your brain power, it's that extra dimension that

Class 8: Living The God Life

provides all sorts of activities that somehow just go in and out and weave a structure all independent of you.

Suddenly you realize that you're not in time. I haven't been aware of time. The road before you is straightened out, the bumps are out of it. Spirit is your guide and your companion and your being. A day like that and you sit back and wonder, "How did it happen? What kind of a day, how can I duplicate it?" They're all going to be that way eventually. And things that no man can accomplish in that normal day are accomplished by the spiritual man, without effort, without looking forward or back; just following the need of the moment. And there's a continuity, there are no gaps. Everything is fulfilled in divine order. The law changes to Grace and when it's working with you it makes possible a new way of life that never tires you out. That's the spiritual way and when you try to describe it, it's sort of sand falling through your hands.

When the Christ stood before the banquet and there was no wine, there were six jugs of wine - of water rather - and the seventh jug the water, went through each one and came out in the seventh as wine. That was a perfect symbology of the seven stages you're going through. It starts as water it ends as wine. As you go through the flesh in the waterpots the flesh is changed and lo it isn't flesh at all, it comes out Spirit.

Now our goal is to find this delicate automation called Grace which regulates the universe of God. And when you're nestled in it you have no responsibility for your life. God lives God's life and it appears as you. So you know God's life doesn't die. It appears in a new form and then a new form and then a body of Light. Each transposition lifts you into a higher level and each one is made possible by the level you're in. You now are building your next body. Christ is weaving your garment. And unless you let Christ weave your next garment your next body will be the same as the one it is now. The same caliber, the same plane. Your body must be in accord with the plane you're in. A mortal cannot live on the fifth plane. That's why we slowly find ourselves changing bodies because the fifth plane demands an immortal body. From the fifth plane on you'll never see mortality again.

Before you enter the fifth plane you will have a fairly good feeling about where you're going and why. A fairly good feeling about, "I don't have to be concerned about it, it's being handled by the Father." But your mind will not be there. It will not be a mind because the mind is excess baggage. Your Christ mind will be there and it will always out picture Christ activity. And then there will be a period in which you are prepared to receive your Spirit. And when you receive your Spirit at that moment, you have been purified of all earthly desires, all earthly hopes, all fleshly ideas, everything that would make you a single individual in search of something. So that what you seek and what someone else seeks would be different and it's not going to be that way. We're all moving in the same direction. The only thing we seek is our spiritual body after we have found our Soul body.

And then our Spirit and Soul will co-create the full identity of the Son of God. Everything you do now makes possible the fulfillment in the now of seeing that you are the complete whole Christ. Every little thing you do that will not be a part of the Christ is unreal. And it will be burned away by the furnace. They always use that expression of the furnace well, whatever we don't need in our future home as the Christ, is burned away. And so you start cooperating rather than waiting to find out, "Oh, Christ doesn't need that third home. Christ doesn't need this fourth car. Christ doesn't need this, Christ doesn't need that." You become quite simple it appears, because the Christ already has everything the Christ needs and then you start to say, "Well if the Christ has everything the Christ needs and I am the Christ then I have. It doesn't look like it in my life but I must have." And then you start to realize that the things you don't see, you have. And your entire attitude changes you're not seeking those things, you're not seeking to acquire, you have.

You remember the blind man? He didn't know he had sight but he was thinking of physical sight. Christ showed us that the sight was in him. Everything that you need but don't see you have, because Christ has everything. Christ is complete whole and I being Christ am complete whole. You must fill the difference with faith. The knowledge that Christ has everything. I am the Christ and then Grace becomes your ally. The Grace that produces what it needs when it needs it, but you don't have it before the Grace does it. This is what happens as you go along and permit the Spirit of God to fill your whole being. You find that Grace picks everything out of the infinite and deposits it at your door. You don't have a single moment without, but that's only after you've attained that degree

Class 8: Living The God Life

of Grace which is the law of heaven operating. Nothing is ever missing and if you can summon enough faith until it happens you will find that your life is always filled. There's no room for doubt.

We worry about the wrong things. The things we worry about, the things we think we need are not the things we need, because when we have Grace living our life that's when we have the things we need. We know not what our needs are. All we know is about our material needs, our material wants, but the real needs, the needs that come and are fulfilled by the Spirit are already established. Right now everyone in this room is complete in Christ if they have Christ. If they are asleep to Christ naturally that appears as a lack, a deficiency. But there's no deficiency in Christ and if you're awake and accepting Christ then the you that needs these things is not there. And that's when all things are accomplished effortlessly.

Let's see if we can feel the power of Grace operating in our lives. It will operate strongly or weakly depending on whether or not Christ is uppermost in your consciousness, you are aware of Christ. You know what Christ can do and you know that Christ can do it at an instant, and then you finally know that Christ has done all the things Christ must do for perfection.

[Silence]

Paul was an exponent of eternal life. He was aware that eternal life was his. He was aware that his students had to learn it and he was aware that every student had the capacity to learn that eternal life was the only life in the universe, anything else was a counterfeit.

Now when you live eternal life you don't attain eternal life it just is the kind of life you live, so that we live eternally because eternal life is like a commodity. That's the nature of life to be eternal. Just as we have accepted temporary life, now we learn to accept eternal life. Eternal life is the nature of the essence of God the Spirit. It is not the nature of material life. And graduating from material to the essence or Spirit of God, we graduate from temporary life to permanent life. Once touching eternal life that's the nature of our life forever. There is no one here who won't attain eternal life. And when we know that, when it's a part of our being that eternal life is the nature of the life that I am, we refuse to wear the temporary life over us as if we've got to do something to be eternal. The temporary life drops away. We simply exist in what we are,

"I am eternal life."

There's no fuss. I didn't have to become good to be eternal life, it is what God granted each of us, and then when you accept it all the limitations that temporary life place upon you are renounced, that all bursts like a bubble. Think of the many things you do because you think your life is temporary.

[Silence]

Do you feel your life in other realms now? Do you know that it is in other realms now? As you feel your sense of body in this realm, if you were let's say an airplane pilot, you would be aware that the atmosphere is always there in the sky and the atmosphere is slightly different than it is on the earth. Just as a deep sea diver knows that the temperature, the densities, the pressures are different underneath the water, they are above in the sky. But you're not in them right now and yet you can feel this on the basis of your past experience perhaps. We're not in eternal life to the visible, but you can feel the nature of it, and when you touch this truth within yourself that the essence of God that I am coming into here, is precisely what the essence of God is, in the Kingdom of God. I'm feeling it at this level and when I feel it at a higher level it feels differently, but I'm aware of something at that higher level that I will one day discover that I am in now. And when I enter this higher realm it's like entering what I already have a knowledge of. So we are slowly being built into that knowledge of what eternal life is.

Now then, with this somewhat awareness of eternal life as my present life now, I can live now a little differently than I thought I could, and if I don't know how, the Christ knows how. And the Christ knowing that I must live on this higher level prepares me in a way that I cannot prepare myself. Christ does everything necessary; it transmutes all of your understandings, all of your beliefs, it prepares the way for you. If things feel strange but wonderful, that's part of your preparation, so that when you say, "Now I am ready," something in you will tell you that the Spirit has completed the preparation you can now walk into the Kingdom of God. That day is inevitable, that moment.

A long time before you arrive you'll have the feeling of being transported to another realm, but you won't be going anywhere, the elevator of your consciousness will be rising.

Class 8: Living The God Life

Something comes along in your life and you can't do it, you just can't do it. Relax a moment and know that the Christ of your being can do it. And learn to drop the feelings of mortality that rise up when tasks become too difficult and learn that Christ can absorb any demand made upon it, provided the demand is a spiritual one. Anything you request is already on the waves of Spirit before you request it, and the answer is coming back to you before the request gets out of your mouth. Sometimes you haven't the ability to see the answers right in the airwaves around you. But always the thing you need is being placed before you in the invisible by the Christ, ever attentive to every need.

I hope you're getting to know that you're a very special being and that you are so important that a table has been reserved for you and you must find the way to prove worthy of being at the table of Christ. Everyone who sits at this table is at the Lord's last supper. Even though only a few were there we are all to be invited. We will be given every need met. The bread will be passed around and we will discover that it is the life of Christ as a symbol. And we will discover that in that life there is my Soul, and my Soul, and my Soul, we're all part of the bread of life. Each one has a built in miracle worker; you must learn to trust it. It won't turn itself on or off because it's running through eternity.

A new relationship begins between the Son and the Father, and the Son goes forth completely secure in the fact that the Father's love accompanies him wherever he goes. That must be your sign that you live in the Kingdom. No matter where you go or what you do the Love of God goes with you. And you must show forth that Love to be worthy of being the Son, you can't hide it. Everyone becomes a pure channel for the Love of God.

Remember when you face your patient never think of yourself as being alone to do the job. You're going to a patient who needs the Love of God and you are that envoy. There's nothing can stop it from flowing from you into the patient awakening the Love that is already in him and coming forth as an individual who has been healed by some power that he knows not of, which you know is the Love of Christ.

Why would sinners be healed if God had not forgiven them their Love? Through his Love he has forgiven them. When a sinner is healed God is showing you that in the Spirit of Christhood which is in a man how could Christ be in a sinner? How could Christ be in a murderer? But Christ is the center of everyone's being. Do the same, forgive as the Father forgives, Love as the Father Loves. Be with each individual a Light, a treasure, a sign of God present and let that individual walk away healed by God. Now the world won't know what's coming at them, but this is a Love army. This is a divine effort.

∞∞∞∞∞∞∞∞∞∞∞ End of Side One ∞∞∞∞∞∞∞∞∞∞∞

What so often happens is that we have a good seminar - and I think this was a good one - people go home, the next thing you know they're caught up into the swirl of activity. The seminar becomes something they think of as a real nice place, we had a good building and we met some nice people and then in two months it becomes a sort of a memory and it thins out. Other people I think the rare ones, have a seminar all the way home and when they get there they're still in it and then they put it to work. I'd like to feel that we have a group here that will always be in a state of oneness that we shared something and that we continue sharing. I'd like to meet with you individually and I'd like to go on with the feeling of being in Christ. If we could depend on ourselves and our friends go into the Christ and stay there and then carry it out to the rest of the world so that we know that they are the Christ even if they don't know it. If we carried all of that with us that would be like a transfusion to the world and an inspiration to our children. So I'd like us to strengthen that before we go.

This was a healing seminar but as you see, it was a healing of ourselves as well as the people we were going to heal. What has happened is that we have renewed our faith in the Father. Faith can be large or small and our faith in the Father has to be infinite. There is nothing that is wrong in God's universe, nothing needs repairs and knowing this our job is to come to that level of consciousness which lives on a par with the Father.

Paul said it was not wrong in his eyes for any man to feel like God. And the implication was that he was God. Anytime you do not feel like God then we are feeling unlike God and those times are the times that we are stepping down in consciousness. You cannot feel like him or unlike him at the same time, you feel one or the other. And every time we digress into being unlike God that's the time we digress into mortality. The Father demands that the Son be like the Father;

Class 8: Living The God Life

"All that I have is thine."

How can you have all of the Father if the Father is separate from you? And then when you realize, the Father is not separate from me, not apart from me, can you truly reach that realization without wanting to do something wonderful to show the Father, "That I know you are my being. I know we are one. I know I am the light. Wherever you are I am, wherever I am you are. I have never denied you. I never will." When you can feel this in you isn't there a surge of triumph, victory? What can happen in a life that is so welded to God that it will live in a seamless garment? There's plenty of space in that relationship for all the kinds of fun you want, but it's held together with the invisible bands of knowing that there is only one being and that is God and that is me. The I in the midst of me is God and he can do anything in the universe. He'll spring up in the middle of the ocean, in the midst of the fire, in the midst of the flood, in the midst of the hurricane, God IS. When you find that to be true so that your faith is deeper than the skin, but it makes your Soul vibrate, then you are ready to go forth and accomplish your mission in life.

Now what is your mission, let's clarify it. He said,

"Feed the hungry, heal the sick, raise the dead. Let your Light shine."

But what is your mission? What are you establishing as the central focus of what you are to do? Have a conversation with the Father and tell him what you have decided your mission is. And ask for his approval, literally ask for his approval. If he turns you down look at it again and see if that mission you have selected is doing the Father's work. It maybe and it may not be. Give him the final option to decide through you that this is what I must do. And if He says this is what you must do you're a lucky man, because that's what you must do and that's what you will do and it will be the most successful mission on earth. You will be working with a million invisible angels who will all do the work for you. Anything the Father wants you to do is spiritual and spiritually endowed, spiritually ordained and is spiritually executed by the Father. The Father will be right where you are. And what you use to perform that mission will be protected by the Father's presence.

If you decide you're going to Africa and build a great hospital and you say to the Father, "Is this what you want?" "Yes I want you to build that hospital." Well let me tell you right now the site is selected. The workers are there. Whatever the Father wants is done. If you have been selected to be a part of any operation that is divine you will do your job well and effortlessly, but you must be sure to have the Father's approval.

Oh it may not be a grandiose mission. You may be a housewife in a small town just smiling at the neighbors going by, appearing in the store, being at the Sunday meetings, nothing very big, but if the Father told it to you, it's big, it's what you've got to do at this point. And you'll find that you get to be a very firm believer in only doing what the Father has approved, because that's only what is protected. It carries with it the law of Grace. No weapon used against you shall have power.

Let's find our mission. Let's find it now! Let your wildest dreams be expressed, maybe they're not so wild. Maybe your job is to take care of one sick man, get permission don't do anything without permission, a divine wink will do.

[Silence]

Sometimes we really hear strange things when we ask for permission we may not even be able to interpret it right at the moment, but everything you get has a meaning. And I assure you that when your course has been established by the Father you had better follow it.

[Silence]

At college they give you aptitude tests. They spread them out in front of you and you fill in all the questions and then some professor tells you what your best aptitudes are and then from that you decide what you're to be. The aptitude tests don't always work. But then the truly wise people who have been endowed from on high don't follow in a general pattern which everyone else follows and the one who stands out as a genius doesn't like to see that he's good at figures and that he's supposed to be in that and so forth. Your talents are divine and you must pursue a mission which matches your divine talents, and nobody knows as well as the Father what you must do.

[Silence]

Do you realize that if everyone in the world were equipped to select the things they're going to do in their life by this method, equipped really, that everyone would be on a divine mission. And our paths would not cross, our paths would not conflict, our paths would be so that we would interweave and help each other, and add to each others mission, and all would be successful. And a successful people are a happy people there's no mischief in them.

[Silence]

Now let's take the next step. Presumably you have been given your mission, the Father may alter it from time to time. What steps are necessary for you to fulfill this mission?

[Silence]

Every child of God has a mission. There's no exception. But I do know this, that you must find the Kingdom of heaven on earth. You must locate it and you must step in it and you must utilize the facilities that are divine. You must wake up. You must help your neighbor wake up. You must help build the divine network on earth so that everything that the Father teaches goes through you and through the network, the wider, the more amplified, the more the world then will be transformed by the Spirit of God. We are now in the transformation process. We must all help widen the process. We must receive the news and spread the news, and the news is that you are the Christ, and you are the Christ, and we are all the Christ of God. The beggar on the street is the Christ, and you teach this in your quiet way, and you teach it by proving it, and you teach it by exposing the untruth that blocks the way. And you can consider that your mission, always, without ceasing.

When you're told to pray without ceasing the real meaning would be:

You are the Christ. Don't ever be anything but the Christ and you have completed your prayer, but without ceasing be the Christ.

People often ask us if we believe in reincarnation. Yeah we do for the slow ones.

(students laugh)

The quickened ones are translated.

I believe our seminar might be over and that we can all thank each other for a job well done. We have come with a purpose, we have fulfilled that purpose. We have done the Father's work, each of us. Let's hope we continue to do so.

To each of you love, blessings, and thank you.

(students applaud in appreciation)

The End

www.ingramcontent.com/pod-product-compliance
Lightning Source LLC
Chambersburg PA
CBHW030108100526
44591CB00009B/327